EBURY PRESS

MURARIRAO GHORPADE

Reeta Ramamurthy Gupta specializes in narrative non-fiction. This is her seventh book. Her previous works include *The Stranger in the Mirror*—the biography of Rakeysh Omprakash Mehra; *Sanjeev Kumar: The Actor We All Loved*; *Savitribai Phule: Her Life, Her Relationships, Her Legacy* and *Win the Battle of Your Mind in the Age of Social Media*. She is a reading coach to India's top corporations. For the last three years, she has built a dedicated following for her weekly book review column on Network18 titled #BookStrapping.

Indrajeet Ghorpade is an Indian businessman primarily involved in mining and commodity trading. He is a descendant of the Maratha clan of warriors of the Deccan. His hobbies include wildlife photography and conservation. This is his first literary work.

MURARIRAO GHORPADE

The Accidental Catalyst Behind Robert Clive's March over India

REETA RAMAMURTHY GUPTA
INDRAJEET GHORPADE

EBURY PRESS
An imprint of Penguin Random House

EBURY PRESS

Ebury Press is an imprint of the Penguin Random House group of companies whose addresses can be found at global.penguinrandomhouse.com

Published by Penguin Random House India Pvt. Ltd
4th Floor, Capital Tower 1, MG Road,
Gurugram 122 002, Haryana, India

Penguin Random House India

First published in Ebury Press by Penguin Random House India 2025

10 9 8 7 6 5 4 3 2 1

The views and opinions expressed in this book are the authors' own and the facts are as reported by them which have been verified to the extent possible, and the publishers are not in any way liable for the same.

Disclaimer: This book attempts to trace links between events that happened in history. Although every effort has been made to ensure that the information in this book was correct at press time and while this publication is designed to provide accurate information in regard to the subject matter covered, the publisher and the authors assume no responsibility for errors, inaccuracies, omissions or any other inconsistencies herein and hereby disclaim any liability to any party for any loss, damage or disruption caused by errors or omissions, whether such errors or omissions result from negligence, accident or any other cause. This book is based on a variety of sources, including published materials, and reflects the authors' own understanding and conception of such materials and/or can be verified by research. The objective of this book is not to hurt any sentiments or be biased in favour of or against any particular person, region, caste, society, gender, tribe, community or religion.

ISBN 9780143472988

Typeset in Goudy Old Style by MAP Systems, Bengaluru, India
Printed at Replika Press Pvt. Ltd, India

www.penguin.co.in

In gratitude

This book would not have been possible without the commitment, patriotism and curiosity of my co-author, Indrajeet Ghorpade, the descendant of Murarirao Ghorpade, who carries in his blood the bravery that defined the fearless Marathas

—Reeta Ramamurthy Gupta

Being Candid

'Indian history has been written in just two languages—Persian and Marathi. The disposition to write and record history has been seen among these two cohorts only . . . Traditionally, Muslims from Iran, Turan, Afghanistan and Arabstan have always had a fondness for writing history. It is upon observing the Mughals that the Marathas realized that they too must record history.

'The earliest among these efforts is the *bakhar* recorded by the Chitnis of Baroda. The Peshwas would hire writers to compile these bakhars. At some point they were embellished by hearsay and artistry and became reading material for the upper echelons of society. Eventually, it became a matter of pride to compose these bakhars and they started being available to the Patils and Kulkarnis in the villages.'

. . . *Ghorpade Gharanyacha Itihaas*,
Shri Baba Raje Ghorpade
(Translated from the Marathi by Reeta Ramamurthy Gupta)

Contents

Prologue

The hero of our story is the warrior nonpareil, Murarirao Ghorpade. His great valour was witnessed and passed down generations orally but never documented.

This is surprising; because the decision of whether Robert Clive would win India for the British or Joseph Francois Dupleix would win India for the French was determined by Murarirao Ghorpade. He was an accidental catalyst! And this had nothing to do with the individual capabilities of Robert Clive and Francois Dupleix—one of them just got lucky.

By all accounts, it would seem that Murarirao created this luck. He couldn't have known the full import of his actions—for generations to come—at that point. After all, who could have divined that all of India would fall to the British after 1757? A mere thirteen years after Robert Clive set foot in India in 1744 and six years after he fought alongside Murarirao Ghorpade.

Now every good story needs a witness,[1] someone who heard and saw things that you and I did not. Someone who can offer possible explanations of gaps in documented history. A silent inheritor to a legacy.

My co-author, Indrajeet Ghorpade, a twenty-first-century gent of royal lineage performs this vital function in our book. Now, when I say that he has royal blood flowing in his veins, make sure you also note that it is the same blood that ran in kings like Chhatrapati Shivaji Maharaj and the great warrior Santaji Ghorpade.

Indrajeet will help us trace the life of Murarirao Ghorpade, by sharing anecdotes from his childhood as juicy nuggets between sections, establishing the time and the context better.

So, let's travel back in time to the eighteenth century.

'We feel Murarirao's blessings even today! He came to Gutti[*] in 1746 and developed both the fort and the area around it. The drought-infested Anantpur Zilla has the gift of water thanks to Murarirao's work. He built several wells around the area that could sustain the people in and around Gutti.'

–Venkat Somaji, historian

---

[*] Gutti means 'cluster' in Telugu. It is actually four forts in one, with the township snuggling in the shallow basin formed by the hills. This basin houses the fort's main water supply, a tank built of dressed stone, about a quarter the size of a football field. At least two massive walls topped by broad sentry-walks surround the perimeter of the complex, and within these walls, each hilltop is a separate fort capable of defending itself, and supported by the other three. The one that towers above the others, soaring 900 feet above ground, is the main fort, and it was as formidable a defence installation of the times as any you can think of, Chittore or Gingee or Daulatabad. About halfway up and after you have passed through the sixth or seventh ring of walls, you notice a tiny white shrine that seems to be riveted on to the living rock of a sheer precipice. This shrine is said to have been Murarirao's favourite place of worship. Predictably enough, it is now bereft of its idol of Gajalakshmi.

Why This Book

When the present-day Ghorpades (three of them with seven big cartons of material packed tight) gathered to tell me the story of their ancestor Murarirao, the one emotion I picked up loud and clear was a sense of pride.

'Murarirao was one of the few warriors in history who broke the "French Hollow Square",' said one. 'The feat can only be understood when equated to the famed Chakravyuh[1] in the Mahabharata, a military formation that can be overcome *only* by the greatest warriors.'

The family shared digital albums, diaries and publications in English, Telugu, Marathi, Arabic and Persian; there was a plethora of information.* Almost anything could spark an anecdote—a picture here, a poem there, a flash of memory or even a favourite dish!

'The Ghorpades are connected umbilically to the Bhosale clan, headlined by Chhatrapati Shivaji Maharaj, the torch-bearer of *Hindavi Swarajya*. For generations, the Bhosales were the kings and the Ghorpades were their loyal military generals. A succession of cousins, marked by generational loyalty; perhaps a unique phenomenon,' said another.

My curiosity was piqued. The available evidence put Murarirao Ghorpade's birth around 1704. His grand-uncle Santaji Ghorpade[2] was already the stuff of Maratha warrior legend; easily the most well-documented[3] member of the Ghorpade clan. Santaji and Murarirao were separated by two generations. Between the two, they shared tales of exciting military conquests, espionage and loyalty from the seventeenth- and eighteenth-century Deccan.

---

* One of the many books to refer to was *Scaling the Heights* by Manohar Malgonkar, which he had bequeathed to Prof. Settar and by Prof. Settar to my co-author Indrajeet Ghorpade. The book became a good base for our discussions.

Granted that Murarirao has fewer mentions, but they are glowing references to his valour. The *Indian Historical Quarterly*[4] says,

> Murarirao kept himself up as a factor of political and military importance for nearly 40 years and was the ancestor of the present ruling family of Sandur[5] and Gajendragadh. He is one of those half-forgotten worthies of the 18th century who, despite his ultimate failure to render permanent, his rich achievements of political organisation and gallantry, was most useful to the struggling English power at a period of critical turn in their fortune.

Really? How was Murarirao most useful to the struggling English power?

Which Britisher did he help, I wondered, at a period of critical turn in their fortune?

Further, author M.Y. Ghorpade[6] credits historian Govind Sakharam Sardesai[7] as saying, 'Murarirao was a name to be reckoned with and his name struck terror in the minds of all those who opposed him! The Peshwas coaxed him, Haider bitterly hated him. In fact, few people in Maratha history had such a romantic career as Murarirao Ghorpade, and fewer still, possibly, experienced such vicissitudes of fortune as he did.'

'Romantic?' I wondered aloud and received a smile from Indrajeet. There were surely some beans to be spilled!

I continued reading the seven cartons of material provided to me. 'Murarirao's was a life of monumental struggle, full of incidents and thrills, of victories and reverses, of statecraft and foresight, all varying with the changing situation but grounded in the highest interest of the nation.'

'How could he help the British if he was acting in the highest interest of the nation?' I asked, nonplussed. 'We are discussing the early eighteenth century and the British are still posing as traders. So what was this help all about?'

Indrajeet spoke softly. 'Murarirao never sought to help either the British or the French. He had one big obsession—to ensure that the land he was born in, remained with the natives born on the land. This was his understanding of Hindavi Swarajya. He toyed with the French and the British, writing them elaborate letters, promising them his loyalty. The turning point that he is credited with, was purely by accident.'

I nodded. Indrajeet continued.

'You have to understand his patriotism, in the context of his time. He kept waiting for orders from his kings, the Marathas. But they were too busy bickering with each other. Like the proverbial brinjal,[8] their minds kept dithering and priorities kept swinging. There was a time when the Marathas made Murarirao the Governor of Trichy. But when the Nizam attacked Trichy, they did not come to his defence!'

This aspect of Maratha disunity is well documented.[9]

'Unsure of what to do for his own sustenance and survival, Murarirao decided that he should build his private army and be an independent force in the Carnatic. He had to do this to safeguard his right to collect the *chouth* and *sardeshmukhi*[10] bequeathed to him by his father. The thing that ruffled him, however, was that even though he was loyal to the Chhatrapatis, he was not interested in being subservient to the Peshwas.[11] Yes, it is true that Murarirao's choices and actions altered India's history forever,' Indrajeet added.

Okay. So Murarirao wanted to be an independent force in the Carnatic region. But what about the rest of his persona? His personal life? I felt that my finger wasn't on the pulse yet. 'Tell me more,' I urged.

Indrajeet smiled, like a man about to reveal a great secret.

'I think the most compelling story never told is that of a warrior hopelessly in love and torn between his duty and his desire. The quiet courtship of Murarirao Ghorpade and the daughter of the Nizam,' he finally murmured, almost under his breath.

'Which daughter?' I asked. And then I blurted, 'Which Nizam?'

'The first Nizam of the Deccan. Asaf Jah I. My grandfather[*] knew the daughter's name; he would call her Saheba. He used to recount tales[12] of Murarirao and Saheba with great nostalgia. Though he never knew how many daughters the Nizam had in total.[13] In those days, rulers had wives and concubines and slaves; all in multiple counts. Often, an accurate number of offspring was a leap of faith.'

---

[*] Read Annexure 7, a tribute to Indrajeet's grandfather Bhujangrao Ghorpade for more context.

I was listening with rapt attention. Aren't unrequited love stories of stoic warriors exciting?

'Saheba was an educated lady of great beauty and fine intellect. But as children, we were told that this love came in the way of Murarirao's dream to build the Hindavi Swarajya he was committed to. And that is one of the reasons why he could not follow through with his great love story.'

That the daughter of the Nizam would be educated did not surprise me at all. Historians have spoken about the liberated Mughal women of the North. Many historians have ascribed strength of character and calibre to the Mughal princesses in India; they received the same education as their brothers[14] and were adept at calligraphy, arithmetic, philosophy and writing. They also had access to large amounts of wealth and were very enterprising. For example, in the north, Akbar's Rajput wife, Harkha Bai, had a prized possession—the *Rahimi*[15]—a ship that carried 600–700 pilgrims to Mecca every year.

At some level, the Saheba angle was extremely difficult to digest, though.

'How did Murarirao even meet the Nizam's daughter? Wasn't it really something of a feat to even be able to see her? What was her life like?' I persisted.

'She was pure royalty. And she remained unmarried,' he answered.

'Why?' I asked.

Indrajeet smiled, 'You won't believe this. But daughters of the Mughals often remained unmarried.[16] A case in point being Humayun's sister Gulbadan Begum, a couple of daughters of Akbar and Shah Jahan and even daughters of their extended relatives.'

Okay. So Murarirao's love wasn't to last. Indrajeet quickly reminded me that Murarirao's life wasn't defined by this love. 'He was the consummate hero,' he said. In fact, Haider hated his guts so much that he even sent a spy to kill him.

This made perfect sense. Obsessed hoarders like Haider wouldn't like other hoarders to prosper.

The question remained, though: How did Murarirao change the course of India's history forever?

Let us understand the lay of the land.

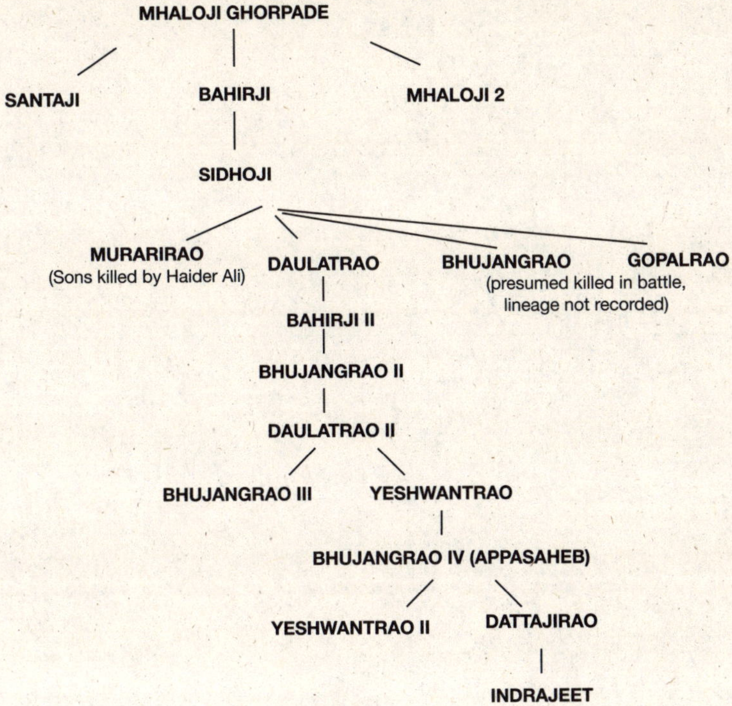

Family tree from Mhaloji to Indrajeet
Source: Ghorpade family

Main Characters

There are six main characters in our story; and I want you to watch out for them when they appear—and understand their context and motivations.

In Part 1, you will meet our hero Murarirao Ghorpade and get an appreciation of his place in the Maratha legacy.

In Part 2, the second character of great importance to our story, the Viceroy of the Deccan, Nizam-ul-Mulk, makes an appearance. You will also meet Chanda Sahib, who, as the son-in-law of the Nawab of Arcot, is supposed to be subservient to the Nizam, but isn't. He's a cunning man who is replete with what can only be described as 'nuisance value'. He literally inserts himself into our story as well. You will then meet the beauteous Saheba, the Nizam's daughter, who becomes the love of Murar's life.

In Part 3, prepare to be introduced to the two men who fought for dominion over India. Robert Clive of the British East India Company and Joseph Francois Dupleix of the French East India Company. You will be surprised to see how close this contest was and how Clive managed to win by a hair's breadth.

In Part 4, as the plot unravels to reveal the chinks in everyone's armour one by one, a new force emerges—that of Haider Ali. A proud warrior and ambitious king, Haider takes our story to its conclusion.

Our story has a fabulous supporting cast. Without the larger tectonic shifts caused by the likes of Chhatrapati Shivaji Maharaj, Aurangzeb, Maharani Tarabai, Shahu Maharaj, Peshwa Bajirao, the Marathas of Thanjavur, Nandraj Dalwai of Mysore, Tara, Bahirji, Siddhoji, his mother and Peshwa Madhavrao, the fertile ground for this story would never have been prepared.

Part 1

The Marathas

Section 1

The Story You Didn't Know

'सवर्प्रथम राष्ट्र, नंतर गुरु, मग पालक, मग देव, सवर्प्रथम स्वत:कडे नाही तर राष्ट्राकडे पाहा.'

–*Chhatrapati Shivaji Maharaj*

(Place your nation first among your priorities. Then your teacher, then your guardians, then God. Your turn comes last.)

1

The Bhosales and the Ghorpades

Period of Rule	Bhosale Brother	Ghorpade Contemporary
Was a Maratha general, not a ruler	Shahaji Bhosale	Mhaloji Ghorpade
1674–1680	Shivaji Bhosale	Mhaloji Ghorpade
1674–1684	Vyankojirajah Bhosale	This is the Thanjavur branch, also vital to our story
1681–1689	Sambhaji Bhosale	Santaji, Bahirji and Maloji
1689–1700	Rajaram Bhosale	Santaji, Bahirji and Maloji
1700–1708	Tarabai Bhosale	Bahirji and Sidhoji Ghorpade
1708–1749	Shahu Bhosale	Sidhoji and Murarirao Ghorpade
1713–1720	Balaji Vishwanath becomes Peshwa	Sidhoji and Murarirao Ghorpade

Period of Rule	Peshwa Line	Ghorpade Contemporary
1720–1740	Bajirao 1	Murarirao Ghorpade
1740–1761	Nana Saheb	Murarirao Ghorpade
1761–1772	Madhavrao	Murarirao Ghorpade

Table 1.1: Generations of loyalty
(refer to Annexure 1 for more context)[1]

The credit for envisaging Hindavi Swarajya goes to Chhatrapati Shivaji Maharaj. Hindavi Swarajya has several interpretations. However, keeping in mind that Shivaji Maharaj was a Hindu king ruling over a small territory at a time when India was under tyrannical Mughal rule, it's fair to say this: enraged by the plunder of local people, places and culture, Shivaji Maharaj defined his life's purpose as making sure that foreign rulers be purged from India and that the rule of the natives of the land be established—hence Hindavi Swarajya. The Ghorpades were a formidable part of its execution.

History stands testimony to the fact that every powerful leader has been aided by a committed, sometimes cross-generational, aide-de-camp. An adjutant, who stands by them, no matter what. The Ghorpades stood as loyal adjutants to the Bhosales, for a long period in history. At a time when brother killed brother for power, borne out amply by Mughal history, this loyalty by succession was unparalleled.[2]

Likewise, the pathbreaking work of the Bhosales,[3] the most famous among whom was Shivaji Bhosale, might never have reached the heights it did without the support of their cousins, the Ghorpades. Both belonged to the Maratha Empire and our protagonist, Murarirao Ghorpade, belongs here.

Let's touch upon their shared ancestry, which itself is argued against by a few scholars.

* * *

As per historian Manohar Malgonkar,[4] the Bhosales and the Ghorpades share 'the same exalted lineage, that of descent from the Maharanas of Mewar'. This theory is advanced by the fact that in a letter to Adil Shah, Shahaji—father of Shivaji—referred to himself as a 'Sisodia Rajput'.[5]

How can this be explained?

In the book *Scaling the Heights–Mired in Their Own Blood: Stories of Loyalty and Treachery from Medieval Deccan*, Malgonkar narrates that in 1334, one Prince Sujan Singh of Mewar[6] was overlooked by his own father to succeed the throne. Miffed, he left for the Maratha lands. Over the course of 200 years, his lineage eventually bifurcated into two brothers: Karna Singh and Shubha Krishna. Karna Singh's descendants came to be known as Ghorpades and Shubha Krishna's descendants came to be known as Bhosales.

It is in the Bhosale[7] line, that three centuries later,[8] the great Shivaji Maharaj was born.

Malgonkar continues,

> Having emphasised that the Bhosales and Ghorpades were not indigenous to South India, it must now be explained that they did not originally belong to Maharashtra[9] either. They were the descendants of a Rajput Prince[10] who emigrated to Maharashtra, put down his roots and made a career as a soldier of fortune.

Many historians disagree vehemently with this 'north-origin' theory; chief among these is the ninety-six-clan claim. The theory goes thus: Marathas are subdivided into ninety-six different clans, known as the ninety-six Kuli Marathas[11] or *Shahānnau Kule*. At some point, these ninety-six clans were apparently misinterpreted to mean Kshatriyas. Anthropologist J.V. Ferreira[12] writes: 'The Maratha claim to belong to the ancient ninety-six Kshatriya families has no foundation in fact and may have been adopted after the Marathas became with Shivaji a power to be reckoned with.'

I met the young historian Indrajit V. Sawant in Kolhapur, who demanded evidence to establish the connection between Mewar's Prince Sujan Singh and Shivaji Maharaj, as laid out in Malgonkar's book. 'How will you prove that Marathas are from the North?' Sawant asked, adding that in 1677, Shivaji wrote a letter to Maloji Ghorpade saying, 'We are both Marathas', as proof that Shivaji never referred to his origins from the North.

Sawant adds further that the probable origin of the Marathas is Halebidu[13] in the South. This is not a view accepted by all historians.

I submitted my confusion to the great historian Jaisinghrao Pawar, who put this dilemma to rest.

'In the fourteenth century, many Rajputs started coming to the Deccan. The ones that came from the North were neither Bhosales nor Ghorpades. They were Rajputs. Similarly, there were many people who migrated from outside India[14] and the other parts of India[15] as well.

Sujan Singh, a sketch
Courtesy of Manohar Malgonkar

'Over the course of 200 years, there was a lot of mixing—it is this mixture that took on a new identity and developed a Maratha character. Look at the variety of features, skin colours and eye shapes among the Marathas. Let me also clarify that there is no doubt that Shivaji Maharaj considered himself a Maratha.'

Indrajeet added that there was also no doubt at all that the Ghorpades too considered themselves Marathas. So, what we are essentially saying is that the Marathas are an intermingled phenomenon. Having considered some aspects to the origin story, let us get to know our brave hero, Murarirao.

2

His Mother's Pet

Sandur was the childhood home of Murarirao; he was born to Sidhoji and Laxmibai. Murarirao grew up with stories about his illustrious ancestors. His mother Laxmibai was both devout and a disciplinarian and she would constantly keep him connected to his roots.

'It was Shahaji[1] who planted the seeds for the Bhosales to become powerful,' she would tell him. 'He was the one who absorbed your great-grandfather Mhaloji Ghorpade in his contingent and gave him the rank of *shiledar*.'[2]

Shahaji also ensured that Mhaloji Ghorpade[3] received a share of his land holdings dating back to the times of the Bahamani Sultans.[4]

Murarirao tried to keep pace with his mother; Bahamani Sultans?[5] Maybe a story for another day. He would get goosebumps listening to his mother and did not want to interrupt her flow. Anything to do with Shivaji or Santaji would get him enraptured.

'Shahaji was compelled by the Mughals to leave Maharashtra and migrate to Kanara[6] as a servant of Bijapur. This was in 1636.[7] He had two sons,' Laxmibai continued. 'His first son–'

'Chhatrapati Shivaji!'[8] yelled Murar, unable to contain his excitement and doing a merry jig around his mother.

'You know all about him. But did you know that he was very close to his mother?' she smiled.

Murarirao could relate to this. He immediately felt that even he was like Shivaji in that regard.

'There was a reason why Shivaji could never work for any Mughal or Muslim ruler. He was away from his father for many, many years and chiefly influenced by his mother. In 1636, when he was just six years old and Shahaji had just aligned himself with Adil Shah of Bijapur, the Mughals captured[9] his wife, Shivaji's mother, under the orders of Mughal general Mahabat Khan. She was brought to the Mughal camp, but her uncle Jagdeorao Jadhav intervened and took her to safety at Kande Fort.'

Murarirao was relieved.

'Even before this,' Laxmibai continued, 'Nizam Shah had killed Jijabai's father Lakhoji Jadhav, brothers Achalji and Raghoji and her nephew Yeshwant, in Daulatabad.[10] This incident forever changed Shivaji's mindset and he could never think of aligning with the Mughals in any way.'

Murarirao could perfectly understand this sentiment.

'And Shahaji's second son, of course, was . . .' Laxmibai paused.

'Vyankoji,' yelled Murar, doing another merry jig around his mother.

'Yes. He was the founder of Maratha rule[11] in Thanjavur.'

'So both Shivaji Maharaj and Vyankoji Maharaj built empires?'

'Yes. Even today, we honour Thanjavur as our brother state. It is our job to protect it against invaders,' said Laxmibai.

'Did Mhaloji Ghorpade dada work only under Shahaji Raje? Was he alive during Shivaji Maharaj's times?'

'Yes. Mhaloji continued his loyalty to the family with Shivaji Maharaj. At the time of Shivaji's coronation in 1674, Mhaloji was almost fifty years old.'

Murarirao took a moment to imagine how grand this coronation might have been. But his curiosity got the better of him and he asked again.

'If Shivaji did not like working for the Mughals, why were other kings okay with it? Why didn't they build their own empires?'

'Why don't you ask your favourite Madullah for an answer? I have to cook now.'

Murarirao's face fell. 'Tell me one more thing, *Aai*.'[12]

Laxmibai smiled. 'The person you admire, Santaji, also saw Shivaji Maharaj in action. Such a huge influence on such a young mind!'

Laxmibai got up to do her chores and Murar went for his *Mardani Khel*[13] lessons, determined to fight better than his progenitors.

3

Multiple Marriages, Multiple Heirs

The next day, Murarirao was engaged in his preferred pastime: sitting with the raconteur Madullah, a sixty-five-year-old man who lived nearby. Madullah had been around since Murar was a baby. As Murar grew and realized that his father was a man of some importance, his tiny hands would try and reach Madullah's shoulder, as he sat next to him. Whether he wanted to show solidarity or assert that he was somehow grown up too, is anyone's guess.

Madullah had spent his whole life making shoes in Agra before circumstances somehow led him to Sandur. Upon reaching this beautiful paradise, he donned the mantle of the local storyteller of Sandur, especially when it came to Mughal history. He could read Persian and was extremely well informed.

He was also close to Sidhoji. Thanks to his knowledge of Persian, he had travelled with Sidhoji, not as a warrior but as an attendant, carrying things and relaying information. He was also something of a philosopher.

Murar's mind was as close to a tabula rasa[1] as Madullah could find. The duo were thick as thieves. A unique relationship, given the massive age gap between them. Curious, absorbent and sharp, Murar would always have questions lingering on his mind, arising from incomplete conversations with his mother or father.

'Tell me Madullah, other than Shivaji, why did none of the other kings stand up for their own freedom?' asked Murar.

'That's not true. Let me tell you about a brave Rajput king, Prithviraj Chauhan from the twelfth century, almost five hundred years before Shivaji, who defeated Mohammed Ghori.[2] However, he made the mistake of not annihilating his enemy—and Ghori was able to recoup and came back to defeat him.[3]

'After this, wave after wave of foreign powers continued to sweep over Hindustan,[4] without a break. Even the shining kingdom of Vijayanagara met their match at the battle of Talikota,[5] in which Ramaraya was defeated. There were barely a handful of Hindu kingdoms[6] around—a few in Kerala, a few in Rajasthan, etc. It seemed that the sovereigns of Hindustan were largely unwilling to raise their head above the flood of Muslim conquest. All but a few kings of Hindustan had accepted defeat.'

Madullah paused for effect.

'Even the ablest king of Hindustan, with all his wealth and power, was at most a feudal baron. Take a case in point; even Maharana Pratap's son entered into a treaty with the Mughals, which required his son to attend the Mughal court. And every generation that bowed to this state made it more and more difficult for the idea of Hindavi Swarajya to become a reality.'

'Doesn't this make Shivaji's story even more important?' asked Murar.

'Absolutely! The very idea of a powerful king born in this land had faded into a dim, distant and almost forgotten memory. So, when a friendless, middle-class young man of thirty-two named Shivaji decided to confront the might of the Mughal Empire (then in its noon-day splendour), as well as the nearer hostility of Bijapur (which had been the 'Queen of the Deccan'[7]), he seemed to be determined not only to go against the grain but also jump in with both feet. His fearlessness inspired thousands of generals to stand by him and bet on a better future.'

'So, Shivaji was very brave?' asked the boy Murar, his small body trembling at the thought.

'Yes. At the time, the Mughals were very powerful. During Shivaji's time, it was not possible to see that the Mughal Empire would sink by 1707. There were other brave men too, like Sambhaji, the son of Shivaji and also Santaji[8] your great-granduncle. They fought like they were possessed,' Madullah said.

'If Sambhaji was also so brave, why didn't he continue Shivaji Maharaj's work?' asked Murar.

'You want a longer story?' teased Madullah.

Murar nodded with an endearing innocence. It was almost as if, if he knew things well enough, he could right a wrong of the past somehow!

Madullah continued.

'Shivaji had eight wives. From his first wife, Saibhai Bhosale, he had a son Sambhaji.[9] From another wife, Soyrabai, Shivaji had his second son, Rajaram. Later, Shivaji had the tough task of dividing his conquests between his sons.'

Madullah continued, 'Sambhaji was unhappy with the division and rebelled[10] against his father. Later, Sambhaji returned to his father but was imprisoned[11] in the fort of Panhala, with his wife Yesubai and family. Shivaji chose your great-grandfather Mhaloji Ghorpade[12] to command Panhala Fort and gave him the title of *sarnobat*. Mhaloji Ghorpade formed a fine bond with Sambhaji. Managing the Chhatrapati's son's temperament and keeping him under arrest could not have been easy. That Shivaji entrusted Mhaloji with handling the delicate task of Sambhaji's imprisonment, gives us a sense of how much Shivaji valued Mhaloji.

'It was during this period of captivity that the news of Shivaji's death came about. It took some time for the news to reach Panhala, where Mhaloji was guarding Sambhaji. In a rush, Soyrabai made plans with various ministers of the administration to crown her son Rajaram,[13] rather than her stepson Sambhaji. On 21 April 1680, ten-year-old Rajaram was installed on the throne.'

Murar interrupted, 'Who was older? Sambhaji or Rajaram?'

'Sambhaji. He was the firstborn and an able contender. And he wasn't going to give up.'

Murar interrupted again, 'But why couldn't they sit together and decide who would be king?'

Madullah laughed heartily. 'Can I tell you a secret?'

Murar nodded eagerly.

'For some reason, brothers and cousins never talk to each other when it really matters! Instead, they go out and ask outsiders for help.'

This seemed very strange to Murar. But he saw that Madullah wasn't laughing any more. The thing with Madullah was that he never spoke without a strong basis in what he was saying. So, it was difficult to ignore him.

'Most kings married multiple times and had multiple[14] children. The problem was that every wife felt that her son was the rightful heir to the throne. This created problems,' Madullah said.

Curious, Murar asked, 'Did we learn to marry multiple times from the Mughals?'

Madullah, alarmed that a young boy should make such a connection, shook his head. 'The Marathas learnt a lot of things from the Mughals. Fashion, for example. Having writers in the court and documenting everything is another. But I don't think that having multiple wives was a Mughal-only trait. Even Prithviraj Chauhan had three wives, many, many years ago.'

'How many wives did Aurangzeb have?' Murar was insatiable.

'Three, I think. There could have been countless more concubines,' responded Madullah. 'Now, shall we go back to Sambhaji's story?'

Murar nodded.

'Wanting to stake his claim on the empire, Sambhaji marched to Raigad, while Mhaloji Ghorpade continued to guard Panhala. One can assume that Mhaloji and Sambhaji might have come to some kind of mutual understanding by this point, because Mhaloji "released" Sambhaji to go and fight for his right. He later appointed Mhaloji as *senapati* or commander in chief of his army.'

'So, guarding Panhala was important?' asked Murar.

'Yes! Just around this time, Sant Ramdas[15] wrote a letter to Sambhaji. He exhorted Sambhaji never to forget Shivaji's spirit, with the following words:

बहुत लोक मेळवावे।
एक विचारे भरावे।
कष्टे करोनी घसरावे।
म्लेंच्छांवरी।

'"Collect all your men. Fill them up with the ideas of Hindavi Swarajya. Undergo the hardship of preparation, to avenge the Mughals." Ramdas thus desired that the son should follow in the footsteps of his father.'[16]

'So what did Sambhaji do?' asked Murar.

'Sambhaji coronated himself with Vedic rites, just as his father had done. This was in 1681.'

'So now, there were two kings?' Murar asked.

Madullah shook his head, but he was getting busy.

A man walked in with a broken shoe and Madullah started to fix it. 'We will continue our story later,' he said with his trademark kindness.

Murar decided to let them be and walked towards his house. His mind was racing. How would the Maratha Empire last if two people fought over the throne? Someone had to compromise.

Murar decided to ask his father.

4

Sambhaji's Valiant Death

Murar knew that any conversation with his father had to be pitched right. Otherwise, he wouldn't get all the information he wanted.

'Sarkar[1], do you like the battlefield?' he began.

'What a strange question, Murar. The battlefield is a brutal place; you either kill or get killed,' said Sidhoji. 'It's not a place to like or dislike, but a place to discharge your duty dispassionately.'

Murar's face fell. He tried another angle.

'Was Sambhaji brave?' he asked.

'Of course, *bal*[2]. Sambhaji took his rightful place succeeding his father as Chhatrapati and denied Soyrabai's premature moves to crown Rajaram. During his nine-year rule, Sambhaji Maharaj never allowed the Mughals to rule over the Marathas. Aurangzeb clearly saw him as a threat. In fact, he set his sights on capturing Sambhaji by evil design[3] and delivered him a cruel death.'[4]

Murar didn't like this one bit! He determined that he would pay more attention to his training so that no one could ever deliver him a cruel death.[5] If only he could see far enough!

Sidhoji was in a good mood, and he continued.

'Ironically, it was Sambhaji's heroism while facing an extremely ruthless death in order to preserve his Hindu faith which fired up the Marathas.[6] It is safe to say that what Shivaji achieved in his life, Sambhaji achieved in death.'

'Why did Aurangzeb want Sambhaji to change his religion?' asked Murar.

'Aurangzeb was very orthodox. This was a continuation of his father Shah Jahan's move away from the liberalism of Akbar.[7] But Aurangzeb took it to an extreme; he wanted to suppress the local people.'[8]

Murar did not like the sound of it. 'Wasn't everyone angry when Sambhaji died?' he asked.

'Of course, bal. And this is the exact point when our family's contribution, as loyal subordinates to their kings, reached an incredible crescendo.'

Murar was excited; almost as if someone was going to serve him a sweet dish. Besides, it was increasingly evident to him that his ancestors were privileged to be able to serve Shivaji and Sambhaji, such heroic kings.

'Within days of Sambhaji's death at the young age of thirty-one, Rajaram,[9] who was now nineteen years old, was proclaimed king[10] at Raigad. The Mughals laid siege to Raigad.[11] Rajaram's closest allies suggested that he escape from Raigad in the guise of a yogi. His life had to be protected at all costs. But Sambhaji's widow, Yesubai, and Shahu stayed on in Raigad.'[12]

'Where did Rajaram go?' asked Murar.

'He went to Panhala first, but then he and his troop of protectors wandered from fort to fort for some time. It was at this time that Santaji Ghorpade and Vithoji Chavan decided to avenge Sambhaji's cruel death.'

Just then a visitor was announced and Sidhoji had to attend to him. Murar wondered why these visitors had to come exactly when the story was getting so interesting! He would have to wait for the next morning now! Murar took a good look around his own house.[13] The Sandur fort was in the centre of a valley, surrounded by a moat—the waters of the Narihalla River—which made it safe. You could not enter Sandur except through one of the passes; there was the Narsinghswamy pass in the south which had small stone citadels that became lookout points announcing suspicious intruders. Murar's home was quite spartan because the fort was built not for comfort but to house an entire community, as most functional forts of that time used to be. There were separate areas for the horses, the armoury, the granary, the cowsheds and barracks for army generals and key soldiers and quarters for the people who worked within the fort, such as the diwan and the household help. The fort also housed the drinking water supply for the 200-odd people that lived within. There was, of course, the common *Devghar* (puja room) and the *kacheri (office)*, where Sidhoji would handle administrative matters. Madullah and Nimbkar both lived inside the fort. Madullah, because he was Sidhoji's man Friday masquerading as a cobbler and Nimbkar because he conducted singing classes for children within the fort. As did Murar's childhood friends Yunus Khan, the son of a warrior, and Bhujangrao Ghorpade, a distant cousin. They were the same age and had learnt everything together. They would also lose their virginity together by being sent to the same place on the outskirts of Sandur, called Kudilgi, where the menfolk were handed over to trusted women for this express purpose. This was called *Gejje Pooje*, or worship of the anklet. Once on the fringes of the Vijaynagara Empire, Kudilgi was the place where virgins, young girls and dancing girls were sent for safety during wars. These women were also subsequently available to the highest bidders and for royalty. Sandur was not a rich principality, unlike Gajendragadh or Arcot. Nor was it a menacing fort like Gutti. No one ever attacked Sandur. Outside the Sandur Fort was the rest of the village, comprising butchers, tailors, traders, blacksmiths, small foundries, etc. Sandur was a quiet, secluded place.

Within the Sandur Fort, the only noisy place was the maidan in the centre of the principality. It is here that the infantry was drilled, activities like tent pegging were taught and horsemen were trained by masters on how to open up the enemy's defence, only for the foot soldiers to launch an attack. Grandmasters would be called from various places as well as elephant trainers from Kellady and Buzkazhi equestrian trainers from Afghanistan.

Young Murar was an exceptionally gifted rider. Murar used to love the days when training became sport. He wasn't old enough to spot when sport became politics.

RAJARAM—CHARITAM

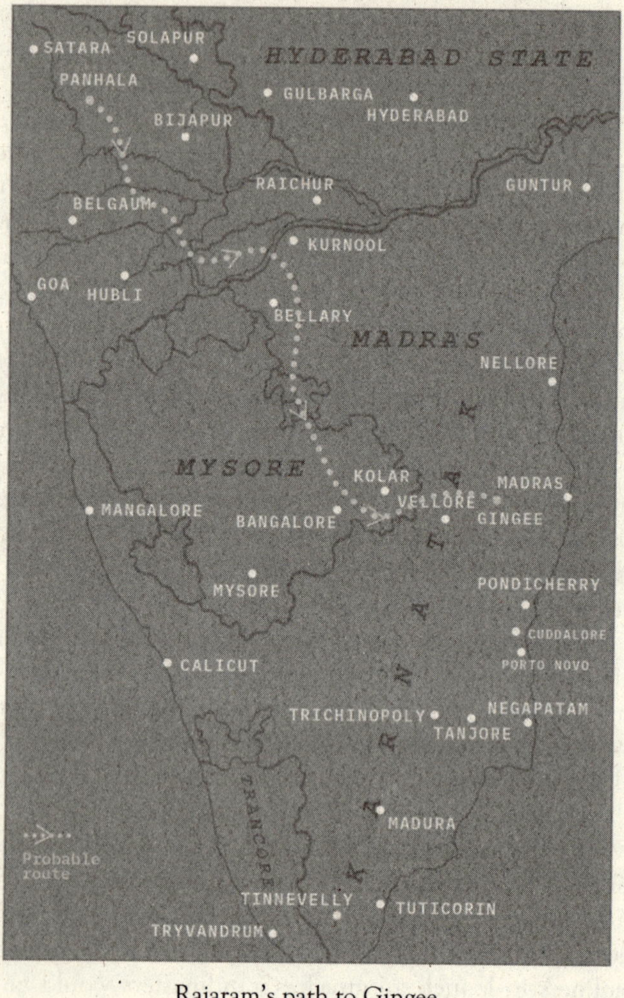

Rajaram's path to Gingee
Source: Ghorpade family

5

The Ghorpades Set Out for Revenge

The next morning, as soon as his eyes opened, Murar ran out of his house, seeking Madullah.

Madullah smiled and called out to Nimbkar, his neighbour, who was known to speak authoritatively about Maratha history. Young Murar and the other children in the fort were a wonderful antidote to Nimbkar's loneliness.

'Have you cleaned your teeth?' said Madullah, already knowing the answer and handing Murar a mix of charcoal and salt and some water.

Murar set about cleaning his teeth, not taking his eyes off Madullah even for a moment as the old man laid out his work tools for the day. He motioned to Murar to sit next to him, as he started sewing the upper and sole together using a hand stitch.

'Was everyone angry with Aurangzeb after the way in which he killed Sambhaji Maharaj?' asked Murar.

'Yes. Your great-grandfather Mhaloji Ghorpade was extremely close to Sambhaji. His sons, Santaji, Bahirji and Maloji swore to continue the Maratha lineage by protecting Rajaram Maharaj and his wife Tarabai, no matter what the cost,' Madullah said.

'What about Sambhaji's family?' Murar asked, spitting out the disgusting mix with which he was brushing his teeth.

'Sambhaji Maharaj's wife Yesubai was a very strong woman. She insisted that Rajaram must not have the same fate as her husband and that he and his wife Tarabai be taken away from Raigad for continuity of the Maratha Empire. Raigad was not impregnable. Yesubai and Shahu stayed back,' pitched in Nimbkar.

'So they were taken to Panhala,' added Murar, who already knew this bit.

Nimbkar smiled indulgently. 'Now, your granduncle Santaji Ghorpade had always been audacious. He decided that instead of reacting to what the Mughals were doing all the time, they must be on the offensive and cause trouble. So he and a small group made their way on a dark night through inclement rain to Aurangzeb's camp at Koregaon—much like putting your hand into a crocodile's open jaw! They stormed into the enemy's house, identified the royal tent, cut down the supporting ropes and the huge cloth edifice came down in a crash, killing everyone inside,' said Nimbkar, keeping the suspense alive.

'Was the tent so heavy? Did Aurangzeb die?' asked Murar in evident anticipation.

'You have to imagine the size of the camp; it was like a city and Aurangzeb's own tent was a sturdy, lavish structure supported by multiple poles, a metallic pinnacle and thick cloth. So when it crashed down, anyone inside would get suffocated and killed,' said Nimbkar.

Murar took a moment to visualize this.

'It was discovered much later that Aurangzeb had spent the night in his daughter's tent and thus escaped death. But Santaji's unit carried away the large gold pinnacles at the top of the emperor's camp and other valuables and presented them to Rajaram at Pratapgad,' Nimbkar said with emotion.

'Aurangzeb must have been very angry,' Murar said.

'Yes. Of course, he was. A Mughal force attacked Pratapgad, where Rajaram was at that point. Santaji Ghorpade oversaw this and launched his own counterattack, routing Shaikh Nizam, the man who was credited with capturing Sambhaji, at the foot of Panhala.'

Murarirao clapped with happiness.

'The Mughals were relentless. Rajaram reached Panhala but had to escape from there, too, thanks to the Mughal menace. His bold aim now was to reach Gingee,[1] a stronghold 100 kilometres south-west of Madras, even as Mughal outposts had been alerted everywhere and instructed to intercept Rajaram at any cost,' Nimbkar said.

'How did Santaji protect Rajaram?' asked Murar.

'Both Santaji and Bahirji did their part, I would say. They stood firmly[2] by Rajaram in his hour of danger. Unfortunately, Maloji, their brother, was captured and put to death. Despite the personal loss, Bahirji remained calm and carried Rajaram on his shoulders while crossing the Tungabhadra River amidst enormous danger.'

'Was Rajaram heavy and difficult to carry?' asked Murar innocently.

'No,' smiled Madullah. 'But carrying someone on your back while crossing the river is a difficult task! Then, Bahirji was also captured by the Mughals near Subhangarh and imprisoned in the Bijapur Fort. He somehow managed to escape and rejoin Rajaram's contingent. To make a safe path for Bahirji and Rajaram, Santaji Ghorpade did what he did best—kept Mughal forces at bay and enabled Rajaram to reach Gingee.'

'Santaji was a true warrior,' Nimbkar added.

It was time for Murar to get up and show a bit of his Mardani Khela skills. He was tired of sitting anyway.

'Rajaram finally reached Gingee[3] in November 1689. The never-say-die attitude of the Marathas gave Mughal Emperor Aurangzeb a foretaste[4] of what was to follow. Grateful for saving his life, Rajaram bestowed titles on all three Ghorpade brothers, Santaji, Bahirji and Maloji.' Santaji was given the title 'Mamlakat-Madar' (pillar of the realm), Bahirji that of 'Hindurao' (Hindu Lord) and Maloji that of 'Amir-ul-Umrao' (chief among the nobles).

There was a time when the three sons of Mhaloji Ghorpade–Bahirji, Santaji and Maloji–were fighting in the same military column.

But after Gingee, everything changed. Maloji was no more. Santaji, already in his fifties, was expecting to be elevated from mid-level commander to chief commander of Rajaram's army. Bahirji, the eldest, also in his fifties, was content to step back and be seen as a mature statesman in Rajaram's court.

Fast forward to 1695, five years after Rajaram's arrival in Gingee. Santaji's temperament and his differences with Rajaram started to come out in the open and become a problem for the Ghorpades; a problem that could not be brushed under the carpet any more.

Section 2

The Maddest of the Mad

6

Santaji the Rebel

Sidhoji would often supervise his son's military training.

One of the silent legacies of Chhatrapati Shivaji Maharaj was that opposing armies learnt to respect and fear the Maratha army. In fact, the Maratha Army moved from place to place with such incredible speed that the bewildered victims credited them with the knowledge of 'black magic'. Shivaji Maharaj's pace was such that Portuguese traveller Cosme da Guarda[1] asked, 'The question is unsolved whether he (Shivaji) substituted others for himself or whether he was a magician or devil in his place.'

With such tall role models, as a child, Murar always wanted to be a great warrior. He was stunned to learn how stones could be used as missiles. Bows and arrows remained popular all through the ages, and there were several types of swords. The Marathas were also excellent horsemen who shocked the enemy with their knowledge of guerrilla warfare and 'shock and awe' surgical strikes.

As Murar finished his training for the day, he went to sit with his father.

'I want to know more about Santaji.'

'Your curiosity is insatiable,' said Sidhoji at first, before continuing. 'Santaji was brave and he was lucky. He knew who his leader was, and he knew who his enemy was. It is unfortunate that after his time, we degenerated to pitting Maratha against Maratha.'

Murar persisted, 'But you are proud of Bahirji Ajoba and Santaji Ajoba, aren't you? Why was Santaji such a great warrior?'

'Santaji was able to cover long distances quickly. He could command large militaries during these long quick marches; he knew that the secret to victory was the element of surprise.'

'Wow,' said Murar, engrossed already.

'But Santaji had his flaws. It is very rare that one man has all qualities, like our Shivaji Maharaj. Along with military might, Shivaji Maharaj was blessed with knowledge of justice,[2] dharma and welfare. Jijabai taught him well and he was truly exceptional. In contrast, Santaji lacked Shivaji Maharaj's calmness, intellect and temperament.'

Murar nodded. There was so much to learn.

'Shivaji Maharaj and Santaji Ghorpade, these were the two people that Aurangzeb and his generals feared the most,' Sidhoji's voice boomed.

'I don't like Aurangzeb at all,' said Murar with some finality.

'Neither do I,' chuckled Sidhoji. 'Santaji was loyal to the Chhatrapati lineage, but rough in his speech. Let me tell you a story. Once, during a meeting with Rajaram Maharaj,[3] Santaji said pompously, "The Chhatrapatis exist because of me and I can make and dethrone Chhatrapatis at will." Obviously, Rajaram Maharaj did not like this tone! So he made Santaji's arch-enemy Dhanaji Jadhav the senapati[4] and ordered him to attack Santaji. Now, Santaji defeated Dhanaji comprehensively and captured Rajaram Maharaj in the process.'

'He captured his own king?' Murar was half-sitting, half-standing by now.

'Yes. Santaji told Rajaram Maharaj, "I am the same loyal servant as before. But you must see that Dhana is not my equal. I will do whatever you bid me to do." Saying so, he set Rajaram Maharaj free. Despite capturing Rajaram, Santaji did not desire the throne. However, Rajaram was completely shaken up by the fact that Santaji should capture him and then stand before him in apparent mock submission—promising to serve him dutifully.'

'Then what happened?' Murar was on edge.

'Rajaram could never trust Santaji again. He released him from service,' Sidhoji's face fell even as he recounted the story.

'But Santaji could have sat on the throne if he wanted to. Couldn't Rajaram Maharaj see that?' asked Murar innocently.

'Yes, but that was not who he was. Rajaram did not want to risk being put in the same vulnerable position again. So suddenly, Santaji found himself demoralized, without a king and without an army. He was free to roam the wild. But this freedom had a flavour of homelessness, not liberty. It was just what Dhanaji Jadhav and Aurangzeb each needed to plot his end; they hated him enough to hunt him down.'

'Did they hunt him down?' asked Murar. He couldn't contain his curiosity any more.

Sidhoji smiled and said, 'Rajaram Maharaj and his loyalists could have done so many other things—such as kept him under house arrest for instance, like Shivaji did to Sambhaji. However, the sorry state of the Maratha pettiness at the time was such that instead of trying to find a way to win back Santaji, he was stabbed in the back. It was during his bathing routine, known only to his own soldiers, that Santaji was killed. Nagoji Mane[5] is considered responsible for the killing.'

Murar felt his eyes welling up.

'Murar, you need to understand what happened here. Santaji's death changed things for everyone. Your grandfather Bahirji was shaken. One of his brothers, Maloji, had lost his life, trying to protect Chhatrapati Rajaram. The second, Santaji, was killed by agents of Rajaram,' Sidhoji paused for impact.

Bahirji's shock and sense of betrayal sunk in for Murar. A part of Sidhoji also wanted to explain why he himself was not in the Maratha court any more.

'Bahirji was aghast that Rajaram should use his resources to finish his warrior brother, instead of focusing on the real threat, the Mughals. It is, therefore, understandable that he didn't feel the same level of loyalty any more,' Sidhoji explained.

Murar nodded. It was natural for his grandfather to feel unsure of what the future held for him, after both his brothers died for Rajaram.

7

Loyal from a Distance

Murar was mourning the memory of Santaji's death that night, as he lay down to sleep.

By all accounts, it seemed that Santaji had definitely been reckless, short-sighted and hot-headed; his anger and his own rancid words betrayed his intense loyalty. But wasn't it possible to rein him in for the benefit of the Marathas, rather than kill him?

Murar learnt from Nimbkar during subsequent conversations that Bahirji's shock and anger at his older sibling Santaji's death seethed at first and then solidified to caution. He didn't trust that the right decisions were coming from Chhatrapati Rajaram's court any more. Generations of loyalty to the Bhosales, it seemed, had come to nought.

However, Bahirji had always been a wise warrior. He continued to profess his loyalty but, subtly, diminished his involvement in the Maratha court.

Murar felt raw about how his ancestors had been sidelined. He sought his father, so he could feel closer to Santaji and quench his own insatiable curiosity.

'Do we have any paintings of Santaji, Sarkar?' Murar asked Sidhoji.

Sidhoji was engrossed in paperwork—after all, he had three principalities to manage—so he didn't respond immediately. But Murarirao persisted, and his father finally answered.

'Murar, we were warriors. We never made our own portraits. We never made jewellery for our women. We never made lavish palaces. We just knew how to fight wars and be loyal,' said Sidhoji.

Murar looked around his own home and acquiesced.

'What does "Hindurao" mean, Sarkar?' he asked, referring to their family title, which Rajaram had conferred on Bahirji.

'It means "the chief of this land". These are our lands, Murar, and we are natives of Hindustan. For the longest time, people from outside—like Aurangzeb—have tried to lay claim to our lands. But Chhatrapati Shivaji Maharaj knew that we had to reclaim our lands.'

'"Hindurao" sounds nice, Sarkar.' Murar seemed happy. 'Even Ghorpade sounds nice. One day you have to tell me how we got our name.'[1]

Sidhoji returned to his papers but Murar had more questions.

'What happened after Bahirji Ajoba moved away from the Maratha court?'

Sidhoji knew that his son was not one to give up. These were uncomfortable questions but sooner or later, he had to answer them. He spoke up, 'Bahirji was untrusting, specifically of Chhatrapati Rajaram. When I was very young, Rajaram Maharaj died after attempting to attack Aurangzeb. He was just thirty when he died of lung disease. His courageous wife Tarabai[2] took the reins. Unfortunately, her senapati was Dhanaji Jadhav—the man widely believed to have been tasked to kill Santaji.'

Murar knew that there were two people he didn't like. One was Aurangzeb and the other was Dhanaji Jadhav.

'Bahirji would never work with Dhanaji! However, appearances were kept up and Bahirji remained loyal to Tarabai.'

'And what happened to Chhatrapati Sambhaji's son Shahuji?'

'Do you remember that the brave Yesubai stayed back in Raigad to save Rajaram Maharaj? She and her son Shahuji were captured by the Mughals. Later, when Aurangzeb died[3]—this was in 1707—the Mughals became very weak. There was no clear succession there either. So, in a last-ditch attempt to weaken the Marathas, they released Shahuji[4] from captivity. They knew it would create a rift in the ranks; divide loyalties and create a civil war-like situation among the Marathas.'

'So Shahuji was released, only because the Mughals who held him in captivity didn't know what to do with him and they thought he would be a bigger nuisance to Maharani Tarabai[5] than to them?' Murar was following the story intently.

Sidhoji nodded. 'Aurangzeb's sons and Shivaji Maharaj's descendants were both fighting over power. There was bedlam all around. The unfortunate thing was that instead of joining hands and routing out the Mughals who were completely dispersed after Aurangzeb's death, Maharani Tarabai chose to attack Shahu.'

'Why?' asked Murar, genuinely confounded. 'They could have instead attacked the Mughals together!'

'If only we had answers to why families behave the way they do, Murar! While preparing to attack Shahuji, Tarabai had a shock of her own. Her designated senapati Dhanaji Jadhav switched to Shahu's side. She had to flee and take shelter in Panhala.'

Murar couldn't believe what he was hearing! 'Dhanaji had cheated Santaji Ajoba also earlier.'

Sidhoji laughed at Murar's choice of words.

'It seems that way to us for sure but there will always be other versions. Dhanaji Jadhav died soon after, around 1708. Before this, Tarabai had carried forward the war of Maratha independence bravely, for eight long years, as Regent for her minor son.[6] All this time Shahu Maharaj was imprisoned, and she was the only one holding a torch for the Maratha Empire. She was greatly skilled in cavalry and strategic movements and was hailed as "Mahishasurmardini"[7] meaning, the slayer of demon Mahishasur.'

'Wow!' exclaimed Murar.

'Shahu tried everything to get Maharani Tarabai over to his side. He attacked her, sent her peace messages. He had the capacity to bring her to her knees in no time.[8] But Maharani Tarabai believed she deserved more than being seen as less in rank to Shahu.[9] The catch was that Shahu had neither the energy nor inclination for it. Besides, his own nobles, generals and advisers were averse to the idea of entirely crushing Tarabai. For, in that case, Shahu would become extremely powerful[10] and their own petty interests would suffer. They needed to have two people they could pit against each other.'

Murar didn't really like what he was hearing.

'Shahu Maharaj occupied Satara and Tarabai was in Panhala. This was around 1709. Tarabai then reached out to Bahirji to be her senapati. But he died around the same time, having consolidated his estates extremely well and being loyal to the Marathas to his last day.'

'Did you ever get to observe Bahirji Ajoba closely?' Murar asked,

'Yes. I used to accompany your *ajoba*[11] on most of his expeditions. So, I was well aware of everything that was happening. In 1710, Tarabai shifted her capital from Panhala to Kolhapur, citing that Panhala, though a formidable military stronghold, was not suitable for a kingdom's growing capital. She installed her son Shivaji II on the throne there. Tarabai is credited with being the founder of the Kolhapur kingdom, more popularly known as "Karveer Rajya" in the vernacular.'

'Whom did you join?'

'As Dhanaji's son Chandrasen Jadhav was with Shahu Maharaj at the time, eventually I joined Maharani Tarabai's army as the senapati,' said Sidhoji.

'Then why did you leave for Sandur?' asked Murar.

'I left Maharani Tarabai's court in 1714. Here, in Sandur, I am an independent ruler of my own kingdom and I am not forced to take sides. When I was in Kolhapur, I was fighting against my own people, not protecting Hindavi Swarajya. My own brethren were switching sides and loyalties for no reason. That's why I left. But no sooner than I did so, than Rajasbai,[12] another widow of Rajaram Maharaj, put Tarabai in prison and took over the reins as regent,' Sidhoji said. He paused and added, 'But enough for today. I am tired now!'

It was around 1716 when Sidhoji received more land from Sambhaji, Rajasbai's son,[13] via a formal *sanad*–a letter that was enforceable like an ordinance. Surprisingly, his branching off made him an independent power, enabling him to strike deals and seek favours, not just for the Marathas but also for other Nawabs, Nayaks or whatever they decided to call themselves.

Our hero, Murarirao Ghorpade, all of twelve years old, fully aware of his past, uncertain of his future, was making sense of his legacy. He constantly tried to reconcile what he had heard about his ancestors and create his own identity. His primary regret was that the Maratha power waned the way it did, and he didn't know what would come of these warring factions.

He did feel let down at times that his father's work had no major cause attached, larger than their own survival. While he was grateful that his father ensured every possible kind of training, in every possible weapon, for him, he wondered–what was he preparing for?

Murar had a lot to think about.

8

Not So Mad, After All

By 1719, the Mughals were a pale shadow of themselves. Aurangzeb's son Bahadur Shah ruled from 1707 to 1712 but after his death, there was a succession of 'blink and miss it' rulers.

Fifteen-year-old Murar was very fond of writing in his diary. He had his own interpretations of everything his father, mother, Nimbkar and Madullah had narrated to him. He lived a comfortable life and was looking forward to shaping a few achievements of his own.

His questions to his father had also become more open-ended and less pointed than before.

One day, after dinner, as the two of them were sitting together, he asked, 'What is happening to the Mughals?'

'They are in their own mad struggle. It is son against son, puppet against pretender[1] and all sorts of consequences. Anybody who thinks they have a chance is jockeying for the throne. Others have created small fiefdoms of their own and pronounced themselves rulers of that place,' said Sidhoji with pure distaste.

Murar appeared dejected.

'Look at the brighter side. I'm taking care of Gajendragadh, Sandur and Gutti for you. Just as the Mughals chieftains are out there grabbing whatever they can, so are many of the Palegars[2] and smaller Maratha chiefs. Everyone is out for themselves. I am choosing to take care of my family,' said Sidhoji in a bid to cheer up Murar.

Later in the day, Sidhoji was watching Murar master the *patta* (sword) and *vita* (corded lance). Murar moved skilfully, making swishing sounds, shifting his feet as if he were defending himself against multiple soldiers who had surrounded him.

Sidhoji watched in amazement. Within himself, he wasn't sure whether he was happy or that he had made the right choice by choosing to move away from the Maratha court. Those who came before him had the honour of serving Chhatrapati Shivaji Maharaj. What would he not give, for a day of serving such a great man. The thing that bothered him though, was whether he was setting the right example for Murar. So much had changed since Bahirji's times. What kind of environment would Murar have to survive in, and would he be ready?

Parallelly, Murar was facing a dilemma about what he must do. After much thought of whether he would be betraying his father by asking such a question, he finished his lessons, walked over to Madullah and asked, 'Why do you think Sarkar had to come from Kolhapur to Sandur?'

Madullah said, 'Moving away from court was not really Sarkar's decision alone. It was your Ajoba, Bahirji, who was disillusioned. Your father also felt that he wasn't serving Hindavi Swarajya because the Marathas had shifted focus from evicting the Mughals to fighting among themselves.'

'Murar, human relationships are not simple,' observed Nimbkar. 'Did you know that Zinat-un-Nisa,[3] a daughter of Aurangzeb who never married, brought up Shahu Maharaj like her own son, during the time of his imprisonment? When Shahu came of age, two brides were found for him and his marriage was celebrated with the pomp and grandeur befitting his rank. Isn't it strange that a Mughal princess should love Shahu Maharaj as her own son?'

Madullah continued, 'Aurangzeb's other daughter Zebunissa; she was very skilled. But Aurangzeb imprisoned her for the last twenty years of her life. If a father could do this to his daughter, then why couldn't Rajaram order the killing of Santaji?'

Murar made a face as if horrified. Then he drew a king in the mud and stamped all over it.

Madullah laughed. 'Whose face are you stomping on?'

Murar winked. 'Guess.'

Murar ran back home, and asked his father, 'When are you teaching me how to use the *baghnakh*,[4] Sarkar?'

Sidhoji raised his eyebrows even as Laxmibai laughed and said, 'If you teach Murar well, he will be as good as Santaji.'

Murar's body was trembling with excitement. He wanted to make his mother proud of him. Even the disintegrating Mughals would need to be pushed out of Hindustan, after all!

If only Murar knew then, who his real bête noire would be. The decline of the Mughals and the disunity of the Maṛathas was the vacuum that created the space for the French and the British to make a play for India.

9

A Matter of Faith

One might draw parallels between the great Shivaji Maharaj and Murar's upbringing. Thanks to his mother's insistence on his education, Murarirao had a wonderful way with words and could write eloquent letters, which he would later employ when he was trying to negotiate between the French and the English.

His mother's strong views on faith had a profound impact on him. As he weighed his predecessors' actions against his mother's teachings, her words rang in his ears: 'No one should abandon their duties because he sees defects in them. Every action, every activity, is surrounded by defects as a fire is surrounded by smoke.'[1]

So Murarirao grew up a very balanced man. However, one trait that he might have inherited from the quick-tempered Santaji was his waspishness. He would say things on the spur of the moment that could well have been avoided and, eventually, this would put him in big trouble with Haider Ali.

As he blossomed into adulthood, here's what we seem to know about Murarirao's physical appearance. Students of history in Madras in the 1920s recall the well-known historian G.S. Srinivasachari[2] creating the following picture of Murarirao in his lectures: 'A grand personality–a tall man with long arms (*ajanubahu*) and long strides, walking majestically up the Gutti Fort, and sitting like an eagle on an elevated spot that is known as "Murarirao's seat" to this day.'

In the initial years, Murarirao fought many a battle under his father's leadership and, above all, developed a daring and independence of spirit that were to distinguish him as one of the bravest soldier-statesmen of his time in the Deccan.

Murar's seat, an artist's impression
Source: Ghorpade family

Writing about military conflicts in the Deccan at the time, Robert Orme[3], the famous historian of eighteenth-century India, has this to say of Murarirao and his troops: 'He soon made himself admired and respected by his neighbours, enlisting none of his countrymen but such as were of approved valour, and treating them so well that they never entertained any thoughts of quitting him: on the contrary, the whole army seemed as one family.'

Aurangzeb exited this world (more than 300 years ago), in the winter of 1707. He was buried in a simple, open-air grave in Khuldabad, Maharashtra. In contrast to Humayun's imposing tomb of red sandstone in Delhi or Shah Jahan's lavish resting place at the magnificent Taj Mahal in Agra, Aurangzeb's grave made no demand that he be remembered. In accordance with Aurangzeb's wishes, the tomb was plain and unmarked, located within a Sufi shrine. Over the centuries, marble floors were added, as well as a marble railing and an identifying plaque. Even with these embellishments, however, the modesty of Aurangzeb's tomb issues a strong contrast to the massive blocks of stone that boldly proclaim the burial sites and earthly legacies of his predecessors.

Aurangzeb: The Life and Legacy of India's Most Controversial King
Audrey Truschke (Stanford University Press, 2017)

Section 3

Kolhapur Mahalaxmi

10

Sidhoji and the Mahalaxmi Temple

There is no date assigned to Murarirao's marriage, but Indrajeet is confident that he could not have crossed his eighteenth year. So, one could suppose that, in the year 1723, he was already married to Sagunabai.

It was on the day of Dussehra, 8 November 1723, that Sambhaji welcomed Sidhoji to Kolhapur to preside over a function to reinstall the powerful idol that had been kept hidden to save it from the Mughal generals. Called 'Ambabai' or 'Mahalaxmi', the investiture of this powerful idol was a privilege being granted by the Chhatrapatis to the Ghorpade family to honour generations of their loyalty.

Sidhoji Ghorpade, wife Lakshmibai, son Murarirao, daughter-in-law Sagunabai—all made the trip. The idol still remains a favourite of devotees all over India. It is one of those monuments that elevates Kolhapur's gravitas; in fact, and one may say that Kolhapur's distinction, in ancient and mediaeval ages too, was that it happened to be the home of Goddess Mahalaxmi. It was a famous place of pilgrimage and known as Dakshina Kashi or the Kashi of the South.

There is no consensus on when this temple was built. Madhukar Shripad Mate,[1] in his book, *Temples and Legends of Maharashtra*, argues that the date of the temple is not earlier than the seventh century. On the other hand, Padma Purana,[2] which is a collection of ancient legends, ascribes the creation of the temple to Lord Vishnu. In fact, Lord Vishnu is believed to reside in it in the form of Mahalaxmi. Since Vishnu is also said to reside in Kashi in Varanasi in the form of Shiva, Kolhapur got the name of Dakshina Kashi. A third version says that the temple of the goddess Mahalaxmi was built by Karnadeva[3] in 634 CE during the Chalukya reign.

Whether this temple was created by Lord Vishnu himself, or by a humble stone carver and installed by one of the later Kadamba kings,[4] the point is that the idol of Mahalaxmi at the temple had always been held in the greatest veneration by all Indians. In Aurangzeb's time, no temple was safe[5] and a temple that was particularly precious to the locals,[6] even less so.

Indrajeet offers perspective. 'Whenever devotees knew that a Mughal ruler was on their way, they would remove the idols from the temple and hide them in plain sight. Mahalaxmi of Kolhapur met with the same fate. Did it happen when the menacing Shaikh Nizam[7] laid siege to Panhala in 1689? Or on some other earlier occasion when a general of Bijapur's Adilshah was camping in the vicinity? What is clear is that the goddess was safe but not in the temple. We do not know when she was taken away. But locals estimate that she was in hiding[8] for almost forty-three years.'

Greeting the guests at the function was Tara, the daughter of the Shrimant Bhattji, the local Raj Purohit, who was responsible for carrying out the ceremony with due procedure.

To be the effectuator of the restoration of the Mahalaxmi temple was a great honour for Sidhoji Hindurao Ghorpade. The investiture ceremony was grand, befitting a revered deity who was coming back 'home' after forty-three years. A sacred and elaborate ritual that marked the consecration of the deity's presence within the temple premises followed. The locals of Kolhapur had begun preparations days in advance, with meticulous purification of the temple and the idol. The main act of investiture involved Shrimant Bhattji infusing life into the idol, symbolizing the deity's manifestation in the physical form. Intricate rituals that included the chanting of sacred verses, offerings of flowers—chiefly the lotus, the goddess's favourite—incense and food, elaborate *aarti*[9] sung with ardent worship amidst the resonance of bells and conch shells, followed–making this a day of great vitality, vibrations and vibrance. It was surreal.

The night of the ceremony, as Sidhoji's family was preparing to rest, Murar could not sleep. What he had witnessed that day shook him to his core. It reminded him of everything Madullah and his mother had told him about the grand coronation of Chhatrapati Shivaji Maharaj. The idea that invoking God's blessings could invigorate the power vested in a place or person was powerful. He was wondering whether history had anything in store for him at all; was he ever going to be put in a time and place where he would be the subject of such a massive infusion of divine blessings? Lost in thought, he heard someone scream. Lakshmibai heard it too and came out of her room immediately.

As they ran towards the voice, they saw the figure of Tara standing and trembling, her eyes bloodshot and her hands holding five lotuses each.

Tara was exactly Murar's age. She was beautiful in a way that those who beheld her felt protective of her. Hers was a gamine, frail beauty.

At this very instant though, there was nothing frail about Tara. It seemed that she could pick up the whole house and throw it if she wanted to. Such was the power exuding from her person.

Not knowing any better, Lakshmibai knelt before her. So did Murar. Both of them closed their eyes. It wasn't uncommon for a deity to possess a person and speak through them, in their culture. Lakshmibai was given to faith, not doubt. There was eerie silence all around for a while. All ten lotuses fell on Murar's head as Tara spoke, 'I will protect you!'

Saying this, Tara went into a trance, shaking uncontrollably till she fell, unconscious. Lakshmibai and Murar never spoke about this to anyone. They did not know what others would make of it and did not want to dilute their own divine moment with the opinion and judgement of others.

But in that moment, Murarirao Ghorpade found a sister he would cherish all his life.

11

Murarirao, the Chief of Gutti

As stated earlier, Murarirao Ghorpade was born sometime around 1704.[1]

He was twice blessed; his grandfather Bahirji and his father Sidhoji were wise observers, not given to impulse. You may recall that Bahirji had served under Rajaram and been the chieftain of Gajendragadh.[2] Later, Sidhoji captured the fort of Sandur[3] and made it his residence; far away from both Satara and Panhala.

Murar's confusion over which faction of the Marathas was stronger was also clearing. On the one hand was Chhatrapati Shahu Maharaj and on the other was Maharani Rajasbai's son Sambhaji. They fought a battle along the River Varna in 1730, during which Shahu's superiority was a foregone conclusion. After all, he had the courageous Peshwa[4] Bajirao on his side.

There is a letter expressing Shahu Maharaj's delight at receiving Murarirao at Satara on 14 November 1730. This could be a conclusive indication that Sidhoji wasn't alive at the time, because the letter addressed him as Murarirao Hindurao Ghorpade. It would be only upon Sidhoji's death that the title 'Hindurao' would pass on to his son Murarirao. Thus it would appear that, around the age of twenty-six, Murarirao had come into his own.

It so happened that Murarirao was reasonably wealthy. He had inherited a Deccan triangle of sorts–Gajendragadh and Gutti from Bahirji and Sandur from Sidhoji. Even as he travelled to all three places routinely, he eventually made Gutti his seat–he was often referred to as the Chief of Gutti.

There is a story behind his choice of Gutti.

In a letter dated 21 January 1731, addressed to Murarirao Hindurao Ghorpade, Chhatrapati Shahu informs Murarirao that he has restored to him the rights that he had earlier annulled, of being entitled to the sardeshmukhi income of the territory stretching from the Panchganga to Kanyakumari.

As he read the letter, Murar felt good but aimless. Mother Lakshmibai was his best counsel, to decide what to do next.

'Aai, I would like us to move to Gutti, There is nothing to do here. Baba has already taken care of everything and one of our cousins can manage Sandur. There is a lot more work to be done in Gutti,' Murar said.

'Why do you feel so?'

'Gutti is more strategic. It is sandwiched between the Nawabs of the Carnatic on one side and the Nizam-ul-Mulk of Haiderabad on the other. It can be attacked at any time by the various self-styled Nawabs and Palegars that are teeming all around. Also, if the Marathas call on me to fight, I can do more from Gutti than from Sandur.' It seems obvious, of course, in hindsight.

When Murarirao took over, Gutti Fort had nine gates. Murarirao built five more. He also conducted several repairs and made strategic fortifications.

Lakshmibai had witnessed Bahirji's and Sidhoji's frustrations before. She could plainly see that Murar wanted his life to be of some consequence. He wanted history to remember him. She nodded and asked, 'What if the Marathas don't call you?'

Murar knew that this was coming. 'I will administer Gutti Fort and its precincts like a welfare state, like Shivaji Maharaj. I will train my own army and protect what we have. I will build horse and elephant stables and an armoury.* I will protect the farmers, the livestock breeders, the traders and the community workers who give us food and goods.'

'What about Gajendragadh?'

'Our cousins are taking care of it well. Besides, their silversmiths and goldsmiths and their riches are made for a life of comfort, not

* Refer to Annexure 5 to study how innovative the Marathas were with their weapons.

for a warrior like me. I will visit Gajendragadh and Sandur from time to time.'

Indrajeet explains, 'At Gutti, Murar would spend days honing his skills on horseback or in swordsmanship. Sometimes, he would sit and meditate under a peepul tree. He would regularly perform the *Surya namaskar*[5] and read all available *pothis*[6] of the time. On days when he had to oversee administration, he would live in the sandstone hills of Gajendragadh. There he would visit temples, go hunting, check on important trading ports such as Hubli, the welfare of the people, etc. The Lambanis[7] would often pass by, getting goods from all over the place.'

Murarirao oversaw the administration and collection of tributes from Raydurg, Chitradurg, Harpanalli, Anegundi, Kanakgiri, Kanchanguda and Bellary, among others.[8] To preserve and protect this, he had no choice but to train and maintain a strong and highly efficient military force. In fact, Sidhoji had also lavished attention on Gutti and built it into an impenetrable fort that could withstand a prolonged siege.

Murarirao would become a power to reckon with in the affairs of the Carnatic. He was guided several times by Tara, whom he sought advice from, from time to time. From 1731 to 1739, Murarirao spent his first eight years as a ruler consolidating his position at Gutti and the surrounding areas.

Watercolour painting in the nineteenth century by Justinian Grantz (1892–62) titled *Gooty Church Garden, Andhra Pradesh.*
Source: Wikimedia Commons

Remember that Murarirao was not affiliated to any Chhatrapati or Peshwa directly; he fashioned himself an independent contractor of sorts—with his own flag and coin (pictures below)—even while his core philosophy was that these lands must be ruled by his own people and no one else.

Flag of the Ghorpades, an artist's impression
Source: Ghorpade family

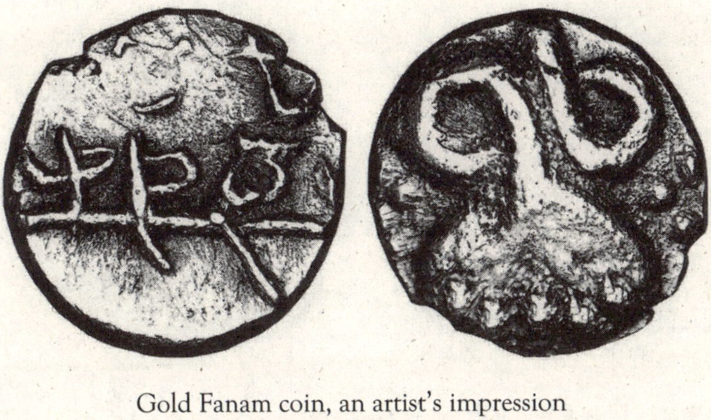

Gold Fanam coin, an artist's impression
Source: Ghorpade family

Yet, thanks to the teachings of his childhood, Murarirao decided to make himself available for any Carnatic expeditions of the Marathas. He was their cousin holding the fort, far away from Satara and Panhala, who could be called upon as an ally if something untoward happened in the South. Murarirao knew that, from a historical point of view, he owed his loyalty first to the Maratha kingdom; a kingdom free from the despot Aurangzeb.

As the wise Chhatrapati Shahu Maharaj[9] of present-day Kolhapur puts it, 'To understand the Marathas, you have to understand the Mughals. Aurangzeb is a key figure in Maratha history. The resentment against him was a pivotal factor that united the Marathas, even after Shivaji Maharaj's death. Think about it; which other king in history has stayed away from his kingdom for twenty-seven years and set up camp outside to defeat his enemy?'

The fact remains that after Aurangzeb, the Marathas suddenly did not have this big common enemy to unite against. So, they became enemies of each other! And into the Maratha mix came the Peshwas.* Chhatrapati Shahu was, in fact, the patron of the Peshwai period, which began in 1713 under Balaji Vishwanath. After 1720, the new brave face of Peshwai was his son, Bajirao.

* Refer to Annexure 2 to understand more about the rise of the Peshwas.

Hindavi Swarajya is a very powerful idea and we must dwell on its meaning a bit. Scholars have weighed in on a letter from Shivaji to Ajobaji Naras Prabhu Deshpande of Rohidkhore on 17 April 1645 where he wished for a 'Hindavi Swarajya'. The authenticity of this letter is doubtful. Historian Setumadhavrao Pagadi** views it as 'Indian rule'. Other historians suggest that since the Mughal rule was based on 'Islam', Shivaji might have also indicated respect for the religion of the land–Hinduism–as a prime objective of freedom. To achieve this, he knew that he would not just have to be a warrior but also a statesman. He was the first to realize the importance of having a naval force,*** and therefore he strategically established a navy and forts along the coastline to defend the Konkan side of Maharashtra. Jaigad, Vijaydurg, Sindhudurg and other such forts still stand to testify to his efforts and ideas. His military strategy included a deep awareness of guerrilla tactics such as raiding, ambushing and surprise attacks on his enemies.*

As a statesman, he created a group of trustworthy men around him. He was a just administrator. He took the establishment of his Hindavi Swarajya identity a step further when in 1674, he crowned himself as Chhatrapati with Vedic rites in the ancient Hindu tradition. It is said that the courtiers and wazirs of the Mughal Empire laughed,

* J.V. Naik, 'The Foundation of Swarajyaya', in *Shivaji and Swarajyaya*, edited by Indian Institute of Public Administration (Bombay: Orient Longman, 1975), pp. 43–57.

** Setumadhavarao Pagdi was an Indian civil servant, a polyglot, an accomplished historian and a distinguished man of letters, who specialized in modern Maratha history, especially the history of Shivaji.

*** Shivaji Maharaj is often referred to as the 'Father of the Indian Navy'.

called Shivaji an upstart. But Aurangzeb understood Shivaji's larger vision and was irked by it. Shivaji represented a direct challenge to Aurangzeb's efforts of converting the entire Indian subcontinent into Dar-ul-Islam.***

---

* Historian Medha Deshmukh Bhaskaran, in her book *The Life and Death of Sambhaji* (Penguin, 2021) writes, 'Aurangzeb was obsessed with thoughts of Shivaji's coronation. He feels apprehensive and vulnerable–despite having hundreds of warrior Tatar women from Russia, trained to kill with their bare hands, all over the place, including on the ramparts fortified with battlements; despite the gunmen and the archers crowding the towers overlooking the streets of Shahjahanabad and the banks of the Yamuna River. Aurangzeb is furious–the sultanates of the Deccan could not handle a landholder. The older sultans of the Adilshahi and the Qutbshahi have died; the new Adil Shah, Sikandar, is just eight years old, while the Qutb Shah, Abul Hassan, the son-in-law of the erstwhile Shah, has twenty thousand women dancers in Haiderabad and remains busy holding lavish parties for his wealthy friends. The Shia kingdom's courts are riddled with conspiracies, failed coups, murders and internal strife among the power-hungry nobles. This has allowed infidels like Shiva to grow strong. For the first time in his life, Aurangzeb regrets throwing out all the soothsayers from his empire.'

** This refers to the dominion of Islam, namely, any structure (be it a home, community or state) that allows the free practice of Islam.

Part 2

The Mughals

'More often than not, whenever a great ruler dies, it creates a vacuum. The line of succession is often unclear. The dead man has no place in Parliament; he cannot bequeath his membership and he can never know for certain who will succeed him after his death.'*

* Nobel Prize-winning German writer Elias Canetti famously said this in his book *Crowds and Power* (Victor Gallant Ltd: 1962).

Section 4

Many a Succession Battle

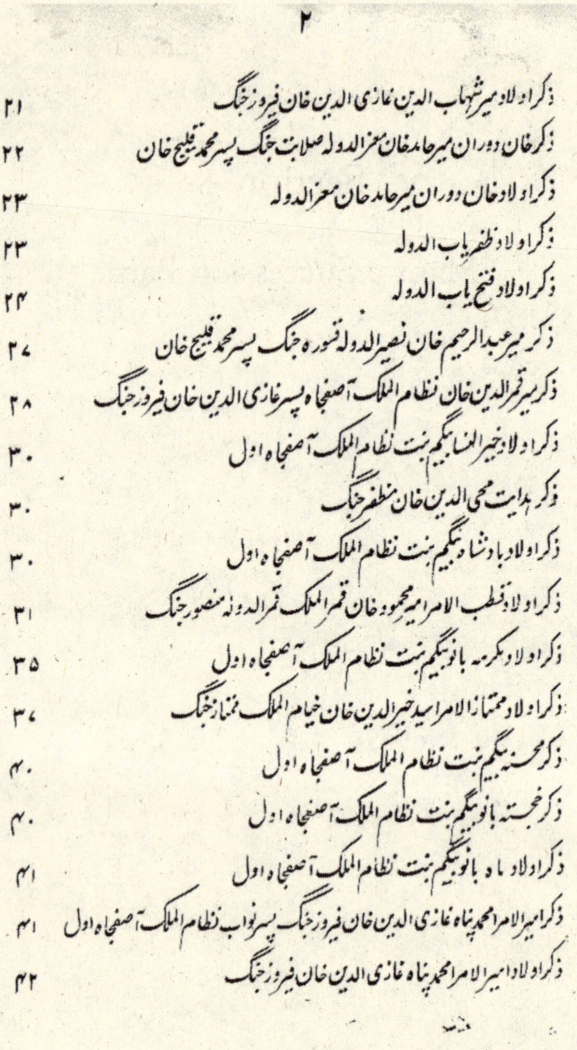

۲

ذکر اولاد میر شہاب الدین غازی الدین خان فیروز جنگ	۲۱
ذکر خان دوران میر حامد خان معز الدولہ صلابت جنگ پسر محمد قلیج خان	۲۲
ذکر اولاد خان دوران میر حامد خان معز الدولہ	۲۳
ذکر اولاد ظفر یاب الدولہ	۲۳
ذکر اولاد فتح یاب الدولہ	۲۴
ذکر میر عبد الرحیم خان نصیر الدولہ قسورہ جنگ پسر محمد قلیج خان	۲۷
ذکر میر قمر الدین خان نظام الملک آصفجاہ پسر غازی الدین خان فیروز جنگ	۲۸
ذکر اولاد خیر النسا بیگم بنت نظام الملک آصفجاہ اول	۳۰
ذکر ہدایت محی الدین خان مظفر جنگ	۳۰
ذکر اولاد بادشاہ بیگم بنت نظام الملک آصفجاہ اول	۳۰
ذکر اولاد قطب الامرا میر محمود خان قمر الملک قمر الدولہ منصور جنگ	۳۱
ذکر اولاد مکرمہ بانو بیگم بنت نظام الملک آصفجاہ اول	۳۵
ذکر اولاد ممتاز الامرا سید خیر الدین خان خیام الملک ممتاز جنگ	۳۷
ذکر محسنہ بیگم بنت نظام الملک آصفجاہ اول	۴۰
ذکر خجستہ بانو بیگم بنت نظام الملک آصفجاہ اول	۴۰
ذکر اولاد ماہ بانو بیگم بنت نظام الملک آصفجاہ اول	۴۱
ذکر امیر الامرا محمد پناہ غازی الدین خان فیروز جنگ پسر نواب نظام الملک آصفجاہ اول	۴۱
ذکر اولاد امیر الامرا محمد پناہ غازی الدین خان فیروز جنگ	۴۲

The name of Khajista Banu Begum, Urfiyat (pet name) Saheba, features fourth from the bottom on page 9 of *Shajarah-i-Asafiyah*. She remained *nakad khada* (unmarried) as per official records. The names of all the daughters and sons-in-law are available in the book *Nizam-ul-Mulk Awal*. Courtesy of Salar Jung Museum

12

Aurangzeb's Breadcrumbs—The Nizam Becomes a Power in the South (1671–1748)

SHAJARAH-I-ASAFIYAH

A Detailed Geneological account of Nawab Nizam ul-Mulk Asaf Jah's Family

Compiled by

Nawab Muazzam-uddawlah Muazzam ul-Mulk Muhammad Badarud-din Khan Bahadur Rafa't Jang, the fourth son of Amir i-Kabir Shams-ul-Umara Nawab Muhammad Fakharuddin Khan Bahadur in 1252 A. H.

and Supplemented by

Nawab Munawwar Jang Mir Jahandar Ali Khan Bahadur in 1301 A. H.

with a Foreword by

Nawab Jivan Yar Jang Bahadur, B.A., Bar-at-law,
Chief Justice, High Court of Hyderabad,

Edited by

Hakim Sayyid Shams-Ullah Qadri,
Honorary Member, ' Societe de l'Histoire de l'Inde Francaise

with an Introductory Note, Historical References and Geneological Tables,

Printed at the Ahd Afrin Press,

Published by The 'TARIKH OFFICE' Hyderabad.

Foreign Agents,

LUZAC & Co., 46 Great Russell Street, London, W.C.1.

1938

Courtesy of Salar Jung Museum

Time to meet Nizam-ul-Mulk, a key actor in Murarirao's story.*

Many historians believe that Nizam-ul-Mulk was brought up in the traditions of Aurangzeb. Probably he resembled him more than he did any other leader; the similarity consisted in their possession of a distinct political aim and their capacity and will to achieve it.

He grew in the ranks under Aurangzeb. In 1702, Emperor Aurangzeb appointed him as the Subahdar (governor) of Bijapur and presented him with a horse. He was also handed the *faujdari*[1] of Azamnagar and Belgaum in the same year and of Nusratabad and Mudgal in 1704.

Following Aurangzeb's death in 1707, his presumed heirs engaged in an accession war, during which Asaf Jah maintained a neutral stance, supporting none of Aurangzeb's sons. This is probably why, on ascending the throne in 1713, Aurangzeb's grandson Farrukhsiyar named Asaf Jah Viceroy of the Deccan region, giving him control of six Mughal governorates and the Carnatic territory, as well as grand titles like 'Fateh Jung'.

The structure of what the Nizam governed in the Deccan looked something like this.

- Direct control of the six *subhas* or provinces of the Deccan—Khandesh, Bijapur, Berar, Aurangabad, Haiderabad and Bidar.
- Overlordship of the five subhas of the Carnatic (formed from old Bijapur and Golconda sultanates)—Arcot, Sira, Cudappah, Kurnool and Savannur, which in turn were headed by self-styled Nawabs.

The three Hindu kingdoms—Tiruchirappalli, Thanjavur and Mysore—called themselves independent. Also independent of the Nizam was Murarirao Ghorpade's territory. And then there were the Marathas, who governed a large territory of their own.[2]

* Refer to Annexure 3 for an extract from an essay about Nizam-ul-Mulk.

Portrait of Asaf Jah I, Nizam of Hyderabad.
The first nizam of Hyderabad with attendants,
ca. 1745. Unknown provenance.
Source: Wikimedia Commons

So far, so good! On the personal front, Nizam-ul-Mulk[3] was from a very illustrious family.[4] He had one legally married wife and four concubines[5] who bore him five sons and two daughters (this is one version of the number of his children). Other versions say that Nizam-ul-Mulk had six sons and six daughters).[6]

Study the Nizam's family tree on page 62.

Khair-un-Nisa was his favourite daughter. However, the names of the daughters aren't frequently mentioned and not much is spoken about them. We will get to know one of them better soon.

Among his sons, the older one was Mir Ghaziuddin followed by Nasir Jang, who were born of his lawfully married wife. Then there were three more sons from his mistresses–Salabat Jang, Basalat Jang and Nizam Ali, in descending order of their age. This is what is documented conclusively.

With a perpetual power struggle[7] in the North, Nizam-ul-Mulk felt the need to maintain some continuity with the evanescent Mughal rulers. Hence, he sent his eldest son, Mir Ghaziuddin, to Delhi.[8]

Map of the Carnatic wars (1746–1760). *From Historical Atlas of India* by Charles Joppen, public domain via Wikimedia Commons.jpg.

13

The Nizam's Departure to Delhi

Among the Nizam's contemporaries, the intrepid Bajirao succeeded his father as Peshwa on 17 April 1720 and was under the employ of Shahu Maharaj. The Nizam fully understood the problems of the Deccan. Now, here was the issue from the word go: from his very first assignment in the Deccan in 1713, the Nizam opposed Shahu Maharaj and supported Sambhaji of Kolhapur.[1] The Nizam also challenged the Maratha claims to the *chauth*–a tax amounting to one-fourth of the produce–of the six Mughal subhas of the Deccan agreed upon earlier by the treaty of 1719.[2] His contention was that the agreement with the Marathas was inconsistent with the authority vested in him in the Deccan.

To resolve this, Bajirao met the Nizam on 4 January 1721 at Chikhalthan. The Nizam was thoroughly impressed by the persona, foresight, courage and reputation of Bajirao. After the meeting, he issued two *farmans*[3] on his own authority as the Viceroy of the Deccan, by one of which he permitted the agents of Shahu to realize chauth from the province of Bidar, and by another to collect sardeshmukhi from the six subhas of the Deccan. Bajirao had started on a good note!

It was around this time that Nizam-ul-Mulk himself was called to Delhi. He helped Mughal Emperor Mohammad Shah get rid of the meddlesome Sayyid brothers, and in return was appointed the Grand Vizier on 21 February 1722. Nizam-ul-Mulk advised Mohammad Shah to be 'as cautious as Akbar and as brave as Aurangzeb'.[4] However, this fell on deaf ears. Mohammad Shah, also called Rangila,[5] was a frivolous and spoilt young man, and the Nizam's relationship with him was tenuous. However, the Nizam kept up appearances, making the nobles of Delhi extremely jealous. They started to plot against him and the following were the immediate fallouts:

- In 1723, Nizam-ul-Mulk was abruptly transferred to Awadh, and in 1724, the entire Deccan region was placed under Mubariz Khan's control.
- Mubariz Khan openly declared that he was not prepared to pay chauth and sardeshmukhi to the Marathas.
- Peshwa Bajirao was enraged. He was well aware of the decrepit condition of the Mughal Empire. He knew that the Emperor was worthless; the nobles were jealous of one another; the government had broken down; and the army was inefficient. He assumed an openly hostile attitude towards the Mughals.
- Bajirao had his own problems too, within Shahu's court. He and Shripatrao, Shahu's *pratinidhi*—representative of the king—were locked in a duel for domination in the Maratha state. Bajirao believed he could strengthen the Maratha state much more by a policy of open war rather than begging for the payment of chauth and sardeshmukhi from the Deccan. Shahu had a different opinion. He felt he should be grateful to the Mughals for recognizing his kingdom and was in no mood for war. He was so against Bajirao's intentions that he even threatened dismissal, if a personal meeting was not immediately arranged to discuss the difference of opinion.
- This personal meeting did happen. Bajirao[6] reminded Shahu and Shripatrao how Shivaji, with far less resources, had defied the Mughals at the height of their power. He had seen the indolence, imbecility and, above all, the wealth of the Mughals and appealed to the religious zeal of King Shahu, urging him to drive out the persecutors of Hinduism from the holy land of Hindustan. He also reminded them that the Nizam was a political genius and never to be trusted.

Meanwhile, the Nizam's second son, Nasir Jung, had taken up more responsibilities in the administration of the Deccan and his seat was in Haiderabad. Over time, there were ideological differences between the father and the son. Nasir Jung eventually wrote a letter to his father, asking him to stay in the North so that he could take care of the Deccan by himself.[7]

However, to Nasir Jung's dismay, in 1724, disenchanted by the lack of purpose in Delhi, the Nizam found his way back to the Deccan and sought Shahu's help to decimate Mubariz Khan.[8] He was successful with this, and he consolidated Haiderabad as his new capital in due course.

We are at a critical point in history now.

The fifteen-year period between 1724 and 1739 was the time when the Nizam was looking to consolidate his power. He knew that his path to further expansion lay towards the south and that, in order to do this, he needed to create dissent in the Maratha ranks. This was also the time when the brave Peshwa Bajirao had convinced Shahu Maharaj that the Maratha Empire needed to expand in all directions.

However, Murarirao Ghorpade, chief of Gutti, had no instructions from the object of his allegiance, Chhatrapati Shahu, to become part of any military campaign. He was focused on running Gutti as a welfare state and shoring up its agricultural output, livestock and water resources.

14

The Nizam's Back and Forth with the Marathas

The Nizam was a wily player.[1]

In the beginning of 1725, he settled down comfortably in Haiderabad. Mohammad Shah, seething at the death of his favourite, Mubariz Khan, decided to cut the Nizam down to size by taking away the 'wazirship' of Delhi and the 'governorship' of Gujarat and Malwa. Therefore, instead of having his attention all over the place, the Nizam decided to focus exclusively on the Deccan. He decided to quietly consolidate his hold for a couple of years, even participating in Shahu Maharaj's twin trips to Karnataka in 1725 and 1726. While he kept up appearances, his real aim was to create rifts in the ranks of the Marathas. He knew when to step forward and when to step back.

First, he told Shahu that he need not maintain Maratha tax collectors—who also kept a check on events—in Haiderabad. He would make an annual payment to them instead. Shahu agreed, despite Bajirao's warnings.

Meanwhile, Bajirao's expeditions south of the Krishna River made the other Maratha regent, Sambhaji II, nervous. He applied to the Nizam for help. In fact, he left his kingdom to his mother Rajasbai and spent the period between 1726 and 1728 with the Nizam.

The Nizam now supplicated to Shahu that Sambhaji II believed that he should have claim to half of Shahu's territories. And that, unless this dispute was settled, he would not be paying up the chauth and sardeshmukhi to Shahu! This was a completely duplicitous move. Even the trusting, non-confrontational Shahu Maharaj was shocked to see what the Nizam was up to. He had bared his fangs in the guise of demanding fairness for Sambhaji II.

This was not all. The Nizam waited till December 1726, when Bajirao went on a campaign to the South, to open hostilities. He exploited the differences between the pratinidhi and Bajirao as well as between Kolhapur and Satara courts to create rifts and weaken Shahu Maharaj. But he went too far when he captured Poona and crowned Sambhaji the Chhatrapati. In April 1727, Bajirao returned to help Shahu. Shahu realized his mistake in not paying heed to Bajirao's advice to never trust the Nizam. With most of his own armies engaged in battles in various places, Bajirao went back to basics, employing guerrilla tactics to trap the Nizam at Palkhed,[2] where a battle was fought in March 1728. It was an astounding win for the Marathas, given the Nizam's extensive planning and the size of his army. But Bajirao's military prowess was exceptional.

Defeated and surrounded by Shahu's troops, Nizam-ul-Mulk restored[3] Shahu's claim to the Deccan chauth and sardeshmukhi and his title as Chhatrapati, also vowing not to support Sambhaji II of Kolhapur. But Bajirao knew that the Nizam's promise was not enough and that Sambhaji Raje II[4] had to be dealt with decisively.

In 1731, the Nizam looked to support another Maratha, Trimbak Dabhade,[5] against Bajirao. However, Dabhade[6] himself died at the battle of Dabhol before anything could come of this. Naturally, other than Bajirao, the Nizam had a few other headaches too, given how large the domain under his jurisdiction was.

15

Connecting Back to the Ghorpades

Let us pick up a couple of threads from Shahu Maharaj's early attitudes towards the Nizam and the Mughal Emperor. In complete contrast to his aggressive Peshwa Bajirao, Shahu did not wish to ruffle anyone's feathers. He was submissive and looking for legitimacy to be granted to him by the Mughals.

Ironically, everything that Aurangzeb had tried to impose on the Marathas, and which they had resisted with such determination and fury, was now happening. The Marathas had always collected their chauth and sardeshmukhi as a matter of right, not as agents of the Mughals. But now, since they were divided into two factions, they were prepared to give up their claim that they were the masters of their land, and both sides were anxious to be recognized by the new Mughal Emperor, Bahadur Shah, as his vassals who had the franchise to collect these taxes in the Deccan. Thus, both Shahu and Sambhaji II sought external recognition for their own freedom and their permission to collect taxes. Even though the Mughals were on the decline after Aurangzeb, it was the Marathas who elevated them.

So, what did the Mughal Emperor do? He refused to take sides. And it was this curious turn of events that brings Murarirao back into the story.

Bahadur Shah Zafar grandly told the respective emissaries of Shahu and Sambhaji II that they would have to fight it out, and whoever won would be accepted as the Maratha king. This person would be subordinate to the Mughals, and a sort of agent authorized to collect taxes on their behalf. Funnily enough, Shahu and Sambhaji took the enfeebled Mughals seriously and set out eagerly to prove that they were the legitimate faction. Instead of attacking the Mughal Empire at its weakest, they were so myopic that they were fighting against each other! They began to gather allies, and both the Maratha sides courted Sidhoji Ghorpade.

What did Sidhoji do?

Indrajeet Ghorpade pitches in. 'Before we come to that, Sambhaji II wrote a letter to Sidhoji, giving him the news that he had granted the villages Mangawati and Sadalge to Santaji Ghorpade's widow, Soyarabai.[1] Sidhoji promptly sent his messenger to say that he should be granted a 3 per cent share of the revenue (*nadgoundi*) of the village of Chikodi. In June 1716, Sambhaji II duly granted this request in a formal sanad followed by a personal visit.'

Did this tilt Sidhoji's balance in favour of Sambhaji II?

Indrajeet continues, 'Not really. Sidhoji had become aware that, in the ongoing war against Shahu Maharaj, Sambhaji had decided to align himself openly with the Nizam. The two of them had planned to crush Shahu's faction. There was a brief period during which Shahu began to look vulnerable and both sides wanted Sidhoji[2] on their side again. Sidhoji realized that a fight could not be put off for long. It is understandable that Sidhoji did not want to be dragged into a war against two brothers.

'Shahu had Bajirao on his side. The final war between Shahu and Sambhaji, which had been going on for all of twenty-two years, was finally decided in March 1730, when the two armies met head on, at the banks of the River Warna, about twenty kilometres north of Kolhapur. Shahu won a convincing victory but imposed surprisingly light terms on his adversary and cousin, Sambhaji,' explains Indrajeet.

So, did Sidhoji manage to maintain good relations with Shahu Maharaj?

'Oh, yes. In fact, Shahu wanted Sidhoji Ghorpade to join him with his contingent.[3] He was preparing for a final onslaught to resolve the ownership of the Maratha kingdom. But Sidhoji still did not take sides.'

Why?

'We will never know for sure. Eventually, north India fell to Shahu's share and the south, including Karnataka, to Sambhaji II's. In accordance with this division, Shahu sent off a dispatch to Sidhoji Ghorpade asking him to hand over the fort of Koppal to a nominee of Sambhaji. Now is when Murarirao enters the story. He and his wife Sagunabai, travelled from Gutti to Satara ostensibly to congratulate Shahu on his victory.'[4]

'Having taken over from Sidhoji, Murarirao now waited patiently[5] for someone to call upon him for war. Ideally, one that did not involve him fighting between two factions of Marathas!

Section 5

Wily Little Kingpins

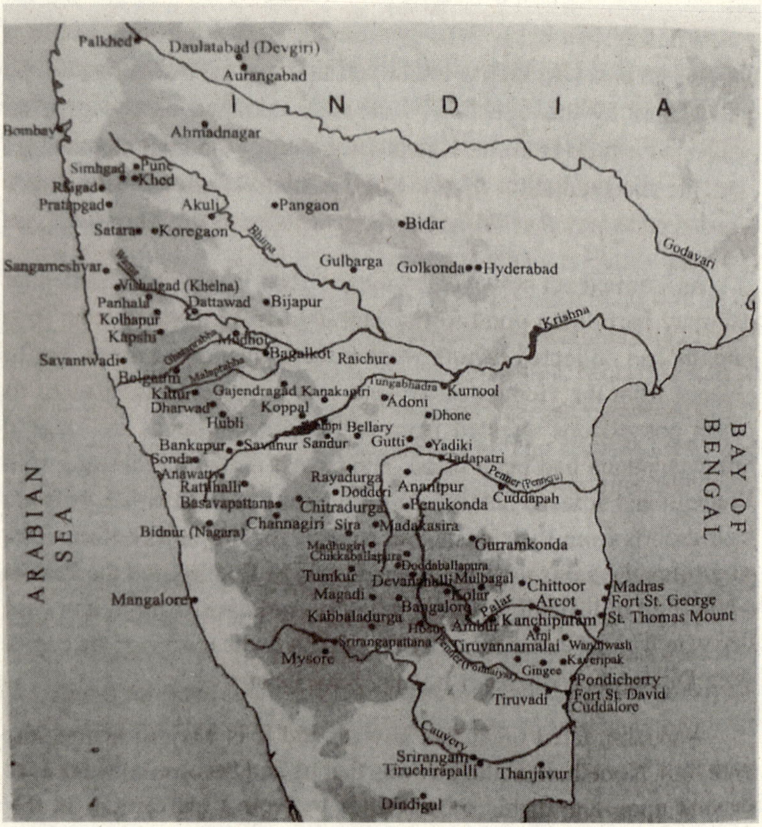

Peninsular India of the eighteenth century
Courtesy Manohar Malgonkar

16

More Headaches for Nizam-ul-Mulk

After 1725, even though the Nizam had all the time in the world to focus on the Deccan, the Marathas occupied most of his time till 1731. Nevertheless, he took seriously his overlordship of the five subhas of the Carnatic–Arcot, Sira, Cudappah, Kurnool and Savannur, headed by self-styled nawabs.

Now, we need to pay attention to Arcot. And we have to pay special attention to a character named Chanda Sahib, who is integral to our story.

Let's back up a bit to understand the situation in the Carnatic, before we come to the 1730s again.

(Refer map on page 76 to see the location of Arcot.)

The Nawayath[1] king Sa'adatullah I had ruled over Arcot since 1710. This was before Nizam-ul-Mulk was made Viceroy of the Deccan, which he was in 1713. By virtue of him having been in power before the Nizam's interest in the Deccan, Sa'adatullah I felt it was all right for him to exercise a certain amount of independence in thought and action.

Thus, he changed a few things.

Arcot was a place where the issue of succession was traditionally settled by 'selection', as opposed to dynastic inheritance.[2] However, Sa'adatullah I had taken over Gingee (in Arcot) in 1715 by war and wanted to retain power in his own family. But he had no children of his own, so he adopted a nephew named Dost Ali and nominated him as his successor.

He obtained the private consent of the Mughals in Delhi but omitted to secure the approval of his immediate superior,

Nizam-ul-Mulk.[3] This was a definite slight to the Nizam. However, it wasn't possible to find much fault with Sa'adatullah I because he ruled with moderation and success, and his death in 1732 was generally considered the loss of a good man.

Dost Ali succeeded him in the nawabship in 1732. But the Nizam had been unsympathetic towards Sa'adatullah I and hence his successors, so no formal sanad[4] confirming this appointment was ever issued from Haiderabad. Despite this, Dost Ali remained in power[5] peacefully.

Dost Ali had two sons, Safdar Ali and Hasan Ali. One of his daughters was married to his diwan, Chanda Sahib, a wily old fox. Within three years of his accession, Dost Ali had devoted himself to religion, leaving the details of government to his son Safdar Ali and son-in-law Chanda Sahib. It is recorded that Governor Benyon[6] offered presents to these two nobles when they visited him in 1735.

Of humble origin but shrewd, capable and resourceful, Chanda Sahib was both ambitious and unscrupulous, and totally devoid of loyalty even to his own father-in-law, who had given him everything he owned. Chanda Sahib also had the foresight to cultivate deep and enduring relations with the French[7] during this time, which would hold him in good stead in the future.

And the opportunity to cash in on this relationship came after 1736.

Chanda Sahib, an artist's impression
Source: Ghorpade family

17

A Problem Named Chanda Sahib

Now, we are in 1736.

Close to Arcot, in Trichy (refer map on page 76), a Hindu kingdom, the raja died, nominating his senior queen Meenakshi as his successor. The raja's sons challenged her supremacy and sought the help of the Nawab of Arcot to intervene. As is the norm, when families fight and call the neighbour to resolve the dispute, only the neighbour wins!

Dost Ali promptly dispatched his son-in-law, Chanda Sahib, with a strong force, which at first subdued the rebellion in some of the disputed territories. Thereafter, Chanda Sahib formed his own designs and sought to gain entry into the capital itself.

Crafty and deceitful, Chanda Sahib managed to persuade the rani that his only purpose in wanting to come into the fort was to help her to consolidate her rule.

The gullible Meenakshi, after making Chanda Sahib swear on a copy of the Koran[1] that he would do nothing to harm her interests, got the gates opened for him. As soon as he made himself secure within the fort, Chanda Sahib seized the city of Trichy and imprisoned the lady, who thereupon died of shock and grief.

Chanda Sahib fashioned himself the Nawab of Trichy and declared himself the sixth Nawab of the Carnatic. Dost Ali, who had a spiritual outlook to life, was deeply saddened at Chanda Sahib's treachery with the queen. Further, it seems he had sidelined his own son Safdar Ali and had no repentance about it.

There is another version, however, which suggests that Dost Ali encouraged[2] Chanda Sahib to wage wars of aggression against the other neighbouring states, including the Maratha state of Thanjavur. Dost Ali knew that Chanda Sahib was a gifted warrior and that his aggressive ways would help him elevate himself from Nawab of Arcot to Nawab of the Carnatic.

Meanwhile, Nizam-ul-Mulk was upset with both Dost Ali and Chanda Sahib. These events dangerously increased the power and influence of Dost Ali, whose objective, it seemed, was to create an independent kingdom in the south of India and to wean himself off all allegiance to the Nizam.

In 1736 and 1737, Bajirao's courageous excursions in the North kept all of the Mughals, including the Nizam, occupied. There can be little doubt that if the Nizam had been free, he could have made a dash for the South and punished both Dost Ali and Chanda Sahib. Instead, he asked the Marathas to take care of Chanda Sahib. The Marathas[3] were absolutely willing[4] to do it.

After all, the Nizam himself, the supposed guardian of the whole of the Deccan, had as good as given them a free hand, and perhaps even his unexpressed blessings. The nawabs by themselves would be no match for their arms. However, the Marathas took their time,[5] as they too were cautious about the threat of a potential invasion to their lands by Nadir Shah of Iran, the winds of which were already being felt by Delhi. With Bajirao campaigning in the North, they did not want to dispatch a column to the South just yet.

In 1739, Nadir Shah attacked Delhi[6] and the Nizam faced humiliation[7] at the hands of the Persian king.

As news of this humiliation spread, an emboldened Safdar Ali Khan, the son of Dost Ali, attacked Thanjavur in 1739, stirring up a hornet's nest. He deposed Shahaji III and placed another son of Tukkoji named Pratapsingh on the throne. With Arcot, Trichy and Thanjavur seemingly under Dost Ali's control, he looked very menacing in the Carnatic.

In hindsight, Thanjavur was a costly mistake by Chanda Sahib. This was the land given to Vyankoji, Shivaji Maharaj's half-brother, by their father Shahaji Bhosale.

Maharajah Vyankoji[8] had been the founder of Maratha rule in Thanjavur, ruling from AD 1676 to 1683. After settling down at Thanjavur, King Vyankoji devoted his entire attention to the improvement of agriculture and the economic condition of his subjects by providing irrigation facilities, digging and widening of channels and constructing new tanks to obtain better yield. Lands lying low were brought under cultivation and harvests of the year were usually rich, excelling the records of many preceding years. Thanjavur, with its temples and its natural bounty, became a rich principality with time.

The Thanjavur Marathas were the original Maratha bloodline and, in 1639, it so happened that, barring the rule at Thanjavur and Murarirao's trifecta of forts, the Marathas had negligible presence in the region.

But an attack on their cousin woke up the Marathas, who had been unable to send a contingent to the South to rein in Dost Ali, up to this point. They would, soon!

The most tragic fallout, however, was the dangerous precedent set by Chanda Sahib. He was the first prince of the Carnatic to secure the assistance of French troops from Pondicherry for the conquest of Thanjavur. He opened the floodgates of armed intervention by the British and French traders-turned-colonialists into the internal affairs of Indian rulers, to tilt the balance between rival contenders for power.

18

The Nizam's Harem

Having met the people forming the public side of the Nizam's life, let us take a peek into his private life—a few womenfolk and his harem.

All the women in Nizam-ul-Mulk's life—his wives, six daughters and concubines—and the other royal ladies, lived in the harem, which was the women's quarters. It had a battalion of people. The thumb rule was that the Nizam's first wife or the wife who bore him his oldest heir would be the head of the harem. It is believed that within the harem, women had a lot of freedom. Historians believe that the unmarried daughters of the Nizam were spared from the purdah.[1] They moved around openly in the residency and the palace.

The harem was a part of the palace precincts.

The life that the royal Mughal women led was opulent. From the moment they woke up right till they retired at night, there was someone at every turn who held up a brush or a mirror for them. In fact, there was a lady whose only job was to brush each princess' long lustrous hair!

The harem would have many *khwaja saras* (hermaphrodites) who would attend to their every need. This would include running errands and procuring things from the market and, of course, providing important gossip! Within the harem, it was possible to kill and bury someone who had brought disrepute to the family or was found to be a spy or even a traitor of any sort. So, it could be a dangerous place. '*Haram ke muamlat haram me hi dafan ho jaate they*,' said research scholar Amena Begum authoritatively. This translates to, 'Matters of the harem were buried within the harem, they never came out!'

Most of the Nizam's daughters would have *majhabi taleem* or religious education in the Arabic language. However, to understand Arabic, you had to learn Urdu, so they knew that as well. Within their harem and certain sections of the palace, there was no purdah. But their arrival to any part of the common royal residences would be announced so that men could clear the area of the palace they were visiting. Their *tassavur*—or glimpse by a man outside—was simply not possible.

The head of the harem would usually decide what had to be cooked in the kitchen depending on the men's schedule and how many people would be in the palace that day. There were designated market days where caravans would come and the women would know in advance whether apples would be available, saffron was being sold or dry fruits. Other than seasonal produce and hunt, the preparation of daily meals was an elaborate pursuit within each royal kitchen.

The other important person within the harem was the diwan, who would make entries of the expenses, money, grains and revenue—both in and out. The diwan had a special role because they had to finance the next war, sometimes suddenly, with swords and steel, as required. The diwan would know how much tax was collected from the land at any given point in time and whose accounts were pending.

The diwan would also share allowances with the ladies—for clothing and jewellery. The royal palace would be visited by Persian jewellers, who would bring topaz, turquoise, rubies, lapis lazuli and jade.[2] Precious stones were used as an aphrodisiac very commonly.

While the afternoon rest was sacrosanct for the ladies of the harem, evenings would be sessions of gossip, matchmaking, hookah and wine. There were several games allowed within the harem, such as Ganjifa cards sourced from Egypt.

With all this happening, the harem was a lively place. The ladies had access to a lot of information because of their network of servants. This information could be as lethal as state espionage! The only challenge was when they fell ill. Whatever could be prescribed locally and any medicine that could be administered without a male touch, was allowed. Preserving health, therefore, was easier than managing illness. It was not uncommon to have hermaphrodites trained in basic medicine to manage the health of the princesses and the ladies.

The royal family ate food in jade plates, because they would change colour if there was poison in the food.

What about their social life?

In fact, not much is known about the pastimes of the ladies of the Nizam's family. But because of the Mughal influence, we can perhaps use this reference.

During the Mughal times, the royal ladies sometimes had the opportunity for outdoor recreations and amusements side by side with indoor amusements. Outdoor recreations were provided in the forms of hunting expeditions such as falconry, visiting palaces for sightseeing or holiday excursions to places of scenic beauty like the Kashmir Valley, and in playing outdoor games like *chaugan* (polo), pigeon-flying, kite-flying and watching animal fights. In all these recreations, the Mughal women participated along with their menfolk.[3]

Hunting,[4] in fact, was pretty popular in the Deccan. Moreover, Mughal daughters born to royalty had to be prepared for a life of uncertainty. They often travelled along with the royal army[5] and they were vulnerable to being captured. Therefore, princesses got the same education as their brothers, not just in statecraft, but also horse-riding, arithmetic, calligraphy and philosophy. The chief requirement was unquestioning loyalty. They had to be prepared to die at any time. They had access to wealth and they had access to the ear of the rulers, who were their fathers and brothers, and were free to bury themselves in academic or artistic pursuits as was suitable to their stature.

But could they mix with the commoners in their realm?

Amena Begum offers perspective again: 'The commoners and the royalty did not mix at all. There was a *zafar paltan*[6] and *dhol-nagada* announcing the movement of a royal carriage at all times. For example, when they went hunting, the path would be cleared, announcing the *khawateen's*[7] arrival, so that all commoners could clear the road, all the way from the palace to the hunting ground. Each lady would be in her own *tanga* (carriage) with heavy purdah—not just in the front as we know it today, but from all four sides.'

Deedar or sighting of a royal princess was not possible at all.

There is a reference to a time when Peshwa Bajirao was invited to the *Zanan Khana*[8] at the Nizam's palace by his Begum Sahiba. This was when the Nizam's base was in Aurangabad. Bajirao travelled with a large contingent, but as he got closer to the palace, he kept deploying people along the way. A hundred people reached the palace, but at the appointed place of meeting the Begum, Bajirao was allowed to take only two of his most trusted lieutenants. They were separated from the womenfolk by a purdah and asked to sit on the other side. The womenfolk were genuinely pleased to see the charisma and vigour of Bajirao. Begum Sahiba had picked a garment as a gift for Bajirao, and she moved the purdah, stretched out her hand and gave him a paan. This was a rare occurrence for them.

The librarian at the Salar Jung museum added, 'An event like the Nizam's daughter's[9] wedding would be like a celebration across the land. Let's call this *paanch jumaagi.*[10] All the subjects would get clothes and there would be biryani for the entire kingdom on the day of the wedding.'

Amena Begum says, 'Marriages of the Nizam's daughters were permitted only with the Paigah families; there was an understanding to that effect. The Paigah palaces[11] were all close to the Nizam's palace. In fact, the rulers would keep an eye on their daughters and not get them married to people more powerful than themselves for fear of being attacked.'

For all their pomp and splendour, the Nizams lived in constant fear. It is documented that not a single Mughal ruler has ever gone on Haj, while in power. '*Koi bhi takht chodke nahin jaata tha*,' explains Amena Begum, which means that no one felt safe enough for religious travel, while in power.

History reveals that the first Nizam, Asaf Jah, was extremely busy with war and had very little time for anything else. It was only from the third Nizam's time that the education system, welfare, promotion of poetry, etc., took prominence.

There is one person in the harem who is of particular interest to us. The Nizam's fourth daughter. Her name, as we have shared before, was Saheba.

Indrajeet elaborates, 'I have known about Saheba since my childhood. Her beauty has been described to me in many ways, by my grandfather, who regaled us with stories about her.'

Of the Nizam's six daughters, he had a clear preference for Khair-un-Nisa, who was the older one. Saheba, much younger, was left to her own devices. This is because by the time she was born, the novelty of 'babies in the harem' was also past. What is known is that Nizam-ul-Mulk had great affection for Khair-un-Nisa and he would speak to her about things closest to his heart.

'Now, the lady of our interest, Saheba, was an extremely intelligent girl and very fond of the arts. Her assistant, the hermaphrodite Rankha, was her best friend and confidante. She would go to the market and get everything that Saheba needed for her paintings. It is believed that, in a moment of inspiration, Saheba painted a brave warrior on a horse and then waited for him to appear in her life!' adds Indrajeet.

To describe Saheba, a beautiful saying by Vladimir Bartol, who wrote *Alamut*, comes to mind:

> A person can spend his whole life between four walls. If he doesn't think or feel that he's a prisoner, then he's not a prisoner. But then there are people for whom the whole planet is a prison, who see the infinite expanse of the universe, the millions of stars and galaxies that remain forever inaccessible to them. And that awareness makes them the greatest prisoners of time and space.

Saheba was a prisoner of her vivid imagination, and she wanted to be set free. And it seemed that the time would come soon.

Saheba, an artist's impression
Source: Ghorpade family

We have already established that a vacuum was created by the collapse of the Mughal Empire and the disunity of the Maratha Empire. Several European challengers were ready and waiting in line. But, eventually, it was a tug of war between the British East India Company (EIC) set up in 1600 and the French Compagnie des Indes, founded in 1664. The latter's main settlements were at Pondicherry, a day's sailing south of Madras, and at Chandernagore, about 24 km north of Calcutta.

For much of the eighteenth century, Anglo–French rivalry in continental Europe would be played out by their respective trading companies in India. The outbreak of the War of the Austrian Succession (1740–1748) and the Seven Years' War (1756–1763) coincided with power struggles in South Indian states that had become independent of Mughal rule. This gave both companies the opportunity to intervene politically and militarily in what were purely domestic affairs.

The architect of this policy was Joseph François Dupleix (1697–1763). Described by the English scholar Lawrence James as 'a man of dynamic energy who combined ambition, cupidity, Anglophobia and belligerence in roughly equal parts', Dupleix would become Clive's chief rival. In 1742, he was transferred from Chandernagore to assume the governorship of French possessions on the Coromandel coast. This is where all our action is.

In 1739, Safdar Ali Khan, the son of Dost Ali, had just attacked Thanjavur and both the Marathas and the Nizam were livid. Foreign powers got involved!

Part 3

The Foreign Factor

Section 6

Foreigners, Favours and Fangs

19

The Foreign Foursome

When it comes to India, there are four European powers that are worth a mention and unfortunately, their invasions were marred by brutal genocides.

If not for the early invasions by the Portuguese and the Dutch, a market for Indian goods would not have been created and the English and French might have never known the richness of produce of the land of Hindustan. But why did it come down to a tug of war between the French and British only?

First came the Portuguese. They dominated all the sea routes between the Indian Ocean and Europe via the Cape of Good Hope for most of the sixteenth century, thanks to the establishment of this route by the successful journey of Vasco da Gama from Portugal. Blessed with superior fire power to intimidate rulers and traders in Asia, the Malabar coast was their initial domain of violent conquest as well as centre of trade. They bombarded and destroyed Calicut[1] to show how dangerous they were. At one point, other than Hormuz at the entrance of the Persian Gulf, they had factories-cum-naval bases established along the west coast of Hindustan, Macau in China, Timor in Indonesia, Malacca close to Singapore and Colombo in Sri Lanka. They started calling their territories *Estado da India*, with Goa as their headquarters.

The Portuguese were so powerful, that other ships had to carry a card or passport[2] issued by *Estado da India*, if they wanted to sail these territories. They also got involved in local political disputes and embedded themselves in Indian society. It was only towards the end of the sixteenth century that the Portuguese monopoly on the Cape of Good Hope began to be challenged by other European traders. It was the Dutch that came knocking first.

Dutch colonialism was fronted by a joint stock company from the Netherlands called VOC. They started by trying to take over some of the Portuguese locations. Their main interest was in Indonesia, but when they found that the prices of spices in Bantam were higher than they expected, they bombed the city and killed the indigenous people brutally. Evidently, nutmeg, mace and pepper were seen to be more precious than human lives. Similarly, the VOC's conquest of Banda Islands involved a genocide.[3] The directors in Amsterdam had actually instructed officials to repopulate the islands. The Dutch were so strong at the time that when a few servants of the newly founded EIC tried to gain a foothold in the early seventeenth century, they were brutally wiped out.[4] Similarly, the VOC made Java the base of its operations.

India became crucial to the Dutch when they discovered that cotton textiles from Gujarat and the Coromandel were in demand in South Asian markets. While it was easy to get access to Pulicat and Nagapattinam by dislodging the Portuguese, the real battle was for Surat, which was a major supplier of textiles, but also a premier port of the Mughal Empire.

The Mughals encouraged the rivalry between the Portuguese and English because it meant more competitive trade for Surat's merchandise. A market for Indian textiles was being developed in Europe. For example, the Dutch unlocked the potential of Indian trade by finding a market for Bengal raw silk in Japan.

And so it was that when the EIC wanted to put its roots down in the seventeenth century, the Dutch stranglehold over South-east Asian spices was tough to break. The good thing for them was that they had set up a textile factory in Surat in 1613, even before the Dutch, and this, along with sourcing tea from China and indigo from India, was a good start to their trade. Later, a United East India Company was formed, which enabled more traders and financiers to participate in the lucrative trade in Asian merchandise. The first actual settlement of the British[5] began after Andrew Cogan, an agent of the EIC, reached Madraspatnam on 20 February 1640. The British built Fort St George, which led to the creation of what we will refer to hereon as Madras.[6]

The seven islands of Bom Bahia, which were in Portuguese possession till the mid-seventeenth century, were transferred to the English crown by a marital dowry in 1665.[7] With this, Bombay became the western headquarters of the EIC, and they had some presence in Bengal as well. The EIC solidified its trading position step by step. It is to their credit that in the first decade of the eighteenth century, the English organized themselves better towards commercial profitability.

However, they faltered when they decided to show the Mughals their military prowess; the decision to involve their navy and attack the Mughals backfired badly. *The Cambridge History of India*[8] explains the British war with the Mughals, also called the Anglo-Mughal war of 1686–1690:

> The seizure of some Mughal vessels brought about a rupture towards the end of 1688, with the consequence that the factors (sic) at Surat were imprisoned. Child [John Child of the EIC) in retaliation, captured a number of richly freighted ships. Thereupon ensued a siege of Bombay by the Mughal forces until in 1690, the English put an end to the war by a humiliating submission involving the payment of a considerable sum. Child, whose dismissal was one of the conditions of peace, died just as the negotiations were reaching a conclusion.

At this time, the powerful Mughals, led by Aurangzeb, would let nothing untoward happen in their territory. While it took some time for the EIC to recover from the setback of the war against the Mughals, this is probably one of the reasons why the British chose to train their attention first in the south of India, where the Mughals were practically non-existent.

But Aurangzeb's death changed everything.

So much so, that a decade later, in 1716, on New Year's Eve, Farrukh Siyar, the weak Mughal Emperor, was bullied into issuing a farman, granting the British EIC Company full trading rights.[9] The wolfish EIC had finally managed to make political headway into Mughal India, through a direct relationship with the Mughal Emperor.[10]

But by now another European competitor had emerged on the scene: the French East India Company.[11] During the period between the 1720s and the 1750s, the French and the English were locked in a fierce battle to dominate the colonial enterprise of the Indian subcontinent, even as the Dutch company ceased to be a significant player.

Under Pierre Benoit Dumas, the Governor of the Indian territories of the French East India Company from 1735 to 1741, the French started intervening in local conflicts to extend the scope of their influence. This was the time when the encroacher chief of Trichy, Chanda Sahib, became an ally of the French, who were on the lookout for the right bait to hook a prized catch; an entry into the internal affairs of any state.

The French and Chanda Sahib were soon using each other to further their territorial ambitions. Later, when Joseph Francois Dupleix was appointed to succeed Dumas, he looked at Chanda Sahib as an important ally.

Joseph Francois Dupleix
Source: Wikimedia Commons

20

The Emergence of French Ambition

In the seventeenth century, the French established trading posts in the coastal cities of Surat, Masulipatam and Pondicherry. Other French territories included Karikal, Mahé, Yanam and Chandernagore. These territories were governed by French officials and were largely self-sufficient. They also developed a reputation for treating their employees and local partners fairly.

The period was such that the French saw the Dutch as their main threat—the two were also involved head to head in the War of the Spanish Succession.[1] Correspondingly, this was also the brief period during which the French viewed the British as their friends. When French Governor François Martin thought that the Dutch would besiege Pondicherry, he sent French goods to the English settlement for safety. Later, when the French retained Pondicherry in 1699, Martin again reached out to Thomas Pitt,[2] Governor of Madras, a British settlement, to enter into a treaty of neutrality[3] under which the men and ships of Britain and France were not to attack each other. When a French squadron appeared in Indian waters and began to seize English shipping, the Pondicherry Council did its best to limit its captures.[4]

So far, so good.

The French settlement, though, was in its infancy. The population was small, and its presence reasonably feeble. Everything would change forever in 1720, with the entry of the ambitious French general, Joseph Francis Dupleix.[5]

When Dupleix joined his appointment in Pondicherry, he was convinced[6] that it would be possible to make Pondicherry the principal emporium of trade in southern India. And true to his expectations, during the twenty years—1720 to 1740—the development of its trade put a different aspect on affairs. Attitudes started changing as early as 1721, when the French believed that English merchants were jealous[7] of their trade to Manila. In 1725, the French settlement of Mahé and the English settlement of Tellicherry were almost in open war on the Malabar coast.

By 1736, the English believed that the French had become 'our most dangerous rivals'[8] and at the close of the following year, the English directors wrote: 'The most particular intelligence procurable concerning those powerful competitors, the French and their commerce must annually be communicated to us.'[9]

Thus it was that Dupleix saw this relationship changing colour and directed his own charm towards the natives, princes as well as the people, in the manner that was best calculated to gain the esteem of the locals.

There were two people whom he kept a close eye on. One was Chanda Sahib—a man rich with unscrupulous loot—with whom his predecessor had a good relationship. The other was his Maratha neighbour, Murarirao Ghorpade, who possessed a well-trained, independent army. He courted him constantly, given his reputation as the 'invisible' horseman.

Manohar Malgonkar says in his book, 'The lands Murar inherited were peppered over an extensive stretch of the Carnatic . . . and they were looked upon by the various Nawabs and the neighboring Palegars as legitimate hunting grounds for plunder and appropriation.'[10]

In order to administer his domains, Murar had entrusted Gajendragadh to his younger brother Daulatrao and Sandur to another cousin. He focused on Gutti and it was during the construction of the wells around the Gutti Fort that a wandering herd of Lambanis, vagabond traders who sold clothes, appeared to be passing through. During the day, the locals interacted with the Lambanis, offering them food and water and making sure they were comfortable. However, in the stillness of the night, this troupe—

which was actually a bunch of rogue militia—attacked the locals and started killing the residents, appropriating currency and goods from their homes.

As word of this plunder reached the citadel and was relayed to Murar, he and his troupe of fifty highly trained soldiers came thundering down, stopping briefly at the Gajalakshmi shrine inside the Gutti Fort to take the deity's blessings.

Indrajeet says, 'When Murar rode at full gallop, his body was parallel to the ground. You couldn't see him and so you couldn't target him with spears or arrows! He moved so swiftly that the enemy felt that someone invisible had emerged from nowhere and attacked them.'

The rogue militia were routed completely within minutes. Murar defended his people on various occasions with swift, decisive military action. Word spread that if you ever attacked the village around Gutti, the invisible horseman would kill you!

Murar's stature grew and he made sure he kept it that way. He also made sure that he visited his principalities periodically. Sandur, for instance, with its sparkling river and dark forested hills, was a getaway from the oppressive heat of Gutti and also a chance to take blessings at the Kumaraswamy temple. He also visited Gajendragadh, Koppal (a fort he claimed to maintain for Sambhaji II) and Kolhapur, where his sister Tara lived.

It would seem that Murar was everywhere—and he made sure that his movements and his domains were known.

Meanwhile, things were heating up in Madras.

21

The Emergence of Robert Clive

The favourable trading rights granted by Mughal Emperor Farrukh Siyar to the EIC in 1716 was just the beginning. Madras emerged as a key centre for British trade in southern India, attracting merchants, traders and settlers from across Europe. The Company invested heavily in fortifying Madras against potential threats, including the French, local adversaries and random mercenaries, to protect its trade interests in the region.

Moreover, British officials in Madras actively engaged in diplomatic negotiations with local rulers, including the nawabs of the Carnatic, to maintain stability and secure commercial privileges. Local rulers in the South were enamoured by the British and started soliciting their support in their battles against neighbouring kingdoms. A few also solicited the French, which we will explore soon.

One of the major figures vital to our story is Britain's Robert Clive, a part of the British contingent who went out as clerks and became co-opted into the military mentality of the EIC as it expanded across India. In Madras, he worked in the factories but became depressed and isolated in his new circumstances, trying twice to die by suicide. In 1746, when fighting broke out between the British and the French forces in India, Clive gave up his desk and became a soldier. Few can claim to have changed history with a single decision. Robert Clive is one such.

Thomas Gainsborough (1727–1788) painted a portrait of Robert Clive (1725–1774), also known as 'Clive of India' and Baron Clive of Plassey, in a general officer's uniform
Source: Wikimedia Commons

Robert Clive was an extraordinary man. Born in 1725 into the Shropshire gentry, his uncle declared as follows, 'I am satisfied that his fighting (to which he is out of measure addicted) gives his temper a fierceness and imperiousness that he flies out upon every trifling occasion. For this reason, I do what I can to suppress the hero so that I may forward the more valuable qualities of benevolence and patience.'

Given Clive's proclivity to violence, it is believed that, in desperation, his father Richard Clive, a landowner and lawyer, dispatched his unruly young son to India to become a 'writer'—a junior clerk—in the East India Company. Evidently, it was an unlikely calling for such a pugnacious young man. Robert Clive came to India in June 1744, after a very long journey.

He was just nineteen years old when he arrived, not in Calcutta but in the Company's oldest settlement, Fort St George. Here he spent the next two years fidgeting, seated at a high desk, trying to take an interest in the Company's ledgers or in negotiations with merchants. To relieve the boredom, he spent his spare time in the governor's library, reading voraciously, rectifying at least in part the deficiencies in his education caused by his misspent youth.

Here is the big difference. Clive arrived almost two decades after Dupleix. He was incumbent to an environment where conversations about the Mughal Empire were about their weakness and vulnerability. The Mughals lost Delhi in 1739 and were a non-entity.

As he looked around, the other power to reckon with was Nizam-ul-Mulk, who was the de facto ruler of the Deccan. However, his controls were not very tight. Now, Clive had to find something meaningful and hopefully combative to do. His opportunity came with the outbreak of the First Carnatic War (1740–1748), in which Britain and France supported rival Indian factions.

How he met and aligned with Murarirao Ghorpade is the stuff of legend.

The key thing to conjecture is why, despite a very successful stint against the French, Robert Clive and Murarirao Ghorpade did not become a united force thereafter.

1739 is a landmark year for Murarirao.

Up to this point, he was reasonably happy in Gutti. Sitting in his favourite seat (page 41), this phase of his life, as someone who had isolated himself from the mainstream of Maratha history, was at best a plateau. After all, he was trained to be a warrior. To be fair, after a point, Maratha history is a record of the doings mainly of the Satara branch, and, in particular, of its line of hereditary Peshwas, who had managed to seize total control of the affairs of that branch even during Shahu's lifetime. Murarirao was waiting to be called on to a big battle.*

Suddenly, almost as though by divine design, everything began to fall into place exactly as though Murarirao Ghorpade had personally ordered it. While Bajirao was engaged in another campaign, Shahu ordered Raghuji Bhosle, one of his senior-most generals (an embittered rival of Peshwa Bajirao), to take out an expedition into the Carnatic. His explicit orders were, 'Our cousin of Thanjavur is being harassed by Chanda Sahib of Trichy. You are ordered to meet the Thanjavur Raja and chastise Chanda Sahib.'

Raghuji Bhosle, himself in the grip of a consuming ambition to prove that he was every bit as good a general as Peshwa Bajirao, set out at the head of a 40,000-strong army. The Marathas dispatched messengers to Murarirao Ghorpade to solicit his help in this mission. Thus, he who had been waiting with mounting impatience for an opportunity such as this, suddenly became the man who was all but vital to the execution of Shahu's plan; someone who not only commanded his own highly efficient column but who also knew the terrain and the people of the Deccan and spoke their language.

* It was the Peshwas, not the Chhatrapatis, who became the recognized instruments of the supremacy of Maratha power. They functioned as prime ministers and anyone who had managed to isolate themselves from their policies and campaigns found little or no mention in Maratha history.

Murarirao was fortuitously and obviously, the ideal man to represent Maratha interests in this part of the subcontinent, at this hour. He secretly thanked Tara for this opportunity. It was always Tara who had reassured him at his lowest moments, that his time would come.*

---

* This bought back times of the sanad that Rajaram had given Bahirji Ghorpade more than forty years before, and which Shahu had reconfirmed to Murarirao on the occasion of his visit to Satara, and which, for all these years had looked so meaningless, now acquired a semblance of validity. Once the Marathas had established themselves as the supreme power in the South, as they had already done over much of the North, the sardeshmukhi of the entire tract from Kolhapur to the end of the land belonged, by virtue of that document, to the Hindurao Ghorpades.

Section 7

All Hell Breaks Loose

22

Duty Calling Murarirao

'Our cousin' in Shahu's succinct order to Raghuji Bhosle above, was of course, the Raja of Thanjavur, Pratap Singh Bhosale, who had inherited the *jagir* given by the Adil Shahs of Bijapur to Shahaji Bhosle.

Let's recap quickly.

- As we have already seen, upon the death of the Rajah of Trichy in 1736, Chanda Sahib seized Trichy from its widowed rani and proclaimed himself the Nawab of Trichy. He was not only ambitious but also remorseless. Hungry for more, he was watching the happenings in nearby Thanjavur very closely.
- In Thanjavur, there was complete anarchy following Tukkoji's Maharaj's death in 1736. Ekoji, the king's eldest son and heir apparent, succeeded to the throne.
- Chanda Sahib invaded Thanjavur, wanting to take advantage of the anarchy. However, in spite of his poor health, Ekoji offered a determined resistance and forced him to retreat to Trichy.
- When Shahu Maharaj got to know of this, he had just begun his campaign over Miraj. Founded in the early tenth century, Miraj was an important jagir of the Bijapur Sultanate and Shahu wanted to take control of it. So he ordered Raghuji Bhosale to carry on the campaign further south in the Carnatic. He also reached out to Murarirao

to assist Raghuji Bhosale with this expedition. His express orders to Raghuji were as follows:

'You are hereby ordered to ensure proper security of Tiruchirappalli, Chandawar (Thanjavur), Arcot, Shrirangapatnam, Shire, Adoni, Kurnool, Cudappah and various other Mahals beyond the Tungabhadra. Whatever Sardeshmukhi and Mokasa (revenue) is assessed on these regions, you are to take half of it for the expenses of your army, and the other half you need to deposit with Huzoor (central government). Tiruchirappalli and the other places of the Carnatic should also be under Hindu rule and made to yield annual tribute. You and Kusaji Bhosale work together on this and complete the task. The Swami trusts you completely.'

Swami here refers to Chhatrapati Shahu's spiritual guru, Brahmendra Swami Dhawadshikar, a devotee of the god of war, Parashuram.

Ekoji died after ruling Thanjavur for a year and was succeeded by his wife Sujana Bai. The Madras manuscript[1] assigns her three years of rule, during which time the advisers in the court harassed her to no end. At this time, Sayyid, the *killedar*[2] of the Thanjavur Fort, rose to prominence as kingmaker. He imprisoned Sujana Bai in 1738 when the latter questioned his authority. Kattu Raja[3] became the placeholder king for about a year with the help of the French. Chanda Sahib, who was close to the French, asked Kattu Raja to cede Karikal to the French, in return for their help. Initially, Kattu Raja agreed but later, he changed his mind and, in July 1739, did not let the French land in Karikal. This angered Chanda Sahib. The French were his dear allies.

Chanda Sahib invaded Thanjavur, captured Kattu Raja and imprisoned him. 'He is the son of Kuppi[4], a fisherwoman,' claimed the reprobate fomenter Chanda Sahib.[5]

Neither the Dutch at Negapatnam nor the English at Fort St George were keen to help Kattu Raja come out of this. Pratap Singh[6] therefore ascended[7] the throne after Kattu Raja in 1739, against his own will. Pratap was the son of Tukkoji and Annapurna and a legitimate heir. It was Kattu Raja who explained to him, 'If you die and don't accept the government, both of us lose our heads. If on the other hand, we continue alive, we may watch the course of events.'

Soon after ascending the throne, Pratap Singh Bhosale announced the execution of Sayyid the troublemaker. Pratap Singh was soon deposed, and Chanda Sahib was the menace again, taking over the administration of Thanjavur. This was when the Marathas wanted to intervene and help their cousin.

Thanjavur[8] was a significant Maratha base and a very large and culturally rich principality. Everything now depended on how skilfully, how resolutely, Raghuji Bhosle carried out the task entrusted to him by his ruler, Shahu Chhatrapati. Raghuji had a point to prove. He was an ardent campaigner and a fairly successful military leader, but his achievements in the field were consistently overshadowed by the spectacular victories won by Peshwa Bajirao. And this had caused such deep resentment within him as to have provoked him into seeking an armed conflict with Bajirao in which he had come off second best.

Now he had a great chance to duplicate or even surpass Bajirao's achievements.

He could feel destiny calling out his name.

Truth be told, it was the Maratha obsession with conquering the North that had left the Deccan open for battle. It was only in 1740 that the Marathas looked south.[9]

But Raghuji was more a player of the power game than a soldier; no matter how keenly he longed to outdo Bajirao in the field, what he wanted even more was to have a Peshwa at the centre of affairs subservient to him.[10] Raghuji set out in great style and spirit, at the head of an army of 40,000 men composed of cavalry and infantry. About midway through this march, he was joined by a force of 10,000 men under its leader, whom Colonel G.B. Malleson describes as 'the afterwards famous Murarirao'.

En route to Thanjavur, Raghuji Bhosale and Murarirao Ghorpade's team proceeded brilliantly to bottle up Dost Ali's force (Chanda Sahib's father-in-law) and rout them completely. On 20 May 1740, they swooped down on them and gained a quick and decisive victory. Dost Ali was killed in the Battle of Damalcheri.

'No rout could have been more complete,' comments Malleson. 'The account of this defeat spread dismay and consternation in the Carnatic.'

Raghuji thereafter marched upon Arcot and occupied it without encountering much resistance. Then he turned towards the fort of Vellore, where Dost Ali's son and the man who now hoped to become the Nawab of Arcot, Safdar Ali, had taken refuge. As far as Thanjavur was concerned, though, the Maratha invasion brought about the restoration of Pratap Singh.

But before this battle of Damalcheri took place, the Nizam asked for a meeting to be arranged with Murarirao, who was to play such an important part in the mission to oust Chanda Sahib from Trichy. Recall that the Nizam had given the Marathas his wholehearted blessings to deal with Chanda Sahib. Otherwise, there was no love lost between the Marathas and the Nizam! But both were united in their dislike of Chanda Sahib.

Indrajeet says, 'Meeting Murarirao was the Nizam's way of offering his blessings and checking out the capability of this chieftain to whom such an important task was to be entrusted. Was he up to the task of rounding up this pestilential miscreant?'

23

The Nizam Meets Murarirao

Nizam-ul-Mulk was a rich man.

He had divided his kingdom into three parts–one part became his own private estate known as the Sarf-i-Khas. Another was allotted for the expenses of the government and was known as the diwan's territory. The remainder was distributed amongst Muslim nobles, jagirdars, zamindars and deshmukhs, who in return, paid *nazars* (gifts) to the Nizam for the privilege of collecting revenue from the villages under them. The most important of these nobles were the Paigahs.[1] This schema ensured a steady flow of income, even as the Nizam himself was free to rule or meddle in people's affairs, depending on your perspective.

Therefore, when the Nizam invited Murarirao to Haiderabad, he wanted to check two things:

- was he truly as independent as he claimed
- was he capable of taking on Chanda Sahib.

The invitation was not to his home—reserved for only the most elite—but to a bout of falconry. Falconry[2] is the ancient art of catching wild quarry with a trained bird of prey.

The unschooled, rustic Murarirao was escorted to the open area where the Nizam would ascertain more about his character over a few hours of falconry. Now given that this was a royal expedition, Murarirao was dressed in garments presented by none other than the Nizam himself.

'Welcome, welcome, Hindurao,' said the Nizam.

Murar gave an appropriate but not too obsequious reply.

'Do you know that among falcons, the female or "falcon" is about a third larger than the male or "tiercel"?'

Murarirao knew nothing about falconry. It wasn't really a Maratha practice. He was neither overeager nor disinterested. He was a warrior and his stance showed as much.

'Let me show you,' said the Nizam, appraising his visitor.

Murar watched aghast, as high in the sky, a peregrine folded in its wings and tail, becoming the shape of a tear drop. Then it plummeted downwards at an immense speed and a fairly steep angle, before employing its talons to strike its victim in mid-air. The impact[3] was so heavy that Murar imagined the target must have been killed immediately.

'The falcon kills upon impact,' the Nizam said menacingly, with a gesture to boot. 'For any reason, if the prey is still alive and kicking, it will be quickly torn apart using a special notch on its upper bill—the tomial tooth—that breaks the prey's neck and spinal cord. Like the falcon, in war, you have to be fast and you have to see from a great distance. You have to be able to stun your enemy and choke them. Otherwise, the slippery ones like Chanda Sahib will get away,' said the Nizam.

'We Marathas capture and choke our enemies with speed, just like your falcons,' ventured Murar. 'Enemies like Chanda Sahib are easy, because they slip and fall and can be caught easily!'

The Nizam observed Murar's deadpan manner of speaking and was quite taken in.

Now Murarirao was a man of action. He decided that falconry was interesting enough and decided that he would rather learn the skill than pretend to be amazed all afternoon.

He asked if the royal falconer would agree to teach him. The Nizam was happy and immediately said yes.

As the trainer and Murar walked towards where the falcon was kept, to make it sit on Murar's arm, suddenly, from a completely different direction, another falcon swooped down upon its prey in the distance. The entire action was masterfully orchestrated.

Murar asked, 'Was this from our group?'

The falconer responded, 'Saheba bibi is here. She is better skilled than all the rest! Even the Nizam's own entourage.'

Murar was curious. The royal falconer continued, 'I have never seen Saheba Bibi because we are not permitted to. I trained her personal attendant the eunuch and she trained her in turn.'

Murarirao's two faithfuls, Yunus Khan and Bhujangrao Ghorpade, were listening to everything that was being said. Instinctively, they knew that they had to figure out exactly where Saheba Bibi was launching her falcons from.

Yunus Khan immediately came close to Murar and asked, 'Do you actually want to learn this?'

Murar expressed his angst openly. 'Do you know what is happening all over Hindustan right now? The Holkars have routed the Mughals at Rampura and entered Rajaputana. Bajirao has marched on Delhi and raided Kotah, Malwa has become a Maratha province. And what am I doing? Learning how to kill birds!'

Bhujangrao responded, 'Murar, you are here preparing for a battle.'

Murar continued, 'I have waited for nine years. I have the blood of Shivaji Maharaj and Santaji in my veins. I have raised my own army and I have taken care of my people. Is this old man going to decide whether I'm a capable warrior?'

Yunus Khan nodded. With no children of his own, Murar led a lonely life and his conquests had been chiefly limited to ensuring the safety of his own terrains. So when the opportunity to fight presented itself, he was restless and anxious, both. What if this Nizam decided he wasn't up to the task? What would he do? Further, Murar's first wife Sagunabai had died early. The marriage had been a distant, ineffectual one because Sagunabai was feeble and sickly all along.

Bhujangrao decided to lighten the moment. With Murar taking lessons, he said, 'Let us at least find out a little more about this Saheba Bibi. Maybe she can decide if you're a capable warrior or not!' They all chuckled. The two Marathas asked to walk around and were allowed to do so, both because they were guests and there was enough security all around to keep an eye on them.

The day went by uneventfully as prey after prey fell to trained falconers. The Nizam's advanced age and ill health made him retire early to the shade. Murar, who saw value in learning this new skill, continued sincerely.

Meanwhile, Saheba, having finished her dose of falconry, was moving towards a scenery she wished to paint in her well-guarded palanquin. She chose an isolated spot at a height, with a tree that had leaves of every shade of green and yellow on it, all at once. She set up her easel and canvas with paints and asked her guards to leave her and Rankha alone for a while as she wanted to remove her purdah to be able to paint. The guards sat facing away, a bit lower on the incline but within earshot, behind a rock.

'During the course of the day, it was by sheer accident that Saheba and Murar met. And since it was not anticipated, there was no planned resistance to it,' pitches in my co-author Indrajeet.

As Saheba put her brush to canvas, the painting of the brave warrior on a horse that she had created back home seemed suddenly to have manifested before her. Murarirao, on horseback, was following the lead given by his loyals, who had playfully pointed him in the general direction of Saheba. He wasn't sure how far he would be able to go, but the guards had been sent away by Saheba herself and he got a good look.

Murarirao saw the most beautiful face he had ever seen. And before Rankha pulled down Saheba's veil, Murarirao had seen enough. As Murar's horse neighed, the bodyguards rushed forward, wrapping up everything. Rankha put Saheba back into her palanquin and rushed her away. They would be in trouble if another man so much as saw her.

What Saheba saw was thrilling for her too—the normally ordinarily dressed Murar looked extremely regal, as he was wearing fine fabrics that day. These fabrics, of course, had been a present from the Nizam who had invited him!

As the palanquin retreated, the defiant princess opened the curtain to check again how close Murar's resemblance was to her painting.

Only Rankha knew what was happening.

Murarirao smiled. He had just met a feisty princess who tamed predator falcons and hunted at will. He was besotted!

Could he afford to be besotted thus?

Murar's idea of a strong woman was originally shaped by his own mother and Tara.

Tara, what will the gods say?

24

Saheba and Murarirao

'I want to get married to someone who can slice my throat ruthlessly but won't because he loves me,' Saheba would say achingly.

Rankha would feign shock, '*Hai Rabba*! You are a wicked girl, Saheba Bibi.'

Sprawled on the bed seductively, Saheba would say, 'I want you to find me a romance before Abba gets me married to someone of his choice! Abba will choose a weak fool, who can never take over his kingdom; a weak fool who can give me no pleasure!'

Rankha covered her face. 'If anyone hears you talking like this, I will be buried alive in the harem!'

'Rankha, I want to live before I die to marriage.' Saying this, Saheba stretched her hands high up in the air, allowing them to fall behind her head. She bit her lips and hugged Rankha.

Everything, of course, changed after that day of falconry. As it happens with lovers, one look is enough to set the heartbeat at a pace hitherto unknown to it. The chance encounter between Saheba and Murarirao contributed to their subsequent restlessness in equal measures. Both of them tried to ascertain how they could prevail upon their respective assistants to organize another meeting.

To be sure, the advantage was distinctly on Murarirao's side because he knew who she was immediately. It wasn't until two days had passed and Rankha had access to all the possible gossip from every single person who was on the hunting expedition that Saheba found out that the person she had seen was a Maratha warrior, Murarirao Ghorpade.

When Rankha shared the news, there was despondency in her voice. After all, the Marathas were sworn enemies of the Nizam. The meeting organized by the Nizam might have been one of convenience, and in future, such a meeting might not happen. Besides, marriage to a Maratha was out of the question!

Saheba candidly confessed that she was not thinking as far as marriage. She wanted to experience love in that moment and not be bogged down by what would happen to her love and of her love.

'With all the finery he wore, couldn't he have been a Mughal prince?' asked Saheba wistfully.

Rankha knew Saheba well enough. This man who had emerged from nowhere into their lives had an eerie resemblance to the figure Saheba had created from her imagination, on paper. It was too obvious to be ignored. Rankha agreed to support Saheba wholeheartedly, knowing fully well that the harem would never forgive her if they found out. This task had only risk writ all over it.

The first order of business would be to find out if Murarirao was indeed interested in meeting again. Sending a message out and receiving one back was a long-drawn-out procedure back then. Truth be told, finding out Murarirao's name within two days was nothing short of a miracle pulled off by the loyal, devoted Rankha. But finding out more about him meant that every time she left the palace precincts under the guise of some errand, she had to actively try and pass a message to somebody who lived many miles away.

Now how would she find someone who could deliver a letter to Murarirao Ghorpade, ruler of Gutti?

25

Against All Odds

It seemed that Bhujangrao was more resourceful in the matter of re-establishing contact with Saheba.

Having divined that Saheba Bibi liked to paint, Bhujangrao—who knew nothing about painting—began to take a deep interest in it. At the time, most artists of the Haiderabad school of painting used the medium of water colour on paper. These paintings had a distinct style, with most being decorative. They were characterized by flowerbeds, rich colour and Deccani facial types and costumes.

He befriended artists in the market to find out where the finest quality tempered paper and paints came from, which someone like a princess would use. It took him all of three months to find a way to put a box of paints in Rankha's hand, during one of her routine visits to the market.

The box featured a stunning emerald pendant and permanent residence details of Murarirao. Inside, was a line in Persian,

'Send me something of yours if you want me to meet you.'

Now the ball was in Saheba's court. She had no hesitation in sending him the portrait that she had painted, which matched her vision of him.

'I painted you years before I saw you. I have always been waiting for you.'

She wrote and spoke Persian,[1] which at the time was understood by several Marathas.[2]

Rankha could not use any of the normal emissaries to send a message to Murarirao without being beheaded. But she found a way and the correspondence began. And it was this way, for almost a year.

Indrajeet Ghorpade pitches in. 'I roughly remember the conversations[3] this way; Murarirao met Saheba sometime after the death of his first wife Sagunabai.[4] Murarirao Ghorpade was definitely less stylish than the Mughals. But more than anything else, he was a man who appreciated beauty! In Saheba, he found a gritty woman he could respect.'

In his interaction with Saheba, Murarirao was reminded of a saying that his mother instilled in him; it was something Lord Krishna had said to Arjuna in the Bhagavad Gita:

'*A gift is pure when it is given from the heart to the right person at the right time and at the right place, and when we expect nothing in return.*'

Madly in love and unattached at the time, he gave to Saheba the most beautiful things that he looted from the principalities he attacked outside his domain, to sustain his own lifestyle and his army.

Indrajeet adds, 'There's not much we know, except that they met after a year of correspondence had passed and the fire burnt just the same on both sides. They were helped by their aides. Rankha came up with the clever ruse that Murarirao must pose as a eunuch and come to attend to Saheba to relieve her of some pain.'

And so unravelled a joyous illicit interlude, right under the nose of Nizam-ul-Mulk, the Lord of the Deccan.

Section 8

Of Weak Wills and Brandy

Tara's occult powers were now well known. She had a soft spot for Murar and his mother Lakshmibai, who had helped her discover them. She had told Murar after Sagunabai's death, 'I have not come to console you. I know you have lost nothing. I have come to tell you that your tryst with womenfolk has not even begun. You will have three more, very powerful women entering your life. One will inspire you, one will try to kill you and the third will save your life and bear you two sons.'

Murar dismissed this. 'I am a warrior with no battle to fight. You think I'm concerned about women at this point?'

Tara said, 'No matter what you think, these three women will decide your destiny.'

We have already met Saheba, the first woman.

26

The Anticlimax

After the decisive battle of Damalcheri, Raghuji Bhosle had proved that he could be a great warrior.

His Maratha army and Murarirao were now poised for the final onslaught against the fort of Vellore, where Safdar Ali Khan had escaped.

This was exactly the time when news of Bajirao's death reached Raghuji in June 1740.[1] His priorities shifted and he called off the war, wanting to get his own man to be the Peshwa instead—a banker of sorts named Babuji Naik. He began a frantic journey to Satara so he could be on the spot and bring pressure to bear on Shahu.

Suddenly, as though a valve had been released, the pressure on Safdar Ali Khan, holed up in the fort, slackened. Within hours, Raghuji Bhosle's subordinate commanders such as Murarirao Ghorpade were informed that he had decided to call off all operations. He withdrew the entire army to a safe distance and established a camp at Shivaganga, about midway between Trichy and Bengaluru.

Raghuji reached Satara, only to discover that Babuji Naik had already lost the race. Shahu had decided to appoint Bajirao's eldest son, Nanasaheb (refer to picture on page 125), as his new Peshwa. In fact, Raghuji had reached Satara just in time to witness the celebrations attendant upon the new Peshwa's installation, which took place on 25 June 1740.

Raghuji's brilliance on the battlefield was sabotaged by his own fickle-mindedness. He had violated a cardinal principal of warfare and had to pay dearly for it. *To allow a beaten and demoralized enemy a breathing pause was to throw away the advantage of success.* The nawabs and even the French and the English who, as Malleson puts it, had been shocked into 'dismay and consternation' by the resounding victories of the Marathas and their strategic moves, were given time to recover, to think out their moves, to rearrange alliances, even to shore up their defences.

At Vellore, Safdar Ali who, in May 1740, was a demoralized man on the point of surrendering, plucked up enough courage to put out feelers to try and strike a bargain with the Marathas for letting him off the hook, and even to see whether they would accord him recognition as the Nawab of Arcot, given the death of his father, Dost Ali.

The Maratha army that was sitting outside Vellore had nothing to do. So they went on 'loot missions' to the surrounding countryside. As recorded by the indefatigable diarist, Ananda Ranga Pillai,[2] who was then the *dubash*, or translator to the French Governor in Pondicherry: 'News of this pillaging was constantly brought by the inhabitants, who fled from their homes.'

According to Pillai, who lived in Tiruvannamalai and spied on the English in Madras:

> Murarirao plundered Ambur and Vaniyambadi, and later Kanchipuram, against which place he proceeded with 1000 horses and even took away the cloths of gold in its temple, and then advanced against Tiruvattur. Mir Ghulam Husain, an officer of the Nawab, was sent in pursuit of Murarirao; but he only plundered the villages that had escaped the Marathas, and represented that he had taken the booty back from them.

Raghuji Bhosle, dejected that he could not influence the selection of the next Peshwa, was considering his options. Meanwhile, waiting for Raghuji reminded Murar of all the uncertainties that were a part of his life—things he had no sway over. For instance, it had been almost a year since he first met Saheba.

Shivram Chitari's painting of Chhatrapati Shahu Maharaj with Nanasaheb Peshwa on a hunt, mid to late eighteenth century, opaque watercolour and gold on paper
Source: Wikimedia Commons

27

Murarirao Captures Chanda Sahib

Disappointed at many levels, Raghuji returned to resume his quest for Chanda Sahib in July 1740. Murarirao was truly happy to see that once the Marathas made up their minds, they could travel quickly between Satara and the Deccan. He wondered whether, someday, they would respond to his calls for help as quickly as Raghuji returned for the routing of Chanda Sahib.

The landscape had shifted in the Deccan. Safdar Ali, who was stuck in Vellore, showed great ingenuity. With the momentum of the attack gone, he worked out a treaty with the Marathas in August 1741, by which the Marathas agreed to recognize him as the Nawab of Arcot and undertook not to molest him further. In return, Safdar Ali undertook to pay the Marathas a whole crore of rupees, but in easy instalments, to help them in their operations against Chanda Sahib, and also in restoring all the Hindu chieftains on the Coromandel coast to their former positions.

Raghuji then proceeded to shift his gaze to Chanda Sahib, the nuisance maker, the primary target of his expedition. Even after the rout of Dost Ali,[1] when the Marathas had been on the way to Arcot, Chanda Sahib sat pretty in Trichy and sent off his womenfolk as well as his valuables to Pondicherry, which was considered to be one of the most impregnable fortresses on the Coromandel coast. As has been established earlier, the French Governor of Pondicherry, M. Dumas, was a close friend of his. A lot of the wealth that Chanda Sahib sent to Dumas's custody was from the loot he had taken from the Rani of Trichy.

Neither was he bothered by Dost Ali's death, nor was he concerned about Safdar Ali's safety. Chanda Sahib was an island of one.

Meanwhile, Chanda Sahib had taken the fullest advantage of the respite afforded, and strengthened the defences of the Trichy Fort. He managed to raise a new army that was 20,000 strong. This army was to be held in reserve some distance away from the fort and had to be in readiness to turn the flanks of the enemy troops in case they attacked.

Wanting to settle the issue of Chanda Sahib, Raghuji wrote a long letter to Dumas, telling him how remiss the French had been in affording shelter to Chanda Sahib's wife and family, and, even more, keeping his valuables in their custody. '*If you wish that we should be friends, you must give up this treasure, these jewels, these horses, these elephants, as well as the wife and son of Chanda Sahib. I shall send my cavalry to whom you can make them over.*'

Raghuji also threatened that they would meet the same fate that the Portuguese had suffered in Bassein.[2] But Raghuji's reputation and his fickle-mindedness was well known. Hence, Dumas was not intimidated. He firmly but politely told Raghuji, 'What would you, yourself, a nobleman full of bravery and generosity, think of me, if I were capable of such baseness as to hand over to you a lady and her son and her riches she has brought here?'

This was nothing short of an invitation of war. Dumas was telling Raghuji Bhosle in no uncertain terms that he was most welcome to attack him at Pondicherry and take everything he wanted.

Infuriated, Raghuji Bhosle charged on Trichy and brought to these operations a touch of the tactical brilliance that characterized his initial operations. He divided his force into small raiding parties and sent them all over the surrounding country, and then they all suddenly turned in their tracks, became united and surrounded the Trichy Fort. He managed to intercept the reserve army commanded by Chanda Sahib's brother, Bade Saheb, while it was still some distance from Trichy and, in what can only be described as a desperate encounter, utterly defeated it. Bade Saheb was killed.

In a gesture of old-fashioned chivalry, Raghuji Bhosle sent Bade Saheb's body into the fort for burial, 'clothed in rich stuffs'.[3]

The siege of Trichy went on. From the Maratha side, Sardesai tells us, the operations were conducted by Murarirao Ghorpade. Chanda Sahib held on with grim determination for three months. Finally, on 21 March 1741, he decided to throw open the gates.

To quote Sardesai again, 'It was Murarirao Ghorpade of Gutti who showed special bravery and managed to capture Chanda Sahib[4] himself as well as his eldest son Abid Ali.'

Trichy's fort is built on an abruptly projecting 83-metre-high rock believed to be one of the oldest rocks in the world. The summit of the fort can be reached by means of 437 steep, stone-cut steps. It was the Nayakas of Madurai who built the rock fort in the seventeenth century and this was to become an exposition of Murarirao's war stratagem.

Murarirao and his contingent were trained in all kinds of mounted warfare as well as guerrilla warfare. Murar was able to take Trichy because of three strategic moves:

- Continuous, strong surprise attacks on transportation routes, halting the passage of essentials into and messages from the fort
- Using camouflage to capture the weapons of the enemy and then using those against them
- Establishing channels to seek information through deception and espionage, keeping pressure on the enemy while not going close enough at all.

Chanda Sahib was caught completely unawares. He was expecting a full frontal attack, but it seemed that one by one, his own soldiers were just dropping off mysteriously. The stealth, pace and subterfuge of the famous 'invisible horseman', Murarirao Ghorpade, was such that Chanda Sahib's army was completely demoralized, not knowing which direction or what time or upon whom an attack would be launched.

The last mile of entering the fort and capturing Chanda Sahib was the easier part. Raghuji claimed this victory and Chanda Sahib was finally a prisoner of the Marathas. Murarirao Ghorpade won Trichy fair and square, even as Raghuji installed him as the *Subedar* or Governor of Trichy and of the surrounding territory that had been unfairly claimed by Chanda Sahib.

Murar took charge of it, not as a vassal of the Marathas, but as an independent commander. He had answered Shahu's call to join the expedition, but it was done as much to advance his own as well as Shahu's interests. He wished the Marathas well, but had become used to being his own master for far too long to fit into their hierarchical structures. At heart, he was a maverick who refused to be identified as subordinate to anyone else. Standing atop the fort, a frisson of excitement ran through his body; if only he could share this victory with Saheba. But he knew that it was not a possibility. Tara came to his mind, the only other person who understood him best.

As he looked around, his next-door neighbour was Pratap Singh of Thanjavur. To the north and to the west across the width of the Kaveri was the great temple of Sriranganatha, and on both sides of it and beyond were rice fields stretching miles upon miles of an incredible lushness not to be seen anywhere else in the Deccan. This is what made Trichy the granary of the Coromandel coast. Further north was Safdar Ali, the Nawab of Arcot, who, after all, was beholden to him and the Marathas for being made a nawab in the first place. And in the south and east were the red plains that again seemed to merge into Thanjavur.

There was not a dark cloud in the sky. He settled down to the routine of ruling and waited with impatience for the monsoon to be over for Raghuji Bhosale to return so that between them, they could get on with what they had just begun—the process of bringing the entire south of the peninsula under Maratha authority.

Murar had been urging Raghuji that their next objective should be the kingdom of Mysore, and Raghuji had all but agreed. However, the Marathas did not return.

28

Diplomacy by Brandy

Chanda Sahib's capture was a victory savoured by all.

Emboldened, Raghuji sent one of his senior officers to deliver to Governor M. Dumas what can only be termed an ultimatum, informing him, in no uncertain terms, that if he persisted in holding on to Chanda Sahib's treasury and family, Pondicherry would meet the same fate as Trichy.

For some reason, M. Dumas remained unmoved. In fact, he received Raghuji's emissary with the utmost courtesy, gave him a long lecture on the power and resources of France and the bravery and ferocity of its soldiers, conducted him on a tour of his fortifications to show how impregnable they were, and even introduced him to his stock of guns and gunpowder. Then, having impressed him with his state of preparedness, M. Dumas, unyielding as ever but polite to the last, sent a present to Raghuji Bhosle: ten bottles of his best French brandy.

This was an anticlimax of the highest order.

Raghuji Bhosle gave the bottles of brandy to his wife, who found the liquor so much to her liking, that she insisted upon others being procured, whatever might be the cost. According to Malleson, the brandy bottles had given the French an ally against whom Raghuji was but a child. The cordials were to be obtained by any means, and it seemed that they could only be secured by friendly communication with M. Dumas.

In an incredible about-turn, Raghuji mellowed his tone and sent a 'friendly communication' requesting for more supplies. The ever-polite M. Dumas promptly sent another thirty bottles, which so charmed Raghuji Bhosle that he was set to forget all his previous anger against the French.[1] After that, it was just a matter of time before both parties entered into negotiations.

Thanks to some good brandy, the inconsistent Raghuji Bhosle was not able to lay his hands on the treasure that Chanda Sahib had stashed away in Pondicherry, but at least he had defeated Chanda Sahib.[2] He also made sure that the Raja of Thanjavur, Shahu's cousin, Pratap Singh Bhosale, would be left in peace by the new Nawab of Arcot. The job being complete, Raghuji made tracks for Satara which he reached on 24 June 1741. Murarirao Ghorpade was now the Subedar, or Governor, of Trichy.

The news of this resounding Maratha success in the South spread all over India and the credit for being the principal architect of this success was given to Murarirao Ghorpade. The Nizam, who was thrilled that the Marathas had captured Chanda Sahib but were denied access to his valuables, sent a glowing letter of congratulations to M. Dumas along with a 'dress of honour'. The Mughal Emperor, Mohammad Shah, conferred upon M. Dumas the rank and the title of Nawab.

M. Dumas was on the verge of leaving for France. Therefore, he transferred the honour to his successor instead. Hence, Monsieur Joseph Francois Duplex began to style himself as 'Mughal Nawab'.

And then came the most surprising occurrence. Safdar Ali, the Nawab of Arcot, was murdered by his own cousin, Murtaza Ali. The latter set himself up as the Nawab. At this point, it was highly unlikely that Safdar Ali had paid the Marathas the full crore of rupees that he had promised, and there was no guarantee that the new Nawab would honour the undertaking either. This was in mid-1742.

29

The Nizam Wakes Up

After the heroism of 1741 came the lull. Murarirao Ghorpade waited for further orders and expeditions, but there were none.

Neither did Raghuji Bhosle return nor did Shahu send any other Maratha general down south. Soon, Murarirao discovered that the two main armies of the Marathas had gone off on an expedition in Bengal. One under Nanasaheb and one under Raghuji Bhosle. Murar decided to shore up the defences of Trichy Fort on his own. The flag that flew on the mast of the gleaming pink fort[1] was the black and white standard of the Ghorpades.

He was keen to consolidate his gains. He wrote to the English and Madras to supply him with some guns, but those merchants never sold this even to their allies.

Thanks to the Maratha inaction, a surprising event took place. The Nizam had expected the Marathas to replace one nawab with another, not with Murar, who was one of their own. He believed his march to unseat Murarirao from Trichy was legitimate. Hence, he doubled down on Trichy with 70,000 cavalry and 2,00,000 infantry in March 1743

Ananda Ranga Pillai[2] describes this: 'The Nizam, with his sons, kinsmen, and the nobles advanced—as though the sea was rising and flooding the land with horses and foot soldiers and elephants. The camp is reported to occupy an area of about sixteen square miles.'

The Nizam was entirely aware of Murarirao's reputation. And he had prepared adequately to meet his resistance.

Murarirao had his 10,000 cavalry, and he was sure that he would be able to hold on to the fort for months even against the tightest of blockades. He reached out several times to the Peshwa for help, while barricading himself in the fort and manning its defences. Every day he gazed westwards for signs of a cavalry. When he realized that help wasn't forthcoming[3] and that he was alone and unsupported, he decided to change his strategy. Murarirao knew that he already had three principalities to manage on his own. He took full advantage of his familiarity[4] with the Nizam to arrange a compromise and handed over Trichy Fort to the Nizam on 29 August 1743.

Indrajeet adds, 'Murar seemed to know the Nizam only too well. What to propose, what to avoid and which strings to pull. Putting himself first, Murar considered it wise to have got the Nizam to acknowledge his ownership of Gutti rather than risk sacrificing everything he possessed.'

As he led his own dispirited column in the direction of Gutti, he may have experienced a pang of regret at having allowed himself to be drawn into the oil-and-salt mess of Maratha affairs. But not for long. Experience had taught him that survival itself was a matter of making the right alliances. And just like his father before him, he never took sides when it came to the Marathas.

It disturbed him that Shahu was becoming weaker by the day; the bitter rivalry between his two queens, Sakwarbai and Sagunabai, had, since Shahu's last illness, intensified greatly, and both had taken increasingly to dabbling in the day-to-day affairs of the kingdom.

Murarirao had seen an ancient kingdom fall. He had seen nawabs being made and unmade. His pragmatism was such that he knew he could not hold himself against the currents of history. Even to be able to keep what was already his, he had to make alliances. Aside from that, there were the obligations of heredity and religion. And there was also something else—he had tasted power, experienced the intoxication of command in active warfare and the thrill of victories in battle, exchanged talks and bargained for terms with the highest in the land. He wanted more.

Like so many others of his ilk, for whom the game itself was a reward, henceforward he would always find it difficult to ignore the call for action.

The Nizam on the other hand was feeling very bullish. He would always boast that the whole of the Deccan peninsula was his. By capturing Trichy, he had made all the nawabs and the Palegars, who had hitherto paid the Marathas their tribute, his own vassals now. The Marathas were on the path to complete ruin[5] by their own family feuds and internal politics.

When Murar returned to Gutti, there was a familiar scroll waiting for him. It was a letter from Saheba warning Murar about her father's impending attack on Trichy, sent almost two months earlier.

Murar never heard from her or Rankha again.

Part 4

A Valiant Warrior

It is important to take stock of the trajectory of Peshwa Bajirao I, and conjecture how it could have affected Murar.

Bajirao became the Peshwa in 1719 after the death of his father Balaji Vishwanath. Bajirao I, born in 1700, had been part of his father's expeditions since the age of twelve. In 1718, he was also a part of his father's entourage to Delhi. In the Mughal capital, he witnessed unimaginable intrigue and learnt quickly that the Mughals could be conquered. This became even more true with time as he witnessed the gradual deterioration in Mughal politics and wanted to take full advantage of this situation

His own youthful energy, skill and vision prepared him to carry forward the Hindavi Swarajya dream.

Bajirao consolidated Maratha strongholds around Poona, Central India and Gujarat to begin with. From routing Rangeela Mohammad Shah in Delhi to the Nizam at the Battle of Bhopal, Bajirao was unstoppable, expanding the Maratha Empire from the famous 'Attock to Cuttack'. During Murar's growing-up years, he saw Tarabai and Shahu at odds with each other. But with Bajirao's ambition, the pride of the Maratha Empire was all set to return.

One cannot help wonder why Murar did not reach out to Bajirao to become part of his expeditions. Was it possible that to his mind, he was answerable only to Chhatrapati Shahu? Did he consider himself an equal to Bajirao? They were almost the same age; in fact, Bajirao was older and together Bajirao and Murar might have achieved more. The period 1720 to 1740—when Bajirao died—could this have been any different?

Section 9

Murarirao Saves Robert Clive

30

The French Record Some Early Wins

During the period from 1741 to 1748, when Chanda Sahib was under custody, Dupleix built his reputation and recorded some big wins against the English.

It was almost by design that no matter how small the skirmish, the British and the French constantly found themselves on opposite sides. This was a delicate period for Murarirao too, as he was trying to figure out who his allies should be. He had an axe to grind with Shahu, who had not come to his rescue when the Nizam attacked Trichy. However, he was also painfully aware that Shahu was extremely weak. Conflicted on the personal front between his two wives and on the professional front by the discord between Peshwa Nanasaheb and his military commander Raghuji Bhosle, Shahu could get nothing done.

Murarirao opened negotiations with Shahu's rival, the Kolhapur kingdom where Sambhaji was in power. It was Sambhaji's wife, Jijabai, who controlled the proceedings of the court. They were delighted when Murar offered his services, but they had no idea what to do with a warrior like him.

At this time, there were a few half-hearted expeditions undertaken towards the South that failed terribly. Disillusioned with both factions, Murarirao decided to enter the South on his own. By now, the English and French traders were significant players in any action in the South. They were fighting their own race to the finish. It so happened that the French had a few big wins in the beginning.

For example, in September 1746, Dupleix attacked and captured Fort St George from the British. When the Nawab of Arcot tried to seize it back, the French bombarded the Nawab's army with guns so powerful that seventy of the Nawab's soldiers were killed in fifteen minutes and the rest fled in terror. One of the people who escaped from this attack was Robert Clive, disguised as a Muslim.

As Dupleix was rejoicing in this victory, back in Europe, France and England signed a peace treaty. Dupleix was compelled to give Fort St George back to the English.

However, none of these small wins would compare to what was to unfold after the death of the great Nizam-ul-Haq. The towering ruler died on 21 May 1748, at the age of seventy-seven, triggering a war of succession. Nasir Jung, the Nizam's son, who had fought tooth and nail with him when he was alive, realized that succession was not going to be that easy. In fact, Nasir Jung had once written a letter to his father, saying:

> You should remain at Delhi and look after the imperial concerns, leaving me the sole power to manage the affairs at Deccan. I have no desire to go to war with you but if you don't deliver to me the sole management in the Deccan, I will become a faquir and resort to the shrine of the saint Shah Burhanuddin of Khuldabad.

With his father out of the way, Nasir Jung was looking forward to complete control.

However, his own nephew, Muzaffar Jung, was vying for the top job.

Born to the Nizam-ul-Mulk's favourite daughter Khair-un-Nisa, Muzaffar Jung was ostensibly the Nizam's choice as well. Such a major conflict,[1] which involved vast land and wealth, was a prime opportunity for the French and English traders-turned-colonialists to interfere in the succession, as mercenary supporters of rival contenders for power.

31

Murarirao Ghorpade and the French Hollow Square

After the death of the Nizam in 1748, Chanda Sahib somehow managed to pay off a ransom to the Marathas and get his freedom. This was shocking to say the least. A known troublemaker, who had made it his life's mission to destroy the Marathas, was released by the Marathas after seven years in their custody!

Once out, Chanda Sahib wanted Trichy again and he also wanted to gain from the spoils of the war of succession that erupted after the Nizam's death in Haiderabad. The only sure-fire prediction to be safely made in this war of succession was that the British and French would end up on opposite sides.

The other safe prediction was that Chanda Sahib would be the defining factor in terms of whom the French would support. And so, an alliance was formed between Muzaffar Jung, Chanda Sahib, the French and a few other notables.

It was around this time, on 15 December 1749,[1] that Shahu Maharaj expired. Peshwa Nanasaheb became all powerful but did not participate in the events that were rapidly unfolding in the Carnatic.

Murarirao Ghorpade decided to enter the fray. The spoils of such a battle of succession had the potential to fill his coffers for a very long time. Besides, it had been five years since he had heard from Saheba. In the event that she was alive, he wanted to safeguard her interests in this succession plan, even though he didn't really know whether he would be able to make such a difference.

His main desire was to be on the opposite side of Chanda Sahib. Thus, Murar aligned himself with Nasir Jung. The fact that Chanda Sahib wished to regain control over Trichy was unbearable to him. Consequently, when Chanda Sahib and Muzaffar Jung proceeded to besiege Thanjavur, Murarirao was all set to attack. But when Chanda Sahib heard about the size of Nasir Jung's army that was coming towards them, he and the French commander Bussy bolted for their lives, leaving Muzaffar Jung alone to face the music.

Nasir Jung captured Muzaffar Jung and placed him in confinement. Nasir Jung also incorrectly assumed that this was the end of the campaign and that he was the undisputed Subedar of the Deccan and there was nothing more to fight for. He began a debauched celebration of his victory.

Meanwhile, Chanda Sahib and the French were running from Thanjavur Fort towards Pondicherry. Chanda Sahib was panic-stricken but he trusted in the fact that the French were good strategists. Not wanting any part of Nasir Jung's wild salaciousness, Murarirao decided to chase Chanda Sahib down. This is when he faced his ultimate test as a warrior.

Near Pondicherry, the French formed into one of their traditional military manoeuvres called 'The Hollow Square'.[2] Now Murarirao, who did not know the first thing[3] about such a manoeuvre, rode right into it. Suddenly, he saw himself surrounded on all sides.

We have to take a minute here to understand the deadly Hollow Square formation. It was essentially an infantry formation that had been used in wars over several hundred years. The idea was to have an outer square of men, with an inner empty square. Colonel George Bruce Malleson has said that the soldiers facing outwards had a specific task assigned.[4] It was one of the infantry formations of choice against charging cavalry. The men in the formation were tightly packed, facing the enemy in all four directions, whilst the hollow centre allowed the men flexibility to rotate. The centre was also the place to hold reserve arms and supplies.

Now, forming a Hollow Square required some planning. Every soldier had to move as fast as possible to get into place. And the French were adept at this complicated formation.

Murarirao found himself completely out-manoeuvred and was in a fix. The French had built up an intimidating military reputation. Were the next few moments going to be the last moments of his life? Would he lose to that insufferable man, Chanda Sahib?

Eeeesh . . . a blade whizzed barely a millimetre past his ear. Another hissing sound followed almost immediately, as one of his soldiers was slain, his neck bent sideways and bleeding like a tap. At that moment, Chanda Sahib's cavalry further attacked his flank and separated him from the rest of his contingent. There were just fifteen of his soldiers left inside this formation, which he had never seen before.

'Is this going to be the last battle of my life?' he asked himself as four of his loyal soldiers surrounded him, giving him a moment to gather himself.

His father Sidhoji Hindurao Ghorpade had been wise to not take sides within the Maratha fold. After all, no one knew why wars were being fought in the first place! The whims of the Peshwas—who were not in the same mould as the Chhatrapatis whom the Ghorpades had been traditionally loyal to—were barely righteous. Tara's prophecy rang in his ears. He sought strength from her in the moment. His next thought was Saheba; he had to live in the low probability event that she was trapped in the harem, waiting for him.

Schwing! The man on his right collapsed. Murarirao was exposed. He clenched his sword and roared like a lion, joining the fight again. There was no time for philosophy or overthinking on the battlefield. Onlookers might have seen how seamlessly synchronized his hands were with his steed, executing fluid, dynamic strikes while in brisk motion. Each swing precise and devastating, guided by expert control, even as the horse's gallop became an extension of his own intent, delivering blows from varied angles and effortlessly adapting to shifting combat scenarios—allowing him to strike with shocking anticipation of his opponent's moves.

Murarirao focused on what he knew—horsemanship. He assessed the number of soldiers he had to outrun and those he had to outwit and picked up the pace. Swinging with a speed never seen before, he made a dash to the other end of the square, hoping to carve an opening by the force of his strength and his unmatched agility.

Many of the men he encountered were left anxiously clutching their swords, as Murarirao's intense eyes bored into their skulls. Wherever he detected any nervous energy, he attacked ruthlessly and when he found a determined opponent, he used all his training to find a gap that his sword could penetrate so he could emerge at the other end of the square. His pace, his accuracy and his strength, all three had never been witnessed before.

In the matter of a few minutes, he lost nine of his fifteen men inside the Hollow Square. But the rest of his contingent who were riding on the periphery of the square, joined him again as he exited the death-trap formation with his life intact. This was nothing short of a miracle.

The Hollow Square as a military marvel is extremely well chronicled. The complicated formation is described by Colonel William Barriffe in his work *Military Discipline*.[5] As per the book *Life of Crassus* written by Bernadotte Perrin and Plutarch, the Hollow Square formation was used by the Romans. The square was revived in the fourteenth century as the *schiltron*, and later appeared as the *pike square* or *tercio*, used widely in the French Revolutionary and Napoleonic Wars.

A detailed exposition of the square in action and much else is contained in a military manual by the British General Richard Kane, printed in 1745 after his death. It is titled, 'A New System of Military Discipline for a Battalion of Foot on Action; With the Most Essential Exercise of the Cavalry, Adorned with a Map of the Seat of War and A Plan to the Exercise.'

The Hollow Square fell out of use in the late nineteenth century with the advent of modern repeating firearms (which made concentrated formations risky in the face of increased firepower), along with the parallel decline of horse cavalry.

In this instance, however, Chanda Sahib got away. However, news of Murarirao's skill spread far and wide.

Everyone wanted him on their side.

32

The Nizam's Successor

As the French and Chanda Sahib reached Pondicherry, they got down to planning their future moves. The first strategy was to buy time. The second was to bring about a rift in the ranks of the opposing groups. Dupleix also wanted to establish a psychological advantage over his opposition. He moved with stealth. Unlike most local players, Dupleix was strategic in his choices and his was clearly a different military philosophy.

Murarirao, fresh from regaining Thanjavur and beating the Hollow Square, underestimated him at first. Murarirao was camped outside Pondicherry, planning his next move, when Dupleix raided his army and killed 1200 of his men. This setback not only reduced the fighting ability of Murarirao's column but also had a psychological effect on the morale of his men.

The French raid struck terror in the hearts of all of Murarirao's partners. They looked up to him as a great warrior and derived strength from him. Nasir Jung was scared out of his wits and escaped to the safety of Arcot, and the English retreated as well. The French were thrilled to see that the enormous army that had charged towards them was now disintegrated completely. They regained lost ground by capturing Gingee first, post which they set out towards Arcot. Nasir Jung on his part, had collected a few dubious allies, who secretly hated his obnoxious behaviour and his sexual depravities equally and used the opportunity to find and kill him.

The French proceeded to release his nephew, Muzaffar Jung, and proclaim him the Viceroy of the Deccan and Chanda Sahib as the Nawab of Arcot.[1] By now it had become clear that no matter who the nawabs were or who the Nizam was, the real masters of the Coromandel were the French.

Chanda Sahib was not one to forget good graces after victory. After nominally obtaining the permission of Muzaffar Jung, he conferred on Dupleix not only the villages of Villiyanallur and Valudavur but also Bahur along with the eighty-one villages in its neighbourhood. The English resented in particular the granting of the following places, which brought their trade and commerce into jeopardy, namely, Covelong to Monsieur Dupleix, Porto Nova to Madame Dupleix, St Thome to Padire and Alampara to Monsieur d'Auteuil.

Mentioning this to the Court of Directors, they wrote to the following effect: *So that we are surrounded in such a manner as for the French to have it entirely in their power to stop our trade or debar us from any supplies of provisions from the country and we have great reason to believe from what has already happened, they will not be waiting to make use of their advantages*.

To build on the gains of this win, it was important for the French to move in quickly, crown Muzaffar Jung as the Nizam and exert control over Haiderabad. However, a few nawabs were unwilling to accept him as the Nizam, chiefly those of Cuddapah, Savannur and Kurnool. Therefore, during Muzaffar Jung's journey to Haiderabad to be crowned, the armies of the rebel nawabs came face to face with him. In a hand-to-hand skirmish, the Nawab of Kurnool put a knife through Muzaffar Jung's brain and killed him.

The French General Bussy, who was preparing for a ceremonial coronation, was now left without a Nizam to crown. Hurriedly, they picked Salabat Jung, one of the other sons of Nizam-ul-Mulk, to be the new Nizam. A game of *Jeu de morpion*,[2] it was, for the French! Since the Nizam was to be a French-orchestrated puppet, no matter who occupied the seat, the coronation had to happen. Salabat Jung became the new Nizam of Haiderabad and the French had overlordship over his territory.

Being on the losing side of the battle of the Nizam's succession hurt the British tremendously. They began to look for the next opportunity to regain all the advantages they had lost. The strategy was simple–they were going to fight the French by offering to side with whoever happened to be at war with them.

Under such circumstances, it seemed that the latest occupant of Trichy, Muhammad Ali,[3] who had no real claim, was the safest bet to back. Chanda Sahib would definitely come to capture Trichy and bring the French with him.

As expected, they came. It was July 1751 when they reached Trichy. The English had ample time to send their contingent and guns to reinforce Muhammad Ali's army. Unfortunately, in the very first encounter, the English contingent was so panic-stricken by the effectiveness of the French artillery that they turned and fled! The English and Muhammad Ali repaired to the shelter of the fort and barricaded themselves in, and the French laid siege to the fort.

The French knew that taking the fort would be tough, so they waited to starve out the defenders into submission.

Three weeks later, a counter-offensive carried out by Robert Clive worked wonders. Robert Clive had just joined the East India Company and was a writer in Fort St George. He suggested to Governor Thomas Saunders that if Arcot were attacked, it would divert Chanda Sahib's attention away from Trichy and force him to send troops to Arcot, his capital, which he had left dangerously unprotected.

Robert Clive proceeded to set this plan in motion. He gave up his clerical desk and marched from Madras to Arcot in five days. Clive occupied the fort unopposed, secured the fortification, including the cannon, and prepared for a siege. This was a win of his mind, more than his military might.

Dupleix sent a column from Chanda Sahib's army to deal with Clive's forces. This column, commanded by Chanda Sahib's son Raja Saheb, came and laid siege to Arcot, and began the long-drawn-out process of starving out its inmates. Thus, two simultaneous sieges were in progress–one at Trichy and one at Arcot.

33

A Moment of Revelation

Murarirao wanted to act on the sieges that were in progress. However, he was dejected that the Marathas had once again let Chanda Sahib loose; a fiend he thought he had captured for good! This time, he wanted to think though his actions before committing to one side.

One evening, he, Bhujangrao and Yunus Khan were celebrating his feat with the Hollow Square, with some inebriated merrymaking. Murar was a reticent drinker, but the melancholy air of Saheba's certain disappearance was weighing heavily on him. One might say that he indulged that night. The situation was tricky; other than Rankha, there was no one they could trust, and they had no idea where Rankha was either.

Suddenly, the guard outside Murarirao's fort announced a visitor. A bit tipsy, Murarirao felt embarrassed to receive a visitor in his state. When he saw who the visitor was, he was ashamed! It was Tara. She had a halo about her. Almost as if she were commanding them, all three of them got up.

Murarirao spoke first, 'Welcome, sister Tara. Sorry for the state you're seeing me in. It has been a long gap.'

Tara sat down and specifically asked Yunus Khan and Bhujangrao to stay on as well. Like kids caught taking an extra piece of candy, they felt sheepish and did not trust themselves to open their mouths.

Tara looked straight at Murar and sat down on the only comfortable spot she could find. She spoke. 'I've come to tell you a few things. First, about Saheba. About three years ago, the Nizam's begum made independent inquiries about a new eunuch healer who had been visiting the harem. She couldn't find this person. Initially, she was suspicious on an entirely different account. Her grandson Muzaffar Jung was being groomed to succeed Nizam-ul-Mulk against her own son. She believed that the eunuch healer had something to do with it. That this was some sort of conspiracy against her son to distract him from his duties. Worried for Nasir Jung's safety, she tightened the security in the harem. When she learnt that Rankha was the person who let the eunuch in, she believed that Saheba was part of the plot. Rankha revealed nothing about the eunuch healer. Angered, the begum buried Rankha alive in the harem. Saheba was sent away, forever.'

Murar realized there was no point asking Tara how she knew about him and Saheba. Tara was omniscient. Weakened by the alcohol, Murar cried.

'Aren't you relieved that Saheba is safe?' asked Tara.

Murarirao admitted that he was relieved about this. But he felt the pain of missing her.

Tara let it sink in. 'You would not have retained Gutti if you did not know how to negotiate with the Nizam when he attacked you at Trichy. Saheba taught you everything you needed to know. She served her purpose.'

Murar was quiet. He did not like Tara's dispassionate appraisal of Saheba. But Tara could say anything to him.

She paused for a few seconds and then continued.

'Murar. Let me tell you the real reason I'm here. A choice you're about to make in the coming days will shape history.'

Murar did not really feel very confident about himself at that point. He had suffered a setback of sorts; an ugly drubbing by Dupleix due to his own unpreparedness, and he was extremely despondent at having lost 1200 of his men. Murar loved his soldiers like family and frankly, his resources were limited as compared to the others in the fray.

Tara continued. 'Hindustan is going to have a new ruler. The one you choose in the siege of Arcot, will rule Hindustan.'

Murar could not make head nor tail of this prediction. Further, he wanted no part in choosing the future ruler of Hindustan unless it was one of his own people. But there was no such person on the horizon. The brave Bajirao had died as well.

'I'm confused, Tara,' he said.

Tara continued. 'Your destiny will play out whether you like it or not. When you were in Trichy, the Nizam had attempted your assassination by a hashish-influenced contract killer from Persia. I was there. He fell to his own death. You survived because you were meant to do more.'

Yunus Khan was startled. Yes. A body had been discovered outside the fort walls and nobody knew who the person was.

'Be careful. One more person will come to try and kill you. It will be a woman this time. This will be before you turn sixty-five. I may not be able to prevent this but someone else will.' Tara now closed her eyes.

Murar folded his hands as Tara started trembling. She had said all she wanted to say. When she collapsed, Murar bent to pick her up and put her on his own bed. No one dare touch his guardian angel! He slept on the floor, keeping a watch, grateful for her presence in his life.

The next day, Bhujangrao escorted Tara all the way back to Kolhapur.

34

Murarirao Saves Robert Clive

The British and Muhammad Ali (refer portrait on page 157) were in Trichy where the French and Chanda Sahib had laid siege. The British (Robert Clive) were also in Arcot, where Raja Saheb and the French had laid siege.

So, the morning brought with it continued negotiations with the French. Murarirao knew that he had to make a decision fast. He was extremely well disposed to Dupleix. On the one hand, all their personal interactions in which Dupleix had tried to woo him from time to time had been cordial. But on the other hand, Dupleix and his General Bussy were worthy adversaries who loved Chanda Sahib above all else.

Dupleix, on his part, knew that Murarirao was way more reliable than the bunch of allies he had surrounded himself with. The debauchery that folks like Chanda Sahib could stoop to had shocked the living daylights out of him. Because of their unwarranted excesses, he would often lose the advantage of time to build on a victory. It would be a wonderful opportunity to work with Murar–someone sober, less swayed by the pleasures of the flesh, in a world where opium increasingly ruled supreme.

Murarirao consulted two other Hindu nobles at the time, Nandraj of Mysore and Pratap Singh Bhosale of Thanjavur. There was also the question of who would pay him, if he decided to support Muhammad Ali. The latter had declared that he had no money to pay them in advance but that he would pay later. Given that Chanda Sahib was on the opposing side (the complete lack of moral fibre in Chanda Sahib was still a major deterrent to Murarirao), he decided to support Muhammad Ali's cause and align with the British column.

For the first time, he was impressed with what the British had done. They did not have the weapons of the French yet, though that would be a matter of time. But Clive's military stratagem had made a huge impact on his mind.

Murarirao played his cards close to his chest even as Tara's prediction weighed heavily on him. He thought about his wife Ranubai waiting for him back home. With, Ranubai, his relationship was entirely one-sided. He had married her merely to produce an heir, in the aftermath of Saheba's disappearance, but she was entirely devoted to him. Thankfully, she had a large family on her maternal side who would take care of her if anything were to happen to him in battle.

Murar set off from Venkatagiri in November 1751 towards Arcot, where Robert Clive and Muhammad Ali were inside the fort and Raja Saheb was waiting outside.

Robert Clive knew that his move had been brave, but he needed a Hail Mary to capitalize on it. When he heard that Murarirao had come to Arcot instead of Trichy, he sent a messenger to him for help. Murar, who was mildly undecided up to this point, made up his mind that he would respond to Clive's call for help. He conveyed that he would not delay to send a detachment of his troops to the assistance of such men as the defenders of Arcot, whose behaviour had now, for first time, convinced him that the English could fight. At this point, he was 50 km west of Arcot. Robert Orme,[1] possibly the very first historian of the English in India, has recorded the nature of help that Murarirao gave to Clive. The detachment he promised was commanded by his nephew, Bhujang Rao, son of Daulatrao of Gajendragadh (different from his childhood friend Bhujangrao) and its strength was 1000, while Murarirao himself, with the remaining 5000 mounted troops, proceeded southwards, in the direction of Trichy.

Meanwhile, Raja Saheb had given many ultimatums to Clive, also in the hope that Murarirao would choose to support his siege. However, seeing that Clive was not responding to his ultimatums,

Raja Saheb assumed that Clive was feeling safe, thanks to some assurances given by Murarirao nearby. He was convinced that Murarirao would now attack him. He had heard tales of Murarirao's bravery and did not want to be pitted against him. His mere presence was menacing enough for Raja Saheb to withdraw his force at first to Vellore.

This was exactly the kind of providential blessing Robert Clive had been hoping for. After fifty days of being holed up at Arcot, Robert Clive was free to come out and resume his activities to relieve the pressure on Trichy. Clive left a garrison in the Arcot Fort under Captain Kilpatrick and marched in pursuit of Raja Saheb's force. The latter's army had now broken up and some guns for hire had even gone home! Intending to rejoin the siege at Trichy, Raja Saheb had to cross the Poondi River at Arni. This is where Robert Clive and Murarirao's forces met them face to face.

The stage was set for the Battle of Arni. Robert Orme gives an account that reveals the manner in which Murarirao's troops fought in this battle:[2]

> The Morattoes fought in a manner peculiar to themselves: their cavalry were armed with sabres, and every horseman was closely accompanied by a man on foot, armed with a sword or a large club, and some...a short, strong spear: if a horse was killed, (its rider immediately began to act on foot. and if the rider fell and the horse escaped, it was immediately mounted, and pressed on again to the charge by the first footman to seize him. Notwithstanding the difference of numbers, and the advantage of the enemy's disposition, they behaved with great spirit.
>
> They made five successive charges, in every one of which they were repulsed by the fire of the (French-trained) sepoys. (Because of the excessive casualties among the Marathas) two field pieces were sent to support them, and they were ordered ... to attack the enemy's artillery. (The guns of the French) were captured and then this whole wing gave away and retreated likewise, pursued by the Morattoes ... when night coming on, the pursuit ceased... Thus was won the battle of Arni. The final tally of the dead or wounded is revealing: about 50 of the French, 150 of the enemy's

> cavalry and sepoys... The English lost no Europeans, and only eight sepoys. But of the Morattoes about fifty were either killed or disabled.

As news of Murarirao's support for the English and their collective wins spread, the mood in Trichy changed. The gloom of defeat was lifted, as they knew that the combined force of the English and Murarirao had tasted victory.

On 9 April 1752, British reinforcements led by Major General Stringer Lawrence, the commander-in-chief of Fort William, joined the troops sent out of Trichy and made it inside the fort lines. Two days later, he led a military unit against the besiegers, prompting French Commander M. Law to lift the siege and retreat to the area near the Sriranganatha temple.

The successful team of Robert Clive and Murarirao Ghorpade refused to let up. They continued the chase and defeated the French Army once again. Murarirao and his general Yunus Khan were finally happy that they had chosen a man 'who knew how to fight'. Robert Clive too couldn't believe his luck when, on 2 June 1752, the French surrendered to the English. And then, news of Chanda Sahib's death emerged!

It so happened that Chanda Sahib was being chased down by Manaji Jagtap, the commander of a 1000-Tanjorean horse army. He caught up with the truant, in the lush betel and banana plantations near the Sriranganatha temple. With Chanda Sahib's fate in his hands, he did not hesitate to stab him through the heart and sever his head. The latter was sent on a tray to Muhammad Ali as a gift.

Even though this was a local war, it was projected very differently in two different camps. For the English, it was 'their Clive' who won a decisive victory against the French Dupleix, reversing the tide of the latter's many successes. Muhammad Ali became the Nawab of the Carnatic and his men supplanted the French as the real arbiters of the affairs of south-eastern Deccan. The menacing rock fort of Trichy became the possession of Muhammad Ali, and the English left a permanent force to enable him to hold on to it.

Muhammad Ali (1717/1718–1795), Nawab of Arcot, Tilly Kettle (1735–1786), Victoria and Albert Museum
Source: Wikimedia Commons

The French simply did not want this to be seen as an English victory. They clearly maintained that their defeat at Srirangam 'was totally ascribable to the valour and activities of the Morattoes (sic) (Murarirao's) cavalry'.[3]

Unfortunately, in what is known as the 'great fraud of Trichy', the euphoria of victory made Muhammad Ali renege on the promises he had made to Murarirao and the other Hindu kings. He could have negotiated, but he wanted to give them nothing. At first, the British refused to intervene. And later, the manner in which they intervened was nothing short of hara-kiri. Declining to take responsibility, they engaged in dubious subterfuge, betraying a short-sightedness that lost them Murar's loyalty forever.

On the other hand, Dupleix—convinced that Murarirao was the reason for the English victory—decided to woo him with double the force.

Major Stringer Lawrence, who had first-hand knowledge of Murarirao's skills, knew that they had three choices: either they had to pay Murarirao or suffer the threat of him crossing over to the French. The only other alternative was to plot his death. Accordingly, Lawrence devised a plan where they invited both Murarirao and Nandraj—who had also contributed a few troops to the battle–to Trichy to discuss their grievances. The plan was to ambush them in the process. Murarirao did not suspect this in the least. He felt betrayed by the behaviour of Muhammad Ali and his only objective was to make him pay.

Fortunately, Haider Ali, a general of Nandraj who possessed an excellent network of spies, was able to warn them just in time that it was not safe to enter the fort. The invitation to discuss remuneration was but a trap to capture them. At this point, Murar and Nandraj had already passed the first gate, but somehow they managed to get out of that situation. It was even more mortifying to Murar that Robert Clive, with whom he shared such a wonderful history, should not help him in his hour of need. Where was Clive, Murar wondered. Surely as a warrior, he knew that the sustenance of Murar's army depended on him being compensated for the battles he fought and won. There was an outside possibility that Clive was not aware of this trap set by Lawrence, but Murar felt it was highly unlikely.

Haider Ali, commander of the Marathas. French painting from 1762, by artist Pierre Adrien Le Beau.
Source: Wikimedia Commons

The negotiations between Dupleix and Murarirao now gathered momentum. They signed an agreement by which Murarirao undertook to assist in Dupleix's struggles against all his enemies, which other than the English and Muhammad Ali also included the Peshwa. Indeed, in January 1753, when Murarirao visited Pondicherry, the pomp with which he was received left nothing to be desired.

35

Robert Clive's Honour Roll

Let's step back a bit. It was on the solid support of Murarirao's troops that Clive's towering reputation came to be built up. The French swore by the fact that the English would never have been, on their own, able to defeat the French in this war, which came to be known as the Second Carnatic War.

Robert Clive had no formal military training. No one would have taken note of him, if not for his success at Arcot and Arni—both powered by Murarirao. After his astounding wins against the French, he established himself as a brilliant exponent of guerrilla tactics. This was November of 1751.

Praise flowed in from everywhere. The legend of Robert Clive started being populated.

> 'The defence of Arcot produced an immense effect upon the minds of the natives of southern India. They had hitherto entertained but little respect for the English, ranking the French as greatly their superiors in military capacity; but from this time, native opinion entirely changed, and the defence of Arcot may justly be regarded as the turning-point in the eastern career of the English,' writes Malleson.[1]

James Mill[2] writes:

> The fort was more than a mile in circumference; the walls in many places ruinous, the towers inconvenient and decayed, and

> everything unfavourable to defence. Yet Clive found the means of making an effectual resistance. When the enemy attempted to storm at two breaches, one of fifty and one of ninety feet, he repulsed them with but eighty Europeans and a hundred and fifty sepoys fit for duty; so effectually did he avail himself of his resources, and to such a pitch of fortitude had he exalted the spirit of those under his command.

After this, Clive's career was transformed. Murarirao might have also hoped that he could continue fighting with a quick-thinking genius like Robert Clive. It is difficult to imagine why two hard-nosed opportunists, who were strategic, self-made and good at fighting together, Murarirao Ghorpade and Robert Clive, would not agree to collaborate further after this big win.

Let's give a thought to Robert Clive's age at this time. He was twenty-six. And Murarirao at this time would have been forty-seven. Could it be the age gap?

What about their nature? In a modern poem entitled 'Clive's Dream before Plassey',[3] Clive is thus apostrophized:

> *'Violent and bad, thou art Jehovah's servant still,*
> *And e'en to thee a dream may be an angel of his will.'*

What kind of violent and bad habits is he talking about? Robert Clive arguably played the biggest role in laying the foundations of British rule in India.

Yet, as a lad of nineteen, when he disembarked at Madras in 1744, it was to take up the position of junior tally clerk. He was the eldest of thirteen children from a family of minor gentry. As a boy, he was known for being 'out of measure addicted' to fighting. Not something to find fault with if you're going to make a name by winning wars.

His starting pay was a mere £5 a year, but if he survived the climate and life-threatening tropical diseases, he stood a good chance of progressing to a junior merchant, councillor or even governor. In one of his first letters home, the young Clive said his aim was nothing more than 'to provide for myself and . . . being of service to my relations'. Touching honesty!

In 1749, Robert Clive was appointed commissary for the supply of provisions to the troops. Far from the control of London, in British India there were stupendous and fast fortunes to be made. Those who were making them were an increasingly independent breed whose loyalty was to themselves first, the Company second and Britain somewhere down the line. Here, Clive himself made some money. The innocent man was growing up! In 1750,[4] Clive had a health breakdown due to gallstones. At this time, he was sent to Bengal, where he became an opium[5] user; initially something he consumed for pain, but the addictive nature of opium cannot be denied. He returned to Madras in 1751. The siege of Arcot was for fifty days or so, ending in November 1751. Could Clive have anticipated this waiting period and carried his medication? Because there are written records that suggest he had 'biliousness and abdominal pain' throughout his life.

Could it also be possible that he craved medication? Who might have arranged it for him? Did one of his many troops manage it? As far as opium availability was concerned, arranging it while being stationed in office might not have been a problem; but for a warrior on the march, procuring it would require some help. The reputation of the 'ruling' jagirdars, etc., during this period was one of expediency and greed. Did Clive expect Murarirao to arrange things for him, in exchange for money?* Did he and Murarirao clash over this to a point of no return?

Fast forward to the Battle of Plassey where Robert Clive would expect nothing but absolute submission to him and treachery towards his ruler from Mir Jaffar in Bengal. Was he expecting something on similar lines from Murarirao—his help to decimate the Marathas, who were now weakened after Bajirao's death?

'Murarirao is highly unlikely to have offered to help him with opium,' says Indrajeet. 'It was not in his fibre at all! About the other matter of helping Clive to rise against the Marathas, this was even more improbable! As far as Murar was concerned, his alliance with Dupleix, even though it loosely involved taking a stance against the Marathas, was unlikely to become serious.'

In 1753, Clive left for England. Several versions report different tidy sums of money that he took back at this point, beyond what

---

* Refer to Annexure 4 for context about Robert Clive, opium and Murarirao.

his wage could be. This was also the year he married Margaret Maskelyne in Madras and they went on to have two sons and two daughters.

What happened two years later, in July 1755, when Clive returned to India, is extremely significant. He landed in Mumbai en route to Madras, to take office as deputy governor of Fort St David at Cuddalore. He took up an assignment before assuming his charge; commanding the land force that captured the Fort of Gheria, about 300 miles south of Bombay, the stronghold of the Maratha pirate Tulaji Angre. Supported in the task by Admiral Charles Watson of the British Navy, Clive helped himself generously to the loot. Clive added this victory to his previous conquests. Trouble broke out in Bengal soon after and the horror of the Black Hole[6] unfolded in 1756. Over a hundred British prisoners died of suffocation and heat exhaustion when they were placed by Siraj-ud-Daula in a cramped dungeon called the Black Hole of Calcutta. Both Watson and Clive were dispatched around Christmas of 1756 to attack Siraj-ud-Daula's army and remove him from Calcutta by force.

A master strategist, Clive bribed various members of the Nawab of Bengal's army during the Battle of Plassey in 1757. The Nawab's own army opted out of fighting entirely. It was an act of theatre, a political coup and a victory on an enormous scale and one that allowed Britain to establish its dominance in India.

Clive's reputation soared further.

'We had lost our glory, honour, and reputation everywhere but India: there, the country had a heaven-born general. He had never learnt the art of war, nor was his name enrolled among the great officers who had for many years received their country's pay! Yet he was not afraid to attack a vast army with a handful of men. Here's to Lord Clive and England,' said William Pitt the Elder, the prime minister of the United Kingdom.[7]

Aged just thirty-two, Clive found himself the conqueror of Bengal and a very rich one at that. Despite strict instructions from London to repulse French attacks and not pick fights with local rulers, Clive had taken things into his own hands, seeing the opportunity for personal enrichment and political and economic gain for the Company. With Plassey, in a single stroke, he had netted £2.5 million for the Company and £234,000 for himself, making him one of the wealthiest men in England.

Clive returned to England in 1760 a hero.[8]

My questions are:

- What if Murarirao had chosen to support Dupleix on that fateful day?
- Did Robert Clive reach out to Murarirao again to go into battle together?
- Did Robert Clive and Murarirao build personal differences after their victories at Arcot and Arni?

The biggest question is this.

What triggered Robert Clive, who owed his reputation to Murarirao, to not come to his rescue while Lawrence was plotting his ambush in Trichy? Was he worried that Murarirao would take the limelight away from him? Was there any personal slight that Clive would have endured that made him antagonistic towards Murarirao? Was the fact that Murarirao survived the ambush, the reason why the two of them never spoke again?

This is history that isn't written.

36

Dupleix Returns to France

Thanks to the treachery shown towards Murarirao Ghorpade, the English seemed as if they would have a setback. Murarirao, in turn, shocked that the English would betray him thus, was completely dejected. He wondered how his decisions were going to change the course of history, as Tara had promised.

For the moment though, he allied with Dupleix. The first order of business, of course, was to punish Muhammad Ali, who was protected by the two-faced Major Stringer Lawrence. As Dupleix prepared a plan, he was delighted to see that Murarirao did not waste time on any wanton pursuits. He went briskly in the direction of Thiruvadi to inflict damage on Muhammad Ali. However, despite an excellent strategy being in place, the French military did not fight at all. Their shocking meekness made Murarirao lose his trusted Bhujangrao Ghorpade to a cannonball. Even his own horse got shot from under him. All Dupleix could do was express regret at the manner in which the French fought.

The reputation that Robert Clive had built and his success had travelled to France and taken the wind out of Dupleix's and his army's sails. But Murarirao persisted by driving the English out of Thiruvadi and Muhammad Ali from his camp and hoisted his own flag on the site.

Almost immediately, the governor of Madras tried to placate Murarirao. Orme observes:

> Murari Rao had made himself admired and respected by listing none of his countrymen, but such as were approved and treating them so well, that they never entertained any thought of quitting him. On the contrary, his army seemed as one family... the spirit of exploit he contrived to keep up amongst them, by equitable partition of plunder... what is more is that, besides the qualities common to the rest of the Maratha nation, such as activity strategy, great dexterity in the management of their horses and sabres, they by their conflict against Europeans had surmounted in great degree, the terror of fire arms.

It was true that, by now, Murarirao's contingent had tremendous experience in fighting against European forces. One dream remained to recapture Trichy. And it was towards this that Murarirao's first experience of fighting alongside Haider Ali materialized. He allied with Nandraj of Mysore to regain the fort.

Murarirao and Haider were experts at warfare, but they did not get along from the word go. As far as Murarirao was concerned, Nandraj was his ally and Haider worked for the latter. So, he treated him as a junior. The *Haidernama* reveals that a prized gun that had been captured by Murarirao's cavalry was appropriated by Haider and that Nandraj had to make him return it to Murarirao!

Despite this, a victory at Trichy might have made them friends. However, their attempt to capture the fort ended in a stalemate. It seems that Dupleix had less and less support over time for his activities in India and there was no vigour in the French contingent. It seemed unlikely that the French would fulfil their commercial promises to Murarirao. When Major Stringer Lawrence attacked the French at Trichy, they retreated and Sardar Balaji Ghorpade of Murarirao's army and thirty of his troops were killed. Once again, both Governor and Madame Dupleix* expressed their regret, but they knew that the end could not be far.

Murarirao was losing his brothers and comrades to French inaction. On the other hand, despite committing to warfare, he was not being paid regularly. Dupleix began to borrow personally to pay Murarirao and managed to hold out as long as possible. The last straw was when Dupleix was peremptorily recalled to France and a new governor was sent. When Charles Godeheu took over, he promptly told Murarirao's agents that he had nothing to do with the liabilities incurred by Dupleix. Not only this, Godeheu entered into a treaty with the English, conceding to them virtually all demands that they put forward, giving the English a new hero, Major Stringer Lawrence.

In his memoir, Dupleix wrote, three days before he died, '*I have sacrificed my youth, my fortune, my life to enrich my nation in Asia. I am treated as the vilest of mankind. I am in the most deplorable indigence compelled to ask for decrees for delay in order not to be dragged to prison.*'

At the end of 1754, Murarirao found himself in Gutti again.

* Refer to Annexure 6 to know more about Madame Dupleix and her impact on Dupleix's fortunes.

Section 10

Regrets and Rebuttals

Ironically enough, Haider Ali,[*] (refer portrait on page 158) who had been directly instrumental in saving Nandraj Dalwai and Murarirao Ghorpade from certain captivity and probable death, was to make it his business to destroy them both.

A lot of literature[**] is dedicated to the persona of Haider Ali. His memory was strong, and he remembered all the events of his childhood, recognized every soldier of his army and remembered a person after having seen them just once. He would make decisions on administration and war instantly, and legend was that he took decisions without pondering on them. He passed on the instructions to his commanders fighting at different locations as though he were present there.

While his mother tongue was Persian, he could speak in Dakhni Urdu, Kannada, Tamil, Marathi and even Telugu. Kannada had the distinction of being the language of Mysore. He could even speak a little French. One of his favourite sayings was:

'My Holy Prophet (peace be on him) is illiterate and I am too an illiterate and upon the Grace of God Allah, I am able to perform such deeds you the learned people cannot.'

---

[*] Haider was, at the time of saving his King Nandraj and Murarirao, thirty-two years old, a man of astonishing energy and enterprise and few scruples, earthy and yet with an ambition that soared above the clouds, a restless savage who was so illiterate that he had yet to learn to sign his name. He had risen from humble beginnings. His family had been rendered destitute by his father's early death, so his mother had brought her brood to Mysore, and sought the protection of a relative who served in the king's army. Haider had been taken on as a common soldier but within a year, he had won a shooting competition and thus come to the notice of Nandraj, who rewarded him by raising him to the command of 'fifty horse and 200 peons'. From here, he kept growing in strength.

[**] Anwar Haroon, *Kingdom of Haider Ali and Tipu Sultan, Sultanat-e-Khudadad*, 2013.

37

The Marathas Wake up Again

It was in 1755 that Peshwa Nanasaheb and the Marathas woke up again. He attacked Savannur–one of the subahs of the Carnatic–with the support of M. Bussy, the French general, who had stayed back as mentor to Nizam Salabat Jung. The Peshwa won a decisive victory and decided to woo Murarirao, to further this advance.

The Peshwa also appointed two people, Gopalrao Patwardhan and Malharrao Raste, to be his agents in the South, and they constantly came in contact with Murarirao. However, Murarirao knew that these trips by the Peshwa were just a means to fill his coffers. There was no purpose to it, and he kept up the charade by choosing to write long letters to the Peshwa committing his purpose, while skirting his calls to be involved. In effect, he was extremely lukewarm towards the Peshwa.

The Peshwa's next move was against Nandraj of Mysore. He demanded such a ridiculous sum from Nandraj that the latter had no choice but to defend his capital with whatever means he possessed. However, by sheer accident, one of the Maratha shells hit the top of the Sri Ranganatha Temple. This was considered a bad omen and both parties decided not to prolong hostilities; Nandraj offered some money and a few territories to the Peshwa.

The Peshwa returned to Poona. The astute Haider Ali felt it safe to drive out Maratha agents from Mysore and reclaim the territories around the rainy season, so that the Peshwa could not retaliate immediately.

As Murarirao watched these happenings in the Deccan, he received news about an old friend. On 23 June 1757, Robert Clive won the Battle of Plassey and became the master of Bengal. Murarirao thought wistfully about the times when they had fought together. Oh, to fight with someone who actually won the war in his mind, way before it played out on the battlefield!

Back in Mysore, when the Marathas returned to reclaim the territories, they found that they were met this time by Haider Ali, who agreed to pay them if they would let go of the fourteen districts they had originally taken. Nandraj did not have the money, but Haider gave his personal security, and such was his reputation that the bankers in the Maratha camp paid on his behalf. Now Haider took over these fourteen districts and started to administer them. His larger plan, of course, was to oust Nandraj.

Haider Ali was an imposing man. He was six feet tall and well built. He possessed a commanding and brisk personality. He used to shave his beard, moustache and even eyebrows. He would wear a large turban on his head, which was decorated with flowers. His army had to wear a certain kind of uniform, while Haider used to wear a white satin outfit, embroidered with golden thread. His socks were velvet and yellow and his waistband was made out of white silk. He would carry a cane decorated with gems at one end.[1] His conviction of his own importance led him to dress distinctly. Within three years of taking over these fourteen territories, Haider became the virtual ruler of Mysore. Soon, he ousted Nandraj and envisioned the expansion of Mysore.

At the time of Haider making himself the master of Mysore, Murarirao's Gutti included a contiguous strip of territory all the way to Sandur and Chitradurga in the West. It could be said that Murarirao possessed a domain that was as large as that of some of the Nawabs of the Carnatic. In the South, it extended all the way to Chikkaballapura and in the East it went in and out of the hilly terrain touching Dhone, Tadpatri and Cottacotta. Murarirao also held many of the important ports in this area, including Sandur, Madakshira, Gundikonda, Koppal, Penukonda and, of course, Gutti, while Gajendragadh was held by other members of his family.

This was a substantial property, and it could be said that Murarirao became rather indolent, despite the fact that he never expected the Marathas to show up for him. Ever. At this point, he wasn't worried about Haider either. So he became a man of letters,[2] favouring elaborate correspondence with one and all for a large period after 1755. From time to time, he would offer military help to both the English and the French. He wrote to the English Governor Lord Bigot on 16 December 1759, '*There is no difficulty in my sending you the army and artillery; in reality my government is your own.*' He wrote similar letters to the French as well, assuring them of his readiness to help.

However, two things happened in 1761. On 14 January, the Marathas lost the Battle of Panipat. On the same day, the French surrendered to the English, making many French soldiers and officers jobless. Haider absorbed 300 of them in his army.

Panipat was an extremely severe blow to the Marathas. So much so that a devastated Peshwa Nanasaheb breathed his last in June 1761. Imagining a weakened Maratha army, Haider was emboldened to extend his power and influence rapidly and quite considerably.

38

Murarirao Waits for the Inevitable

Murarirao was cleaning his sword. It was something he preferred to do himself. One of the men in his unit, Sakha, approached him and asked, 'Are we going to fight somewhere today?'

Murarirao shook his head. He was uncertain about his future with the Marathas after the death of Peshwa Nanasaheb. 'No, but we have to prepare. Things will never be the same again. Haider will come for Gutti.'

Sakha said, 'Yes. But Haider is afraid of you. After all, you are capable of fighting like your grand-uncle Santaji.'

Murarirao thought about all the battles he had fought alongside his own father Sidhoji. Then he smiled abruptly and said with concern, 'Haider is coming for some imaginary treasure, which he feels I have hidden under the fort. Haider has hired many of Dupleix's trained Frenchmen and built a formidable force.'

Yunus Khan did not contribute to this conversation. He knew that Haider was now a disquieting enemy. About the treasure, there *had* been a treasure at one point, but a very amorous Murarirao had lavished the choicest, most resplendent rubies and emeralds on Saheba. And thanks to 'household spies', there was a very high probability that Haider had heard of these overtures and suspected there was more.

Sakha laughed. 'Treasure? Where is it?'

Everyone laughed. For the most part, Murarirao had always maintained complete transparency when it came to managing the affairs of his kingdom. His loyal troops respected the donations he made towards the temples and the personal attention he lavished on them. Nobody suspected the presence of any treasure.

'Do you know, Sakha? We believe Gutti is secure. But brave warriors find ways to pull down the most impregnable defences. Do you remember the way Tanaji Malusare captured Sinhagad fort with *ghorpads* (monitor lizards)? Many years before Tanaji, my forefathers Karn Singh and Bhim Singh had done the same at Vishalgadh for Mohammed Gawan. At that time, we were servants of the Bahamani kingdom.'

Sakha responded, 'At least you and I have the good fortune to fight for people of our land! Your forefathers must have had no choice.'

Murarirao said, 'We always have a choice. It's only when a large number of people think we have no choice that it becomes reality. I'm saying that the idea of using a ghorpad does not belong to Tanaji. It belongs to Karn Singh, who was the father of our Ghorpade clan.'

Sakha was listening intently.

Murarirao's face was animated. He continued, 'So you tie a string around a ghorpad and make it climb to the top of the hill where the enemy fort is. It gets a firm grip on the surface and sits there. The other end of the string is with the men below. One man, light and lithe, climbs to the top first, making sure that he does not put excess weight on the ghorpad. This is a matter of pure prayer and it is the tricky part. This person may lose his life if the ghorpad changes its mind and starts climbing down or moves unexpectedly. If he succeeds, then he finds a new anchor and throws a stout rope for his fellow warriors to climb.'

Sakha said, 'When you say it like this, it sounds possible. Otherwise, the first tendency is to ask how a man can sit on the back of a ghorpad and how will the animal bear his weight.'

Murarirao nodded. 'There are tricks that only warriors know. Santaji, for instance, had some incredible tricks and his philosophy was to first "embed fear" into the heart of the enemy.'

And now you know how the Ghorpades got their name!

Sakha ventured again, 'Santaji had the fortune to fight many battles. How many battles does a good warrior have within him?'

Murar was surprised by the question. But a part of him was excited. 'A warrior just needs to find something worth fighting for, all his life.'

Sakha realized that he had touched a raw nerve. He retreated.

39

Senapati

By 1762, Haider's position and military capability were now much stronger than those of Murarirao, who was perhaps the only power in the Deccan who still dared to openly defy him, from his principality at Gutti. He also knew that Murarirao was skilled at balancing powers in order to hold his own; a tireless correspondent, Murar's messengers kept in touch with the Maratha courts, the Nizam and the nawabs, and the English and French in Madras and Pondicherry.

Haider's absolute plan of expansion made him acutely aware that he must either come to terms with Murarirao Ghorpade or finish him. Murarirao was extremely difficult to deal with, for he valued his freedom and self-respect more than anything else. The only exception he would make was to risk everything if the new Peshwa, Madhavrao, decided to make a determined effort to curb the rising power of Haider. After the drubbing at Panipat, this seemed to be wishful thinking.

At first, Haider decided to send a spy to poison Murarirao. Zahira arrived in Gutti, posing as a trained dancer. She caught Murarirao's eye and became a close confidante. She played chess with him, regaled him with her unique stories and took interest in all the art, dance and other routines at the Gutti Fort. Murarirao, of course, was thrilled to play chess; he had learnt it from Saheba, after all. Until one day, Murarirao's second wife, Ranubai, saved him from his own delusion and caught Zahira red-handed, about to feed him a bowlful of poisonous kheer.

Zahira's failure angered Haider further. He took it upon himself to destroy Murarirao and become the lone ruler of the Deccan.

Haider Ali started to assert himself. He started with Sira,[1] the de facto Maratha depot for provisions and military stores for their Karnataka expeditions. This was easy, but then he immediately attacked Chikkaballapura, one of Murarirao's domains. Needless to say, Murarirao had to send help. At this time, both sides suffered huge casualties. But Haider made peace and withdrew.

What happened next was entirely unanticipated. As soon as Haider turned back, he was shocked to learn that the Palegar who had resisted him bravely, immediately welcomed Murarirao's soldiers to guard Chikkaballapura and himself took shelter at Nandidurg. In his book on Haider Ali, Narendra Krishna Sinha says, 'Haider became furious at this deception.'

Slighted, he surrounded Nandidurg with troops to starve out its inmates and declared an all-out vicarious war against Murarirao.

The breadth of Murarirao's domain was such that his principalities were too scattered to be successfully defended against the kind of army that Haider had built—his French recruits were highly effective. Haider was not only able to take Chikkaballapura back from Murar's soldiers but also captured Murarirao's forts of Penukonda and Madaksira. He also took many of Murar's men prisoners, including Khanderao Ghorpade. It was a series of big wins for Haider.

'The troops of Murarirao were scattered like a grain shaken out of a slit bag,' records Haider's Persian biographer Hussain Ali Kirmani. 'They did not pause even to drink water until they had arrived at the walls of Gutti.' While the latter may have been an exaggeration, the fact remains that Murar's reputation suffered a setback.

Taking full advantage of the dislocation caused by Panipat and the internal dissensions, intrigues and the preoccupation of the Marathas, Haider pursued an aggressive policy of extending his domains towards the Krishna River. He attacked Maratha strongholds like Dharwad, changed the name of Bidnur to Haidernagar and encroached upon regions such as Raidurg and Chitradurg, too. Mark Wilks, a contemporary chronicler, estimates that loot from Bidnur alone brought Haider '12 million sterling'. Bidnur had immense hoarded wealth contributed by the rice trade that supported the whole of Malabar and some parts of Muscat.

The Frenchman Maistre De La Tour, who accompanied Haider in the expedition, observed: 'Haider caused pearls and precious stones to be measured in their sight with a corn measure and when two heaps of gold ingots and trinkets had been piled up, they surpassed the height of a man on horseback.'[2]

Murarirao stayed put in Gutti through these expeditions. Past sixty years of age, he was circumspect about his chances against Haider. But when he was brought news of Haider Ali's triumphs and progress through northern Karnataka, it made him very happy. The Marathas may not come for him, but surely they would come for themselves! Peshwa Madhavrao[3] was all of sixteen, and yet he had an energy, enthusiasm and willingness to deal with problems head-on, which was a welcome surprise. Peshwa Madhavrao wrote to Murarirao, requesting him to proceed on his own and launch an attack on some of Haider's conquests.

Portrait of Peshwa Madhavrao Balajirao
(Thorla Madhavrao or Madhavrao 1st) (1763), by artist Bhoj Raj
Source: Wikimedia Commons

Murarirao responded gladly. He didn't want to lose out on working with Madhavrao closely; God knows he regretted not working with Bajirao in the past. Murar captured Doddaballapura, believing fully that the Peshwa was marching towards Bangalore. Murar sent a message to the Peshwa, 'Knowing that your army is on the march, Haider Ali has retreated towards Bangalore.' While it is true that Madhavrao was on his way to join Murarirao, he learnt that his meddlesome uncle Raghunath Rao was trying to oust him as Peshwa and he turned in his tracks and rushed back to Poona.

Peshwa Madhavrao sent word to Murarirao that he had every intention of resuming the Karnataka expedition, but Haider took full advantage of the interim lull and made more conquests in turn. The reality was that most kings in the Maratha region would fold at the mere approach of Haider's column.

In the meantime, the Nizam at Haiderabad, Mir Nizam Ali Khan Siddiqi, the fourth son of Asaf Jah, declared war against the Marathas, which further delayed any chance of the Peshwa coming to save Murarirao against a potential reaction from Haider. The Peshwa defeated the Nizam but it was not until 25 September 1763 that he was able to return to Poona. Murarirao was growing increasingly impatient. His mind went back to the time in Trichy where he had waited for the Marathas and they never came.

However, this time, Haider had to be taken to task as the Peshwa's own dominion was at stake. Madhavrao assuaged Murarirao's sentiments in his own interest. In February 1964, when Madhavrao crossed the Krishna River and took Haider's port of Honnavar, Murar was overjoyed. Over the next three months, Peshwa Madhavrao's army had a highly successful military encounter against Haider's forces and inflicted a severe defeat on him. First was the Battle of Rattehalli, an open battle where Haider was baited and routed. Then was Annawady where Haider had laid a trap for the Peshwa, which was foiled by the latter's spy network. Immediately, Haider counter-attacked at Varada River, where Shahaji Bhosale and Murarirao were able to defeat him. Meanwhile, Madhavrao took the fort of Dharwad and proceeded to Savannur. Here, at some distance from each other, Madhavrao, Murar and two more Maratha contingents were camping. Haider attacked again; the forces under Murarirao effectively blocked the attempt of this surprise attack from reaching Madhavrao. Even under murderous fire, Murarirao's forces stood their ground till the reinforcements from Maratha Huzurat (household troops) under the personal command of Madhavrao came to support him. In this battle, according to Eloy Joze Correa Peixoto's Portuguese book,[4] *History of Nawab Haider Ali Khan Bahadur*, 'In order that he might escape being taken or known, he took off all his clothes and a *topas* and a *caffree* brought him safe back to camp.'

The Peshwa now promised to stay in Karnataka throughout the monsoon. He also offered Murarirao the jagir of Bhagalot as well as the sentimental value of the title 'Senapati', which his grand-uncle Santaji Ghorpade had enjoyed.

The treaty of 1765 followed, which Haider signed as an act of tokenism; he would neither read nor follow it. For all his nonchalance though, Manohar Malgonkar in his book *Scaling the Heights* suggests that Haider only resisted giving back the lands to Murar as part of this treaty. 'Murarirao is a constant source of danger,' said Haider at the time, while never intending to honour the treaty anyway.

Murarirao's deepest desire at this point was to share this joy with Tara.

Section 11

Pushing up Daisies

We quote from the Anantapur Gazetteer (1905):

Gutti's main hill is a huge, precipitous mass of bare rock which towers hundreds of feet above all the others. The fort was completely impregnable; the summit of the fortress is about 2,150 feet above sea level and probably nearly 1,000 feet above the surrounding country.

The fort is supplied with water from a number of reservoirs which have been made in the clefts of the rock to catch the rain. One of these is traditionally declared to be connected with a stream at its foot. However, it is only the large, deep wells in the old town at the base of the fort which normally took care of the needs of the garrison. One of these wells has a spring which does not dry up even in the height of summer. But the main citadel of the Gutti fort, which was considered impregnable, had to depend, in an emergency, on a number of reservoirs or rock-cut tanks or pits which stored mostly rainwater.

40

Murarirao's Last Hurrah with the Marathas

Peshwa Madhavrao (refer picture on page 178) kept coming back to Karnataka to hurt Haider. At times, the Peshwa would draw Haider out via stealth. At other times, he would entice him, saying that he had come to see for himself what kind of a soldier he really was.

We have already spoken about the first battle of 1764.

Then came the 1766 campaign against Haider. Murar wrote to the Maratha court, 'The Peshwa is fully aware that I have no thought of differing from his plans. I shall waste no time in saddling my horse and presenting myself.' As Murarirao's contingent joined the Peshwa at Raidurgha, Madhavrao Peshwa captured Madgiri Fort, and released the erstwhile king and the dowager queen of Bidnur imprisoned there by Haider. Maratha forces also took Chennaiadurga, Madaksira, Chikkaballapura, Doddaballapura, Devanahalli, Hosakote and Kolara and forced Haider to sue for peace.

As the Peshwa returned to Poona after a successful bid, Murar found himself on the right side of a Nizam-English alliance, who wanted to attack Haider. This was to be called the 'First Mysore War', which took place from 1767 to 1769.

Cassel's *Illustrated History of India* gives the following account of the action that followed:

> Morari had been urged by the colonel to encamp within the advanced pickets of our army; but replied, with a confident smile,

> that he knew how to manage Hyder, and pitched his tents a mile to the right. The Mysorean leader formed a plan to penetrate into the Maratha camp, and on the night of the 22d of August, two infantry columns with 6,000 horse and some elephants set out with this intent, and with special orders to bring the head of Morari Rao to Hyder, who was to remain in reserve with the main body to support the attack or counteract any movement on the part of Smith. But Morari had his corps of spies as well as Hyder, and was quite aware of the coming event. He gave strict orders that none of his cavalry were to mount but that each man should remain stationed at his horse's head. His further orders were that they were to be on the alert and attack all mounted men, without waiting for any password or countersign.
>
> The cavalry of Hyder was followed so closely by his infantry, that the Maratha camp would have been assailed in force but for a curious episode. The battle elephant of Morari Rao, irritated by receiving an accidental wound tore up the chain by which he was picketed, and seizing it with his trunk, he swung it madly aloft and around him and while rushing wildly through the camp he dashed with it at the advancing cavalry of Hyder. These, supposing that the Marathas were charging them, recoiled and rushed over their approaching infantry supporters... The Mysoreans fled.

In the battles that followed, Murarirao dealt a personal defeat to Haider, penetrating right up to his tent where he and his son Tipu had a narrow escape. Haider's chapter would been well and truly over then. The other sad part is that he lost Yunus Khan here.

As soon as Madhavrao left, Haider's brother-in-law Mir Reza tried to please Haider by taking back Doddaballapura from the Marathas. The pattern was that every time the Marathas gained advantages and would return to Poona during the rains, Haider would use this opportunity to get everything back.

So during Madhavrao's next march in 1769, as soon as Haider heard about it, he reached out to Murarirao, to present himself at his camp and agree to become his vassal or face the consequences.

Murar was curious and he decided to meet Haider, despite warnings given to him against it.

To be sure, he had taken all possible precautions too, such as keeping a force under Shivarao Ghorpade poised in the vicinity to launch an attack against Haider's encampment at the slightest sign of treachery. But Haider made no attempt to arrest Murarirao or assassinate him; on the contrary, he received him with honour and pressed presents on him of three elephants, a jewelled turban clasp, a pearl necklace and rich robes, as well as a purse of Rs 25,000 in place of a banquet. He urged him to become his vassal and to pay him only a token tribute of Rs 5000 a year.

To this, Murarirao agreed. This was obviously a pretend pose. Even Haider could not have believed that he was being sincere, for he, too, knew full well how Murarirao had acquired something of a reputation as an accomplished negotiator, with an ability to disarm the opposition by appearing to give in under pressure. But it must not be supposed that Haider was being altogether earnest either. Once the Peshwa returned to the Carnatic, their relationship would automatically fall into its old groove. Meanwhile, if, by a show of sweet reasonableness, he could win over Murarirao to his side or at least ensure his neutrality, it was a ploy worth trying or so Haider convinced himself.

At this meeting itself he may have got an indication that Murarirao had reservations about being his vassal, for when Haider requested he send a force under Shivarao Ghorpade to accompany his army, Murarirao had firmly declined. Thus, having pretended enough, Haider and Murarirao parted ways.

Haider went off towards Savannur to discipline its Nawab, and Murarirao to Gutti, to prepare to welcome Madhavrao back.

41

Missed Opportunities

The same pattern of easy conquest of Haider's territories was repeated when Madhavrao arrived. Murarirao finally told the Peshwa, 'Unless the Maratha army stays on, Haider will never be vanquished.'

So, this time, he appointed one of his brave generals, Trimbakrao Pethe, to stay back in Karnataka during the rains so as not to lose the advantages of the campaign.

Murarirao and Trimbakrao Pethe continued to deal blows to Haider at Melkote, a valley near Srirangapatnam. As Trimbakrao Pethe reported to the Peshwa, 'Hindurao Senapati's force and Daulatrao Ghorpade's son Anandrao were with us . . . and later they made a furious cavalry charge. There was desperate fighting and the Rao Senapati (Murarirao) captured all the guns.'

Haider tried to make the best of a desperate situation and fought with grit. But the Marathas pressed home their attack with undiminished vigour. The battle reached its climax when, as Sinha describes, 'Haider had to quit his horse in a rush and was carried up the hill. Standing on a millstone, he viewed on all sides with helpless anger. The Marathas charged and pursued his troops. (Then) he fled, attended only by fourteen good horsemen . . . to Srirangapattanam.'

Trimbakrao's report to the Peshwa has the authentic, on-the-spot ring:

'Thousands of the enemy troops came with twists of straw held between their teeth in token of surrender and I let them go.'

There are various versions of how Haider escaped. It is said that he affected a beggar's garb, and this may well have been true because once before, too, he had eluded capture by casting off his rich robes for some humble disguise. Anyway, it is easy to see how he or, for that matter, his son Tipu could have got mixed among the thousands of others who, because they were holding twists of grass in their mouths, were allowed to go.

The Marathas seldom made prisoners of enemy troops or even of their lower ranking officers, and certainly did not punish them as Haider often did. According to Sinha, Haider left in the field '40/45 guns, 20/25 elephants, and 7/8,000 horses, besides baggage and treasure'. This is called the famous battle of Moti Talav or Chinkurali.

Why didn't Pethe and Murar continue to Haider's capital where he was hiding and take him down? Surely, such a drubbing as Moti Talav deserved to bring the final downfall of Haider. Not only had he suffered defeat, this was a very big public blow to his reputation! Remember, that we are still in 1771 and at almost sixty-eight years of age, Murar is fully capable of outwitting Haider.

During this period, Madhavrao was all set to launch a final charge against Haider, while also dispatching some of his able soldiers up north to recover the losses incurred during Panipat.

However, Madhavrao's health started deteriorating and it was discovered that he was infected with tuberculosis. He had to return from Miraj as the effects of the disease had started becoming prominent. Despite taking treatment from an English doctor, there were no signs of improvement and slowly, the disease affected his intestines. There was no cure for tuberculosis in those times. Madhavrao decided to spend his last days in his favourite Ganesha Chintamani Temple at Theur.

The bravest of the brave Peshwa Madhavrao died on 18 November 1772. Murarirao was truly shattered. There was a time when Murarirao was indifferent to the Marathas, but this young man had given him everything he could have ever hoped for.

The inconsistent and untrustworthy Raghunathrao, who was under house arrest at the time of Madhavrao's death—Madhavrao suspected Raghunathrao of attempting to murder him and oust him several times—became the chief adviser of the Maratha kingdom.

No sooner did Madhavrao die, than there was utter confusion[1] in the Maratha ranks. The English declared war against the Marathas. With the Marathas trying to hammer out a treaty with the English, Haider saw this as the perfect opportunity to move in on Murarirao. His beloved Peshwa Madhavrao was no more, and Haider knew that no one would come to aid Murarirao.

Haider sent a message to Murarirao to surrender the guns he had captured from him at Moti Talav and pay him a token tribute of Rs 1 lakh in acceptance of vassalage, and to send a contingent to serve under his overall command.

Murarirao saw red when he received the message. He was now in his seventies, but as waspish as ever when slighted! He sent a spirited and somewhat explosive reply: 'I have seen you when you were a mere Naik, with but five men under you. I, Murarirao Hindurao, happen to be the Senapati of the Maratha kingdom. You may have risen since then but I can always take you on. As to the tribute you ask, I am in the habit of levying it, not paying it.'

Expecting Haider to come straight for him, Murarirao sent the women of his family and the families of the other commanders in the citadel to the safety of his fort at Madakasira, 160 km from Gutti.

It was here that Murarirao's father, Sidhoji Hindurao Ghorpade, had been laid to rest.

42

The Death of a Warrior

Haider laid siege to Gutti towards the end of December 1775. Murarirao seemed quite confident of resisting Haider's formidable force long enough to defeat his plan and save Gutti. He had about 4000 of his handpicked men to defend the fort, which was well provided with guns, ammunition, food and fodder. However, a large number of non-combatants had also to be protected within the walls of the fort.

While he was prepared to fight, Murarirao was also a skilled diplomat. He never completely closed the door to parleys. As some arrangement was being discussed for truce, one of the conditions was that Murarirao be permitted to send away the sick and the wounded. According to Wilks, this was a ploy to prolong the defence of the fort by 'dismissing the greater part of his garrison'.

The fewer the people he had to support, the fewer provisions that would get used.

Murarirao also offered to give half the sum demanded by Haider, Rs 6 lakh, in the form of jewellery, and provide hostages for the remainder. Accordingly, the jewellery boxes and hostages were taken to Haider's camp by Pale Khan, the son of Yunus Khan.

Haider treated Pale Khan 'with such a show of consideration that the young man was thrown off his guard and revealed that Murarirao would never have agreed to the truce terms if the fort had not been reduced to only three days water supply'.

This was enough for Haider, who had an excellent ability to draw out and pick up clues in every sentence. By 10 March 1776, the last drop of water in the fort had been exhausted and, for the next four days, the defenders of Gutti managed to live and fight by eating uncooked rice with some moisture from scraped, wet mud. A protracted siege during the hot months was always going to be critical. This was, in fact, the secret of Gutti–its Achilles heel. Murarirao decided to call it a day and stop hoping for the capricious shower!

One can picture him dauntlessly walking down to his fate, having bid a gut-wrenching farewell to the fort that had not let him down, and after a last prayer at the altar of Shakti (locally known as Satyamma–the goddess of truth and power), which still stands carved in the cliffside of the fort, he strode down with only five men accompanying him.

Once within sight, Haider, with his reputation for mercilessness, had Murarirao Ghorpade dragged out unceremoniously. Defeated in body, his spirit yearned for his own brothers–the Marathas–especially the young Madhavrao with whom he had fought so many memorable battles.

In his mind ran a tumultuous flashback of memories–things he had left undone. So many of them.

Haider at once had him surrounded by his guards. Meanwhile, Haider's son Tipu Sultan went up to the fort with more soldiers who were placed at various gates and vantage points within it. On 15 March 1776, the black-and-white flag of the Ghorpades was hauled down from Gutti's flagstaff, never to fly there again.

Interestingly, Haider made a desperate effort to locate the treasure that Murarirao was believed to have hidden in Gutti. Murarirao himself was subjected to the most intensive questioning and interrogation, which must have been more brutal than the act of being captured itself. He lived through the ordeal and succeeded in maintaining that there was no hidden treasure. Even to this day, the myth of buried treasure at Gutti persists, and will always be associated with the place, however stark and spartan it is and has always been.

To this day, Murarirao remains one of the most enigmatic figures in Indian history.

43

Murarirao's Survivors

Here's what is known about Murarirao's survivors:[1]

The black and white flag of the Ghorpades was hauled down from the flagstaff. The date, as estimated by Sardesai, was 15th March, 1776. Two days later, Haider sent a force to take Madakasira where, it will be recalled, Murarirao had sent his family. It was captured without difficulty, and Murarirao's wife and sons—Venkatrao and Narsingrao—were taken prisoners. However, his nephew, Shivarao Ghorpade, was able to make good his escape. Two weeks after the fort had fallen, Haider sent off Murarirao and family to his capital, Srirangapatnam. A Maratha newsletter of 16th April gives a glimpse of how they were conducted.

> Silver chains were brought up to fetter the Senapati with. He remonstrated to Haider that he had come to him as a brother and asked: 'What is the need for fetters?' whereupon they were taken away. But, after they had travelled another ten or fifteen miles (about twenty four km), a halt was ordered to put fetters on Murarirao's two sons, Venkatrao and Narsingrao. Both boys, their eyes brimming with tears, kept staring beseechingly at their father, who protested at this treatment. Whereupon, the fetters were first put on the Senapati himself and after that on both his sons.

A few weeks later, Haider returned to Srirangapatnam and gave orders for Murarirao and his family to be sent to Kabbaladurga, a fort which stands about 25 km to the east of Srirangapatnam, built on a hill 3500 feet above sea level. Mark Wills comments that 'an imprisonment at Kabbaladurga, was, at all times, equivalent to a sentence of death'. Thus, the curtain drops on Murarirao. No one other than his guards, or perhaps some other men serving Haider Ali, ever saw him again, and even the writers of newsletters were reduced to reporting rumours.

Murarirao was certainly alive till the middle of the following year because his name crops up in the negotiations between a Maratha commander Haripant Fadke and Haider Ali. Was a prisoner exchange for Murarirao discussed? Fadke had brought a force into Karnataka, and even though he did not have much success, Haider was keen on patching up his differences with the Marathas.

Later, the womenfolk of Murarirao's family were being shifted from Kabbaladurga to some other place when their party was attacked by a patrol belonging to Muhammad Ali, the Nawab of Arcot. It would seem that they were later brought back to their relatives, and that Ranubai, as well as Shivarao Ghorpade's wife Sububai, were granted pensions for their maintenance by the Poona court.

In November 1777, there was a rumour that Murarirao had subverted his guards and managed to escape from prison, but even at the time, few people gave much credence to it. He is said to have died towards the end of 1777. Nothing more is heard of his two sons, and it is almost certain that they too died in Kabbaladurga before long.

Here he must have suffered privations and insults and perhaps even torture. And yet one cannot help thinking that his real ordeal already lay behind him; that nothing he had endured in captivity could have been as terrible as those last few days in his own fort where he must have been tormented by the dreaded 'what-ifs'.

These are the questions that linger:

1. What if the Marathas had conquered the South and consolidated the empire in the Deccan when they had the chance to? Why were they facing north most of the time? What could have been the reason that Bajirao

and Murarirao did not work closely together to make this happen?

2. What if the two families of Satara and Kolhapur had united and set aside their differences and become an impregnable empire?
3. What if the latter-day Peshwas had understood Shivaji Maharaj's emphasis on a strong navy and continued to control access to India via the oceans and seas? Would this have prevented India's eventual colonization?
4. What if the Marathas had finished the jobs they started—from Chanda Sahib to Haider Ali—on time?
5. Last but not least, given that the Nizam's refusal to take sides between the British and the French was well known, does Murarirao's timely support for Clive therefore become his biggest regret at the time of his death?

Epilogue

Murarirao's Present-Day Relevance and the Expedition to Gutti

We were an interesting group that decided to scale Murarirao Ghorpade's beloved Gutti Fort one afternoon.

Vijay Bhasker of the Gutti Samrakshana Samiti, Venkata Somaji, a young historian, my co-author Indrajeet Ghorpade and I. There was also a seventy-year-old village elder, Kale Ramanaji, who walked with us and put us all to shame; he was faster than all of us!

Venkata Somaji shared eagerly, 'We feel Murarirao's blessings even today. He came to Gutti and developed both the fort and the area around it. The drought-infested Anantpur Zilla has the gift of water thanks to Murarirao's work. He built several wells around the area that could sustain the people in and around Gutti.'

As we reached the foothills of the fort, Vijay Bhasker said, 'First, let us visit the Ramasamy temple in Guttikota.'[1]

At the foot of the Gutti Fort was a Ram temple, featuring idols of Lord Ram and his queen Sita. Somaji said, 'This temple was built before all Ram temples started having Hanuman as a standard feature. Also the inscriptions suggest that the temple dates back to the time of Lord Rama. We believe that one round of renovation happened in the second century AD.'

I was amazed. Could one assume that Murarirao, his troops and family came here to worship, I wondered.

'Murarirao built several temples,' Somaji continued. 'An Anjaneya[2] Swami temple, Sree Nageswara[3] temple, Sree Renuka Yellamma[4] temple outside the fort and Sree Satyamma[5] and

Vinayaka temples inside the fort. But the most striking feature of Gutti is that at all eight entrances of the fort, he made Hanumanji temples. This became the *Ashta digbatdan*[6] protecting Gutti fort. Particularly, the temple at the south entrance called "Hanuman Gadi" is said to have unique powers.'

By now we had reached the summit of the fort. Looking out at the path we had climbed, I could see that there was ample provision for water at various places within the fort and additional hollows that could collect rainwater. A natural depth became a jail for prisoners, there was a performing arts studio and living quarters. As we looked down, we could well imagine how difficult it would be to scale the fort. There was an infamous snake well and even a crocodile perimeter that made a deadly trap for enemies who would accidentally fall in. Neat!

I wondered about the name Gutti itself. What does it mean?

'Gutti or Gooty means "bunch" or "cluster" in Telugu. Like a bunch of flowers,' said Vijay. 'This is a bunch of small forts; not one single fort. Hence, Gutti.'

Indrajeet Ghorpade remarked, 'I'm sure there are books in Telugu about all this.'

Somaji said, 'There is a book[7] about how Gutti was named. Also another book[8] that talks about all the rulers[9] that Gutti has had down the ages. But the locals here celebrate Murarirao's reign even today.'

Vijay Bhasker pointed to a place atop the fort, and we went to stand there. He said, 'For us in Ananthpur district, the enduring image of Murarirao is that of him playing chess at the head of the fort with his concubine. This particular concubine was a spy sent by Haider to infiltrate the fort.'

Wow, I thought. And a rather unrelated question popped into my mind. 'Did Shivaji Maharaj ever visit Gutti? Before Murarirao's time?' I asked.

'No, but Maharani Tarabai visited Gutti. Shivaji, however, visited nearby Srisailam[10] in 1677, much after his coronation. He visited a Shiva-Parvati temple[11] in Srisailam and sat down for a ten-day meditation. As it turns out, Shivaji became so lost in meditation that it was difficult to bring him out of it. Finally, he came to consciousness; to everyone's surprise, he said that he did not wish to continue as Chhatrapati. He would like to spend the rest of his life in prayer. That night, it is believed that Goddess Parvati herself whispered in his ears and asked him to continue the work of Hindavi Swarajya. It is believed that she also gave him a word to continue his work.'

'How much of this is true?' I asked.

'I know people who would swear by it, but nothing is documented. What is known is that Shivaji left 70,000 gold coins at the hands of a Brahman Pandit to build the south entrance gate to the temple. This is still called the Shivaji Gopuram. A few Maratha soldiers stayed back to supervise and defend the temple. He also built a ghat (steps to a river) in the name of Lord Ganesha for devotees to have a bath,' added Somaji. 'From here, Shivaji went to Thanjavur to meet Vyankoji, his half-brother, never to return to the South again.'

'Thanjavur was a big part of Murarirao's life too,' I murmured.

Indrajeet had his own 'aha' moment. 'Yes. But I'm glad we discussed the connection between Vyankoji and Shivaji—both sons of Shahaji. Now, for some reason, the story of the Marathas down south is not discussed much. In 1676, Shivaji began the last great campaign of his life—to capture the South and meet his step-brother Vyankoji who had inherited Shahaji's estate in the South. Now, Vyankoji was an active man himself, he had led an army to Thanjavur in 1676 and imposed his own rule, evicting the Nayaka ruler of the place. Thanjavur, a fertile plain with its own sea ports, was a place eyed by every ruler worth his salt.'

'Okay, so when the Marathas reached out to Murarirao to save Thanjavur many years later, it was on account of this fraternal bond?' I ventured.

Indrajeet nodded.

We were walking down the fort now. Upon our descent from the fort on the other side, we stopped at Thomas Munro's[12] samadhi.

'Folks at Gutti refer to Thomas Munro with affection as Munro Aiyya,' said Vijay Bhasker. 'Even Haider's senapati—Mir Qasim—has been laid to rest at Gutti.'

Evidently, the Gutti Fort had stood witness to many an unheard tale and deserved preservation.

Annexures

Annexure 1: Bhosales and Ghorpades, Brothers-in-Arms

As per Manohar Malgonkar's theory that the Ghorpades and Bhosales are cousins descended from Mewar, their common ancestors served the Bahamani Empire from the time of its formation. As servants to the Bahamani kingdom, the descendants continued to participate in wars against the Vijaynagara kingdom in the South–something they were forced to do. They earned respect and favours, in terms of jagirs and titles from the Bahamani sultans as they were brave warriors.

One person in this lineage, Bhairav Singh, started being referred to as Bhosaji. One of the descendants of Bhairav (Bhosaji) Singh took the name Ugrasen Bhosale. He had two sons, Shubha Krishna Bhosale and Karna Singh Bhosale. This Karna Singh famously helped the Bahamani Sultan, Mohammed Gawan capture the fort of Vishalgad (Khelna). He did this innovatively, by tying a string around a ghorpad.[1] This ghorpad–about 4–5 ft long and 15 kg in weight–was capable of climbing up an almost vertical incline, a feat not possible by humans. Once it got to the top, by virtue of its nature, it got a firm grip on the surface and sat there. Now, Karna Singh sent a few ghorpads up in this fashion, hoping that at least one of them would support the weight of a man who would follow them in their climb. The other end of the string, would be with the men below. The lighter and lither of the soldiers would follow the ghorpad's climb to the top with the support of this string.

Two variables that anyone could not control were:

- What if the ghorpad moved? The ghorpad had to remain stationary and not lose its grip. For instance, if this ghorpad started climbing down, the soldier would lose his balance, fall and probably die.
- Would the ghorpad be able to bear the man's weight? This was vital. The ghorpad had to be able to bear the weight of the man who was climbing.

The magical outcome Karna Singh was hoping for was that even if a single soldier climbed up successfully, he would then find an anchor and help the others to climb. The advantage of this method, of course, was the ambush element. The enemy would be guarding all other sides except this one, which no human being could climb. A handful of soldiers could then enter the fort, proceed straight for the guards who manned the main doors of the fort and kill them. On the other side, of course, a garrison of soldiers would be lying in wait to launch a full frontal attack.

In recognition of this wondrous feat, Karna Singh Bhosale was given the title 'Raja Ghorpada Bahadur'[2] by Mohammad Gawan. This is how the surname Ghorpade remained with Karna Singh's descendants, whereas Shubha Krishna Bhosale's descendants retained the surname Bhosale.

Looking at the same story, with the counter view that Shivaji Maharaj did not owe his ancestry to Mewar, let us summarize the above in a slightly different way. In the inter-mixed population of the Deccan, a confluence of many races and cultures, were two brothers Karna Singh (who got the title of Raja Ghorpade Bahadur) and Shubha Krishna Bhosale who worked for Mohammad Gawan. Both of whom lived in Devgiri before their genealogical lines forked apart.

Now, after the death of Mohammad Gawan (1481), the Bahamani dynasty imploded. There were now five separate sultanates:

- Imad Shahi of Berar
- Barid Shahi of Bidar
- Qutub Shahi of Golkonda
- Nizam Shahi of Ahmadnagar
- Adil Shahi of Bijapur

Now, Shubha Krishna Bhosale swore allegiance to Nizam Shahi of Ahmadnagar. His descendant was the famous Chhatrapati Shivaji Maharaj. Karna Singh Ghorpade swore allegiance to Adil Shahi of Bijapur. His descendants were Santaji, Bahirji and Murarirao Ghorpade.

This maintained continuity of the Maratha presence in the Deccan.

Annexure 2: The Rise of the Peshwas

The office of the Peshwa was first created by Shivaji, and its seventh[1] occupant was Balaji Vishwanath—the true founder of the Peshwa lineage.

In Shivaji's council of *Ashta Pradhans*, the Peshwa was regarded as the first of the ministers and the head of the executive. Next in importance came the Senapati or the commander-in-chief. The *Pant Amatya* had the charge of the revenue and accounts. The *Pant Sachiv* controlled all correspondence and the records department. The *Dabir* was in charge of foreign affairs. The *Mantri* was more or less the private secretary, and had the charge of the household. There were two other purely civil functionaries, the *Nyayadhish* and *Pandit Rao* in charge of the judicial and ecclesiastical.

So far, so good, but when and how did the Peshwas become so powerful under Tarabai and Shahu?

When Shivaji created the Ashta Pradhans, he paid their salaries in cash.[2] There were no jagirs and no hereditary offices. Sambhaji continued his father's practice. It was during the time of Rajaram that a change was made in the old system. Rajaram decided to follow a policy of systematically plundering the Mughal territories and for that purpose, he assigned the different parts of the Deccan to his loyal commanders. These commanders established their headquarters in their own areas and also ruled over them.

Out of their revenues, the commanders paid a tribute to Rajaram and kept the rest for themselves. They acted on their own initiative and did not depend upon Rajaram for anything except the grant of territory to them. They considered the parts of the country granted to them as their jagirs, which were won and maintained by them entirely by their own strength. The commanders did whatever suited their interests and were not in any way obedient to Rajaram. On the contrary, they took pride in their independence.

This blunderous system continued not only under Rajaram but also under Tarabai and Shahu. After 1707, when Chhatrapati Shahu wanted to strengthen his hand, he had to ask for the help of the Maratha chiefs who held big jagirs for him. These jagirdars supported Shahu on the condition that their jagirs were not to be touched. The tables had already turned. But there was nothing he could do. If he tried to confiscate their jagirs, that might have resulted in trouble. All the high officials surrounding Shahu themselves had big jagirs and obviously they were not prepared to part with the same.

Balaji Vishwanath himself had huge jagirs; no wonder he did not raise a finger to abolish the system of jagirs, which had now become hereditary. Thus, the rise of the Peshwas and other jagirdars is neither phenomenal nor accidental. They gradually worked their way up from an ordinary position to the headship of the state and eventually to de facto sovereignty.

Balaji Vishwanath also made the office of Peshwa hereditary in the family and paralysed the power of his other colleagues and, ultimately, that of the king. *This transfer of authority from the master to the servant is so gradually, silently, carefully accomplished that the successive steps important as they were in relation to the whole move, escaped all contemporary notice.*[3]

It is an irony of fate that most Peshwas did not, even once, look back to the great Shivaji for ideals, for inspiration. And at a time when they were learning to outlive their old predatory habits, another nation stepped in, a more irresistible power than any that India had seen before, and the Peshwas went down meekly before it.

Annexure 3: An Extract[1] from an Essay about Nizam-ul-Mulk

Nizam-ul-Mulk's early experience in Deccan warfare had accustomed him to danger and hardship. No wonder, the greater portion of his life was spent in the saddle and under arms. His restless blood, which he had inherited from his Turani ancestors, never allowed him to sit idle. The funny thing was, even though he was always at war, he was essentially a lover of peace—all his wars were of a defensive nature.

Work was his greatest pleasure. His genius shone forth in action. His love of power was tempered with prudence. No dangers were too threatening for him to face, no obstacles too formidable, no tasks too laborious. And yet his soundness of judgement and great common sense saved him from recklessness or from rash attempts to achieve the impossible. In fact, he was gifted with a pronounced political genius and an astounding power of foresight. He possessed, to a supreme degree, a deep and lively sense of reality in politics.

He was as gifted a tactician in diplomacy as in war, and in both he knew how to profit by experience. He was quick to perceive and utilize his enemy's errors. He is the only statesman in the early eighteenth century in India whose tactical aims have been completely fulfilled and whose insight was not belied by subsequent events.

Nizam-ul-Mulk was greatly fond of the company of the learned with whom he used to hold discourses every afternoon. He knew Turkish perfectly well and took delight in speaking this language with his Turani officers. He was a scholar of Persian and composed poetry in it under the pseudonym 'Shakir', which means 'the

Resigned One'. He has left a 'Diwan', which has been published by Mirza Nasrullah Khan, Daulat Yar Jang, Fidai.

Tolerant towards other religions, Nizam-ul-Mulk was a devout upholder of Islamic principles with which he had been fed from infancy. He took great pains to the effect that all religious rites and practices should be performed punctiliously and with the greatest decorum. He endeavoured to follow the teachings of the Quran and the Sunnat in every detail of his personal conduct.

But he was far from being a fanatic. In sharp contrast to Aurangzeb, he respected other faiths, and did not hesitate to appoint non-Muslims to high posts of responsibility, a policy that was usefully followed by his descendants. His boundless good temper and unfeigned humanity were such that everyone, irrespective of their religion, who came in contact with him, admired and loved him. At a time when the charter of the rulers and other public men of India had sunk to an extremely low level, Nizam-ul-Mulk stands out as one the few really good men of the evil time.

Nizam-ul-Mulk believed, and with reason, that he was destined to bring the Deccan, with whose destiny he had completely identified himself, under his beneficent sway. No sooner did he arrive at Aurangabad in 1713 as the Viceroy of the Deccan than he started reorganizing the administrative machinery of the government in order to undo the bad effects of the treaty entered into by the Marathas and Zulfiqar Khan.

Similarly, when he finally established his sway there in 1720, he consolidated his position by the most masterly management of his power and succeeded in completely ousting the Marathas from this part of the country.

The Maratha agents collected chauth and sardeshmukhi and exacted heavy tolls from the merchants and travellers throughout the Deccan. Nizam-ul-Mulk suppressed the authority of the Marathas and openly declared that he was not prepared to tolerate the imperium in imperio. He repudiated the obligations created by the treaty entered into by the Amir-ul-Umara and Raja Sahu by alleging that its observance was inconsistent with the authority invested in the Viceroy of the Deccan. Thus, he succeeded in abrogating this arrangement, the maintenance of which was not only disgraceful to the imperial authority but which also tended to lead to the oppression and impoverishment of the people. His skilful initiative in this connection is a masterpiece of diplomatic manipulation that resulted in the re-establishment of the imperial authority in the Deccan.

Being against the defeatist policy of abdication of the Deccan to the Marathas, Nizam-ul-Mulk had realized that the aforementioned treaty was a direct contradiction of the principles on which the authority of any government worth the name subsists.

When he brought the Deccan under his sway, the Mughal Amils were utterly unable to discharge their duties and the condition of the peasantry was far from satisfactory. There was no justice and no redress of grievances. The authority of the State was treated with contempt and had been perverted into an instrument of oppression.

Nizam-ul-Mulk not only restored the Mughal conquests in the Deccan but also brought back peace and order. He rescued the people from their helpless state and replaced the chaotic conditions with an orderly administration. He reorganized the revenue system, which had become corrupt and iniquitous. He made it a rule that his 'Amils should practise benevolence to the peasantry, inquire into their condition, and exert themselves tactfully to induce them to bring more land under cultivation, assuring them the fruits of their labour'.

The taxation was reduced by rigid supervision and punishment of those servants of the State who made dishonest gains by their exactions. He made it a consistent aim of his policy that the government should exist for the security and welfare of the governed. He seems to have been deeply conscious of the sacred character and the solemn responsibilities of a ruler as is shown by the contents of his testament. His dominions extended all over the Deccan from the River Tapti to the frontiers of Mysore and the Carnatic, right up to Trichy.

There were political advantages for him in getting in touch with the European powers that had established their settlements on the Coromandel coast. He, therefore, consulted his interest to remain on good terms with them, thus preventing the Marathas from seeking an alliance with them against his authority in the South.

On their part, the English and French solicited his favour in order to further their commercial interests. The representatives of both the nations were anxious to enlist the support of the Subedar of the Deccan for their own benefit.

But Nizam-ul-Mulk purposely declined to take sides in their struggle for commercial ascendancy on the grounds of prudence. Although much inclined to favour the French, his position remained so vague up to the last that the representatives of the two European nations at his court failed to know exactly whom he favoured more—a course of action he deliberately adopted as an obvious political convenience. His policy in this regard has since been abundantly justified by the subsequent political events in which the English and French intervened as allies of one or the other of the warring neighbouring states. He had the sagacity to perceive that it was dangerous to get involved in the politics of these foreign settlers who, as he had half suspected, were sure to take full advantage by interfering in the affairs of the Indian rulers.

What he avoided, his descendants could not. They, like other rulers of the country, were impelled by the blind force of destiny to eagerly seek European aid in their internecine struggles and thus give an opportunity to the English to establish their Empire in India.

Annexure 4: Robert Clive, Opium and Murarirao

Robert Clive's death is believed to be an opium fatality.

Upon his death, his old enemy Horace Walpole[1] wrote, 'There was certainly illness in the case, but the world thinks more than illness. His constitution exceedingly broken and disordered, and grown subject to violent convulsions.'

But Robert Clive is hardly the only British gent to be blamed for an opium addiction. The famous William Wilberforce[2] (1759–1833), the philanthropic politician who campaigned against slave-trading, in 1788, suffered such agonizing intestinal pains and digestive system breakdown that his friends despaired of his survival. After a physician, with the utmost difficulty, convinced him to take small doses of opium, he recovered, but for the remaining forty-five years of his life, the drug remained indispensable to him. He feared that if he abandoned opium, he would relapse into intestinal troubles, but stomach pains perhaps provided him an excuse for his habit.

Once, when asked why his fingers were so black, Wilberforce explained that it was from taking opium before making a long speech: 'To that (opium),' he said, 'I owe all my success as a public speaker.' He was too sane and fulfilled in his work to submit to the urge for increased dosages, but though he was never broken by his habit, he was untruthful about it. 'If I take but a single glass of wine,' he claimed, 'I can feel its effects, but I never know when I have taken my dose of opium by my feelings.' This is hard to believe.

Funnily enough, Wilberforce's opium habit was never used to besmirch him. Robert Clive wasn't so lucky. The great tactician, also known as Lord Clive of Plassey, whose military prowess and political ruthlessness entrenched the East India Company's power in India, has been denigrated ruthlessly for his opium use. His consumption also began with a health problem.

In the 1750s, Clive fell ill with severe spasms of abdominal pain, accompanied by acute biliousness; he suffered from gallstones exacerbated by chronic malaria. These abdominal attacks, which continued through his life, often had bouts of nervous prostration as their sequel. He was given opium to kill the pain of the gallstones, and resorted to the drug when depressed. In the initial days, he does not seem to have taken it constantly, in escalating doses, like an outright addict.

At the time of his interactions with Murarirao in 1751, he was an opium consumer—habituated to it to alleviate his pain. So much so, that people who provided him a way to relieve his suffering earned his favours.

When Clive returned to England in 1760, he was a hero who held huge sway with the East India Company and the British government itself. Clive was made Baron Clive of Plassey and knighted in 1764. He reaped vast wealth in diamonds, emeralds and gemstones, too.

In 1772, Parliament opened an inquiry into Clive and the EIC's actions in India. When questioned on the vast sums of money[3] he had received in India, Clive famously replied, 'Mr Chairman, I stand astonished at my own moderation.'

The counter-view[4] was strong too. 'I own I am amazed that private interest could make so many forget what they owe to their country, and come to a resolution that seems to approve of Lord Clive's rapine. No one thinks his services greater than I do, but that can never be a reason to commend him in what certainly opened the door to the fortunes we see daily made in that country.'

Despite this, Robert Clive was granted an Irish peerage. However, in the end, the wealth counted for little. Clive became increasingly ill and depressed at the vicious attacks on his character in the British press. People worried not only about corruption in India but also about how this new wealth might affect national policy in England, if used to corrupt effect at home. All of this put to rest Clive's political aspirations.

On 22 November 1774, he was playing cards at his house in Berkeley Square, when he excused himself from the party and went to his study. There, he took a substantial dose of laudanum and is alleged to have opened his own throat with a penknife. However, there was no inquest.

The papers, hitherto so unforgiving of his actions in India for over a decade, suddenly fell silent and the body was entered at St Margaret's Church at Moreton Say in Shropshire, near his birthplace.

His tombstone bears only the indisputable legend—'Clive, Primus in India'.

In the words of Horace Walpole again, 'He came to town very ill last Monday. On Tuesday, his physician gave him a dose of laudanum, which had not the desired effect. On the rest, there are two stories; one, that the physician repeated the dose; the other that he doubled it himself, contrary to advice. In short, he has terminated at 50, a life of so much glory, reproach, art, wealth, and ostentation.'

Annexure 5: The Weapons of the Marathas[1]

The Marathas have always been a source of inspiration particularly to students of warfare. The geographical ruggedness of Maharashtra made its sons brave, heroic and patriotic. The Maharashtra region was ruled successively by the Mauryas, Satavahans, Chalukyas, Vakatakas and Rashtrakutas, among others.

Hsuein Tsang has famously said, 'The inhabitants (of Maharashtra) were proud spirited and war-like, grateful for favour and revengeful for war.'

The dawn of the seventeenth century found Marathas occupying high military positions in the adjacent governments and in the eighteenth century, they became a terror to the rulers because of their successes in military campaigns and guerrilla tactics in warfare. The arms and the equipment of the Maratha Army were of a heterogenous character. While they adopted the new, they did not reject the old. Consequently, says Prof. Sen,[2] 'the weapons used by the Marathas, represent all stages of civilisation and some them were certainly down from the early stone age.'

The military organization of the Marathas of early times is rather hazy. No evolution is visible, no development perceptible and no chronology is traceable for their weapons.

One sees 'hybridization' of both the old and new types. Though this tendency is not easily perceptible, weapons have been broadly classified as follows:

1. **Stones:** Stones were certainly used as missiles, and Fryer says, 'On the top of the mountains, several fortresses of Sivaji's were only defensive by nature, needing no other artillery but stones, which they tumble down to their foes,

carrying as certain destruction as bullets when they alight'. Again in the battle of Udaigiri, *hat dhonda* or stones were used as missiles and in matchlocks.

2. **Bows and Arrows:** They have remained popular all through the ages and have frequently been depicted in contemporary Maratha paintings. John Henry Grose[3] observes, 'The (Marathas) have also among them excellent slingers and archers.' Nearly forty years later, Colonel Tone[4] confirmed their use by Marathas was in vogue even in 1761 in the Battle of Panipat. The Afghan cavalry under Ahmadshah had more musketeers and archers than the Maratha Army. In this battle, Shejwalkar points out that 'by Ahmad Sultan's good fortune, an arrow struck Vishwas Rao, killing him outright.' Krishnaji Anant Sabhsad, who wrote the life of Shivaji in 1695, said that in his property there were, among other things, 4000 quiverfuls of arrows. Bows were of bamboo and steel. The Marathas could wield crossbows as well.
3. **The Sword:** The Marathas as a rule relied more on swords that were generally of good temper. The most-used weapon in Shivaji Maharaj's siege of the fortress of Phruida in 1675 was the sword. In the third Battle of Panipat, 3000 Duranis were laid to rest by the sword and the rest fled, unable to withstand the fury of the Maratha charge. Confirming their swordsmanship, Tone says, 'They are also excellent swordsmen and these are usually employed in making a charge upon any confusion in enemy.'

   The cavalry charge sword was more reliable than a musket or *bandook*. Maratha swords were both straight and curved. Nanasaheb Peshwa's sword in the National Museum in Delhi is slightly single-edged at the beginning and double-edged towards the end. The hilt is of a *gilota* type with its straight quilt and round pommel. The knuckle-guard was a common feature in the Maratha swords.

   The straight swords were generally very long and double-edged. The Maratha school of painting depicts many varieties of swords. The National Museum has in its collections seven paintings. The *patta*, a long, straight sword, double-edged with a long knuckle-guard, was also popular. Sometimes, we find the narrow-bladed straight rapier with a gauntlet hilt, in which a Western influence could be traced. The most peculiar variety was the *khanda*. Many types of khandas had been used by the Marathas: khandas with a broad blade, with an open-work brass mount, having a curved blade towards the end, etc. A beautiful specimen in the National Museum collection, with a long double-edged blade, mount-gilt and a long knuckle-guard, is of particular interest.

4. **Types of Daggers:** In daggers, too, there were several varieties. The most common ones were with a fluted blade and a small knuckle-guard. The *chilnum* was an adaptation of the Mughal *kapwah*, a curved dagger with a tri-pronged hilt and globular end. The *khanjar*, a curved dagger with a triangle-shaped hilt, was commonly used by the Mughals and the Marathas. The double-edged dagger with an H-shaped handle was also known to them and was called *jamadhar*. When bifurcated at the lower end, it had the name *danlicanch*. Often, we find two *jamadhars*, one within the other; the upper one forming the hollow sheath for the other.

   Another dagger called *katar*, deeply curved, groove-bladed and with a damascened handle, was also used. Frequently, it had three to five portions, with each brought into operation with the help of springs. A special type of dagger known as *bicchwa* generally had a bifurcated blade. The other type of dagger, known as *bhir chir*, was used to rescue a surrounded soldier. The National Museum has a beautiful specimen of this type made of horn. In it two blades are fixed in the opposite direction with a grip in the centre. The *sainti* dagger, a proud possession, had the grip protected by a padded basket of steel from the centre of which projected a small dagger. This weapon, introduced in Spain by the Arabs, was successfully adopted by the Marathas. Evidence of this belonging to the fifteenth century AD is found in *Armerian Real de Madrid*.[5]

5. **Spears:** The spearmen or the *atekari* were personally selected by the rajas. Later, Pindaris were also recruited to the Maratha Army, whose favourite weapon was the Maratha spear, 12–18 feet long. Spears were of three types: the javelin, barachha and spear. The first two were hurled at the enemy while the third one was used as a thrusting weapon. Generally, it consisted of a steel blade attached to the top of a wooden shaft but there are several examples where the shaft of the javelin and barachha is made of steel. During Shahu's period, spearmen used to march just behind the king. The banner, *jari patta*, was always carried before the king. Lances were popularly called *aiti*. The Third Battle of Panipat (1761) was one of cavalry fought with lances and swords on the Maratha side against the musketry and archery of the opposing side.

    'Each Maratha of note,' says T.S. Shejwalkar, 'had possibly a handgun by his side but he had neither love for it nor expertness in use. He preferred lance and spear at a short distance to the clumsy bow and arrow or heavy, long matchlocks of those days.' That the Marathas were superb spearmen can be judged from the account of General G.C. Mundy:[6] 'On our way thither we were preceded by a band of chosen spearmen, who played their elegant exercise before us with long lances tipped like foils with a button.'
6. **Tiger Claws:** Tiger claws or baghnakh attained considerable importance as Shivaji Maharaj killed Afzal Khan with them. In such a weapon, five claws are attached to pointed plates of steel, lining the palm of the hand. The weapon is fastened by rings at the wrist and fingers.

    There is a second variety of baghnakh, where five curved scythe-like blades are attached to an iron sheet flanked by two fingerholes and a curved double-edged blade projecting to the side of a fingerhole.
7. **Maces:** In between the king and the artillery were the mace-bearers. The mace generally had a knob on a ball with sixteen ridges. The handle was cylindrical at either end and octagonal in the centre. The second category was known

as *garj* or *gurj*. It consisted of a pike, rectangular in section and with a globular head of seven with leaves of acanthus design at the upper end of a cylindrical rod with a knuckle-guard, surmounted by a tapering rod. In certain cases, the globular head of the mace was topped with a quadrangular arrowhead of steel and several steel pikes projected from it. It was used to strike people on the head. Dr Edgerton[7] has included *khunli-phansi* in this list, which had a curiously shaped head of open-steel scrollwork and was more akin to a *bairagi* crutch.

Instances of maces with two globular heads, one over the other, are also found in the sculptures from Badami and Halebid. Sometimes, the *gada* (mace) was heavy, long and barrel-like with a clumsy handle or its lower end was a fluted shaft with a star-shaped cross-section. This type of club appears in the early sculptures at Badami and continues in late Chalukyan sculpture and afterwards. The Persian type or the simple mace was also in common use.

8. **Helmets and Armour:** Maratha soldiers did not have the elaborate and comfortable equipage of the Mughals. They were not encumbered with heavy baggage and equipment. Men wore a turban, a simple jacket and tight-fitting trousers. Officers, no doubt, were better protected with a helmet and an armour of chain. The helmet was known as *top* and was generally made of Damascus steel. It was a recurved pointed cap of steel springing from a circle of conventional gilt leaves. Sometimes plume-holders were also attached at the top. In one case, the top had a rectangular arrowhead of steel. The helmet was generally decorated with rich floral arabesques chiselled in low relief.

   Cuirass or *chaniani*, composed of four plates of steel, was used for protection of the front of the soldier. A complete suit of arms consisted of steel coat mail, a pair of arm guards of embossed steel and a cuirass or broad belt composed of strips of steel. The *sirh bakhtar*, a steel skull cap from which chains hung, was commonly made of small steel rings. In the third Battle of Panipat, it is said that both

Sada Shivarao Bhau and Vishwasrao were fully clad from head to foot in armour. Shields were made of rhinoceros skin and some of complete steel were also in use.

9. **Firearms:** The Marathas not only used firearms but manufactured them too. Captain William Gorden[8] says that Bajirao had his own foundry in AD 1739. Maratha guns were generally large and heavy. Gun carriages were clumsy beyond belief, as the wheels were low and were formed of solid pieces of wood. Locomotion of a few days usually made the carriage rickety. Guns were of all sorts and dimensions and were named after gods. 'Cannon,' says Tone, 'are never made of any precise calibre but are cast indifferently by all diameters and the ball afterwards adopted to the bore.'

Instead of cast shots, they used wrought iron and could never get the precision they required. Maratha artillery was no object of pride. Lieutenant Moor, an English observer, writes, 'A gun is loaded and the whole of the people in the battery sit down, talk and smoke for half an hour when it is fired and if it knocks up a great dust, it is considered sufficient.'

The Marathas were quite conversant with the use of pistols and revolvers, and they knew about three to five-barrelled revolvers. They also used mortars and the projectiles were of the same composition as that of ordinary fireworks. A straight sword blade was also frequently fixed to the mortar. Another offensive weapon used by the Muslims and Marathas was the matchlock. The long barrel was usually attached to the stock by leather strips and strengthened with side plates of steel. In fact, firearms could not be fitted into the Maratha system of war. Apart from the main weapons separately discussed, the Marathas used certain other varieties too. Axes were equally popular. These were of several varieties, such as the battle-axe and pickaxe.

The *pharsa* generally contained a single-edged concave blade attached to a long iron handle. There were double-headed pharsa and pharsas attached with gurj too. *Maru* was another peculiar weapon. It generally had two double-edged blades serrated at the end. The knuckle-guard had a small spearhead attached to it.

Gupti was very commonly used. Walking sticks of many designs that concealed blades have been found. A gupti could be divided into many pieces and sometimes a knife, a pistol, a *churra* and a long blade were all assembled in one place and gave the gupti its real shape.

Annexure 6: Meet Madame Dupleix

Joseph Dupleix married a métis (mixed blood) woman, Jeanne Dupleix (née Albert) (1706–1756), whom he met in Chandernagore.

Madame Dupleix had been raised in Pondicherry, the daughter of a Frenchman, Jacques-Theodor Albert, and a métis mother, Rose de Castro, who was believed to be of Portuguese and Indian parentage. While Dupleix and Jeanne did not have children of their own, Dupleix is to this day remembered as the father of Pondicherry; while he was not the founder of the colony, he was the man who gave the sleepy town life. Madame Duplex is revered as a key figure in her husband's success as Governor, and in the building of Pondicherry as a rival to British power in India.

Madame Dupleix spoke Tamil as well as French and English, a common trait amongst the métis population. While her familiarity with the local landscape and population as well as European customs and languages made her a useful and necessary person for the European settlers, her reputation among the local people was largely negative.

The tensions between Madame Dupleix, other métis in the area and the local, mostly Tamil, communities, are evident in the diaries kept by Ananda Ranga Pillai (1709–1761), the Tamilian who served as Governor Dupleix's dubash (interpreter). In his diary, Pillai wrote extensively of his dislike of Mme Dupleix, especially concerning her involvement with politics, which he believed would be better left to the Governor. His writings also suggest that he resented her for what he saw as the persecution of Hindus through the destruction of their religious practices. While Pillai had respect for the power and authority of the Governor, who came from France and had no knowledge of local customs, he saw Madame Dupleix as a traitor to the lives of the local people. She was given to deriding Hindu and Muslim customs and suggesting the superiority of European ways. While Governor Dupleix could be excused, there is a sense in Pillai's writing that the métis community were passing off as white Europeans when they were not.

Despite her inability or lack of desire to form friendships with non-European and non-métis people in Pondicherry, Madame Dupleix has become something of a local hero in Pondicherry, at least among the Francophile community. She has captured the attention and imagination of many Francophone authors who have written about her life in eighteenth-century French India. Sometimes called Johanna Bégum or Jeanne Albert, Madame Dupleix has been mythologized in Francophile Pondicherry, portrayed as a strong woman who was actively involved in the political affairs of her husband and of French India.

The two major French works that have attempted her biography have made her power over the dubash and her influence on Governor Dupleix, a centrepiece of her life story. These works have also noted the importance of her métis heritage.

The 1934 work by Yvonne Robert Gaebelé, *Métis et Grande Dame: Johanna Bégum, Marquise Dupleix (1706-1756, Imprimerie Moderne)*, carries a title that clearly implies that her métis heritage was her primary identity. Gaebelé's book suggests that Dupleix depended on his wife's mixed background to help him negotiate with local princes as well as local people, including the dubash Pillai. It was more logical, these books suggest, for the governor to trust his wife than his dubash. While Pillai may have been loyal to the Governor, his true interests would have lain with his Tamil-Hindu community, not with the values and goals of the Europeans. The divisions between Madame Dupleix and Ananda Ranga Pillai, two people separated by gender, race and religion, are indicative of the boundaries formed as French colonialism came to Pondicherry.

Despite the overlaps in their lives, they were born in the same location, spoke the same languages and knew many of the same people. The arrival of Dupleix and the colonial system reordered local communities in such a way that, instead of working together, they could only compete to be the most useful to those with the most power, who were, in this case, the French officials, military officers and settlers.

To what extent did their rivalry spoil Governor Dupleix's prospects in India? This is worth thinking about.

Annexure 7: A Tribute to Bhujangrao Ghorpade

In the prologue to the book, we have written this about Murarirao, 'His great valour was witnessed and passed down generations orally, but never documented.'

Who was the person who passed this down to Indrajeet? And what were the descriptions he used? Meet the raconteurs to our story. In Indrajeet's words:

It is said that the conversations we witness in our childhood have a lasting impression on us. I grew up amid tales of warriors, conquests, great loves and great losses.

They say that there are no seven wonders of the world in the eyes of a child. There are seven million.[1]

And so it was that my grandfather awakened every one of these seven million wonders with his stories. My loving mother Chandravati[2] and father Dattajirao were also evidently proud of our legacy—I lost two brothers early and grew up with a sister and a brother—but my grandfather Bhujangrao (we will call him Ajoba[3]) was my north star. He would wake up at 4 a.m., perform his morning ablutions, finish his walk and some stretches and have a cold water shower. I miss the natural 'manly' deportment he had. It was both effortless and undeniable.

When I woke up and pottered about, idly biting on the neem twig in my mouth while my mother ambushed me from behind and put some charcoal additionally to clean my teeth against my wishes, I would find Ajoba at his typewriter. Yes. You read that right. He would record the events of the previous day on his personal typewriter. I found it fascinating. He was a self-taught man and had learnt the English language by sheer willpower.

Everyone was scared of him, but he always made time for me, no matter how busy he was. He made me feel special (Ajoba also had a way of cuddling me that was very tough) and I willingly convinced myself that he was a friend to *me and only me*—for everyone else, he was an authority figure. He would make me sit on his lap and tell me stories. Ajoba always made me feel I was part of something larger than myself.

Like many powerful men, there was a constant threat to his life. So when he took me on excursions to the hills, my mother feared for my safety in the event of an untoward, unexpected skirmish plotted against Ajoba. She didn't like these trips. But Ajoba's word was final. And he travelled with an entourage—there was Kalkappa,[4] Ramrao[5] and Vithappa[6]. There was a fourth one too, Durgappa. Durgappa, the orderly to my father—he had trained under Ajoba—was entirely at the service of my father Dattajirao. Durgappa was alive even as late as the 1990s and my interactions with him are quite vivid in my memory.

Many of my most enduring memories have been formed on these hills. Ajoba had a favourite spot; once we reached it, he would survey the area, find a comfortable place to sit and enjoy the view, with his "walking stick gun". I remember a day on which Ajoba was very upset. He had just seen a child with blue eyes and golden hair, and his blood was boiling.

'Kalkappa, do we even know what blood runs in our veins?' he asked, with disgust.

Kalkappa knew exactly where the conversation was headed. The topic of the plunder of Indian women by foreigners would get Ajoba riled up like nothing else could. And he knew I was old enough to understand. In those days, from Ajoba's perspective, being ten years old meant I was old enough to get married.

'These tyrants; the Mughals, the British, the French. They have outraged our women. Maratha women have been taken as slaves all the way to Baluchistan. Are we a pure race any more? Who are we, really?'

Even though I could fathom Ajoba's concern, it was only when I grew much older that I could grasp the full import of his anger and consternation better. Kalkappa would present his own theory, 'Was sati so bad after all?[7] It was a practice to protect the widows from being assaulted by these invaders. Sometimes even by their own people.'

I spoke emphatically, 'But Kalkappa, you can't burn women alive.' Even though I called him Kalkappa, it seemed that it was a name and a gesture of respect, all at once. Ajoba had created a version of his name that had respect embedded within it, even as all of us called it out.

'Would you rather have our widows raped by the Sultan's men instead?' asked Kalkappa.

This was a completely new angle to me.

'The tragedy is that when a man is in love, he cannot bear to hurt the woman he loves. Like Murar[8] loved Saheba. But where there is no love, there is plunder and outrage. Men take women who do not belong to them and outrage their modesty. We are a mixed race, Kalkappa,' Ajoba would say ruefully.

'Who was Saheba?' I asked.

'She was the great love of Murar's life,' Kalkappa explained. 'Saheba was the daughter[9] of Nizam-ul-Mulk. She was very enterprising and like many Islamic princesses, she was very skilled in painting and hunting.'

Ajoba ventured to add, 'With a busy father and even busier brothers, it seems that Saheba's happiest days were those when she got to hunt. It was on one of the large trips to the open greenlands, where her father, the Nizam, welcomed Murar as a guest to a bout of falconry, that he encountered her.'

Indrajeet wanted to know more.

'Saheba was a bewitching beauteous woman on the outside, but a gushing girl at heart. She was besotted by our brave Murar. Assisted by her personal eunuch Rankha, Saheba encouraged an exchange of letters.[10] This was maintained in the most dignified manner possible, for about a year. Eventually, we know that Murarirao married[11] again. But there is no doubt that Saheba was the love of his life; a love that his ideals, beliefs and principles could not sustain,' Ajji filled in the blanks.

During dinner that night, away from Ajoba's ears, Kalkappa whispered to me, 'Your Ajji knows only the child-friendly version of the story. The initial interest would have petered out if Saheba had not actively helped Murar with information that was vital to his interests. She trusted him so fully and wholly that it is believed that Murar himself entered the Nizam's palace as a eunuch, taking bold risks to get a glimpse of his lady love.'

What! A Maratha warrior entered the Nizam's palace? These conversations and others continued night after night. Kalkappa would ask questions like, 'How did Murar know that he had to open negotiations even before the Nizam was set to attack Trichy? Where is all of Murarirao's loot? It is true that every chieftain had their own network of spies. Why was he so sympathetic to Nasir Jung, Saheba's brother? Murarirao had found a way to access a lot of information, eventually culminating in a very long life. He had to contend with the Mughals, the Nizam and other nawabs, the French, the English, Haider Ali, Palegars and chieftains, Peshwas and Marathas. For the most part, he was one step ahead.'

Ramrao, by now fully inebriated, said, 'Murarirao was a master of letters. He knew exactly what to write to whom to keep everyone happy. It is believed that during their meetings, Saheba passed on vital information to Murar. It was only when the harem had doubts about this, that Saheba disappeared. Don't ask me what else happened inside Saheba's room.' Saying this, he gave me a wink.

Ajoba added, 'Saheba and Murar played chess. This is also known. It was she who taught him the game; pointing out how the king is restricted and helpless. He needs protection, aggression, stratagem; more than anything else, he needs the queen's manoeuvrability and power to attack and survive. He also needs the horses, camels and elephants, bishops and cavalry. Warriors have to win—for freedom and dignity. Murar explained to her in turn that Marathas played the battlefield like a game of chess. They never fought battles in open plains like Panipat but were champions of guerrilla warfare in rocky jungles and hilly terrains. Saheba brought masters from Persia and Turkey to teach him to master the moves and out-think his opponents. With her tough love, Saheba inspired Murar to become a better tactician thanks to their chess games over the years; he privately credited her with his ability to outmanoeuvre his enemies and back-stabbers . . . he was, of course, dressed like a eunuch all along.'

Fascinating.

When we came back from these expeditions, we would be greeted with fried pakodas from the fresh hunt of the morning, made out of partridge or grilled quail. Ajji (her name was Tarabai) would also make nimbu pani, aamras, aampanna or pepper rasam, depending on the season and what was available. Ajoba would drink them with relish. Very rarely, Ajji herself would bring the snacks out; that is, if none of the male help was sitting around. She looked like a queen, my Ajji and had a princely lineage herself.[12] I knew this from childhood—that how someone walked or spoke revealed their lineage. And yes, before I forget, there was no electricity back then. As a child, we lived on petromax, candles and lanterns. But we didn't know any better and were far more privileged than others who didn't even have access to these.

Ajoba's sense of righteousness and integrity became the voice of my conscience. 'Multiple marriages and relationships break families,' he would say. Ajoba exclusively focused on building his own family; he respected Tarabai Ajji immensely and worked to make us all secure. 'It was the practice back in the day, that every man, Maratha or Mughal, had multiple wives and mistresses. Murarirao was survived only by his second wife Ranubai and his nephew,' Ajoba would say.

On another day, he explained thus, 'Murar was fired up by two people; one was Chhatrapati Shivaji Maharaj and his patriotism. The other big influence in his life was Santaji Ghorpade. The latter's valour and commitment to decimating rulers foreign to our land would inspire young Murar. It is unfortunate that Murar did not find a mentor of the calibre he deserved. He was completely disillusioned by the Peshwas, who did not have the same fire in their belly. Despite this, he remained loyal to Shivaji's ideological inheritance.'

One day, Ajoba was no more. I was ten (thirteen) years old. I coped with his loss by starting to smoke the same beedis that he used to. He never smoked or drank. All of Ajoba's writings were passed down to my cousin M.Y. Ghorpade. And he has created some beautiful literature out of those memories. But Saheba's story is known to me, almost as if it happened before my eyes.

When I got down to writing this book, I was reminded of what Ramrao would often ask. 'Who will know of our history?'

And then, as if a brainwave hit him, Ramrao would say, 'Someone should write it down. Especially Murarirao's story.'

Now that you have read Murarirao's story, one thing is for sure.

You wish all Marathas before him were blessed with Ajoba's grounded wisdom on the subject of single marriages.

Annexure 8: Murarirao–A Timeline (For the Avid History Student)

1639: The British come to Madras.

1674: The French come to Pondicherry.

1697: Rajaram escapes from Ginjee to make Satara his capital. Santaji is killed by Dhanaji Jadhav.

1700: Rajaram dies. Tarabai, his widow, assumes charge. Bahirji acquires Gutti as headquarters. Ranoji, Santaji's son joins Bahirji.

1704: Murarirao Hindurao Ghorpade is born.

1707: Aurangzeb dies in February.

1708: Dhanaji defects to Shahu and defeats Tarabai. Shahu made Chhatrapati. Dhanaji Jadhav dies later in the same year.

1709: Bahirji dies around this time. Azam Shah, one son, assumes charge of the Mughal Empire and releases Shahu, son of Sambhaji. Tarabai and Shahu also entangle in power play as head of the Marathas

1710: Tarabai declares her son Shivaji as Chhatrapati of Panhala, Kolhapur. Sidhoji becomes Senapati of Tarabai. Sa'adatullah Khan becomes ruler of Arcot.

1713: Sidhoji's attempts to build a bridge between the two warring Maratha claimants fails. He quits as Senapati and Piroji (son of Santaji) takes his place. Nizam-ul-Mulk is made Viceroy of the Deccan.

1715: Sa'adatullah Khan takes over Gingee by force.

1716: Soyarabai, second wife of Santaji who lives in Gajendragadh is given grants. Sidhoji also demands the same. Farrukh Siyar, the weak Mughal Emperor, is bullied into issuing a farman granting the British East India Company full trading rights.

1718: Rajasbai, the second wife of Rajaram, arrests Tarabai and Shivaji and Sambhaji II, her son, is crowned in a bloodless coup.

1723: Sidhoji installs Mahalaxmi idol in Kolhapur in the presence of Murarirao and Tara.

1730: Murarirao becomes independent as around this time, Sidhoji dies. Shahu defeats Sambhaji, ending the question of which Maratha faction is stronger. Bajirao routs the Nizam and Sambhaji.

1731: Murar is thirty years old. Younger brother Daulat Rao is given charge of Gajendragadh and Murar is in charge of Gutti and Sandur.

1731 to 1739: Murar concentrates on consolidating his territories, building his army and putting a system in place to collect royalties.

1732: Sa'adatullah Khan, Nawab of Arcot dies, adopts nephew Dost Ali and makes him successor without permission of the Nizam who feels slighted.

1736: The ruler of Tiruchirappalli dies and Rani Meenakshi is made ruler. Chanda Sahib tricks Rani Meenakshi, imprisons her and takes Trichy. He becomes a self-styled Nawab.

1739: Safdar Ali, son of Dost Ali, attacks Thanjavur. The Peshwas order Raghuji Bhosle to help Thanjavur cousins against this attack. Raghuji Bhosle sets out to Deccan and is joined by 10,000 of Murarirao's troops. Murarirao meets the Nizam and also Saheba.

1739–1743: The period of Murarirao and Saheba's affair.

1740: Bajirao Peshwa dies. News reaches Raghuji who abandons his task of avenging the Thanjavur invasion and rushes back to appoint his own nominee as Peshwa for personal gain. Shahu appoints Nanasaheb as next Peshwa before he reaches.

1741: Safdar Ali recognized as Nawab of Arcot in exchange for ransom. Marathas recapture Trichy and imprison Chanda Sahib. Raghuji asks Dumas, the Governor of Pondicherry, to return the treasures looted by Chanda Sahib or face consequences of war. Dumas entices Raghuji's wife with fine brandy.

1742: Raghuji returns to his homeland and appoints Murarirao as Governor of Trichy, as Murarirao is the main architect. Dumas becomes a friend of the Nizam, for not returning Chanda Sahib's treasures to the Marathas. Nawab Safdar Ali murdered by cousin Murtaza Ali. Raghuji does not return to the Deccan. Both Peshwa Nanasaheb and Raghuji go north to Bengal campaign leaving the Deccan open and unprotected

1743: Nizam sends 70,000-strong force to recapture Trichy from Murar. En route he takes Arcot and makes his Sardar's infant son Nizam with a guardian, Anwarudin. Nizam appoints his grandson Muzaffar Jung as Governor of Eastern Carnatic.

1744: Shahu's health is not good. Not only is there rivalry between Peshwas and Raghuji but also squabbling between Shahu's wives, Sagunabai and Sakwarbai. He appoints Babuji Naik to collect tribute from the South, despite Nanasaheb's opposition.

1745: Babuji was completely inexperienced. Announces intent to take Trichy back from Nizam. Falls flat on his face.

1746: Shahu's health deteriorates. Jijabai and Sambhaji go to Satara and suggest adoption of Sambhaji to make Maratha kingdom one again. Babuji attempts another Deccan campaign and fails miserably. Meanwhile, the French and the English wake up to the void left by the Mughals and the English are at war. Governor Dupleix attacks Fort St George and Arcot gets involved. This was the first time European guns were used in war. Robert Clive, then a clerk, manages to escaped to Cuddalore. The French were on the verge of victory but because the Anglo-French war ended, Fort St George was returned to the British.

1747: Both factions of the Marathas have been wooing Murarirao. He visits Kolhapur and has serious discussions with Sambhaji and Jijabai and news travels to Satara who also invite Murar. The French and the English are preparing for a showdown. Peshwas have taken over completely from the Chhatrapati's as far as the Marathas are concerned.

1748: Nizam-ul-Mulk dies, leaving a vacuum. A power struggle of epic proportions ensues between son Nasir Jung and grandson Muzaffar Jung. Shockingly enough, Chanda Sahib is released after the French pay a ransom of Rs 7 lakh and ask for help to reinstate him as Nawab of Trichy.

1749: Chanda Sahib, Muzaffar Jung and the French rally together. The English take sides with Murarirao and Nasir Jung. Chhatrapati Shahu dies and Poona becomes the new capital of the Maratha kingdom.

1750: French forces kill Nasir Jung. This is the height of the French success in India. Dupleix was now master of the Carnatic. He plunders the riches of Nasir Jung and fills his coffers with the war chests of the nawabs and the Nizam. Muzaffar Jung, eager to return to his capital, requests Dupleix to send a small army escort. Chanda Sahib once again becomes Nawab of the Carnatic.

1751: On the way to his own crowning, Muzaffar Jung realizes he is not accepted as the Nizam. In a hand-to-hand battle with the nawabs, Muzaffar Jung is pierced in the head. The French reach Golconda without a Nizam. They make Nasir Jung's brother, Salabath Jung, the Nizam. Emboldened, Dupleix and Chanda attack Trichy again. Robert Clive enters the scheme of things and plans to attack Arcot to divide the enemy forces from Trichy. Dupleix responds by sending Chanda Sahib's son Raja Sahib to reinforce Arcot and take on Clive. Meanwhile, Murar is still stalling by negotiating with the French and with Nandraj of Mysore who offers to help. This time, he wants to end his old enemy Chanda Sahib forever.

1752: Raja Saheb threatens Clive and calls him to surrender. Clive reaches out to Murar and asks him to join forces, saying he will not go back and retreat like earlier English actions. Murarirao moves in and breaks the siege of Arcot, saving Clive in the process. Robert Orme records how Murarirao with his nephew from Gajendragadh, Daulat Rao, fights the Battle of Arni, with trademark tactical genius and bravery. Chanda Sahib is killed and at the battle of Srirangapatnam, the British and Murarirao win. On the fateful day of 2 June 1752, the French surrender.

1753: Both the English and the French realize that Murarirao forms the key between failure and victory. Meanwhile, due to a personal slight, Haider Ali, a soldier of Nandraj, makes it his life mission to kill and destroy Murar. Haider is thirty-two years old and illiterate, can't even sign his name.

1754: Despite the massive wins at Arcot and Arni, Murarirao is unable to depend on the English. Similar to Srirangapatnam, where he helped the English take the fort, Murarirao delivers Tiruvadi to the French. Sadly, the French nation cuts off funds and Dupleix cannot afford to pay Murarirao any more. Dupleix is sent back. He is humiliated and cannot pay Murar or his debts. The French give in and hand over most of the Deccan to the English and the new hero is Englishman Stringer Lawrence.

1755: Murar returns to Gutti, fed up of being let down, betrayed by almost all his allies at some point, including the Marathas.

1757: The Peshwas decide to raid Mysore for money and demand payment or attack. Nandraj refuses as demands are very high. Haider Ali promoted as Governor of Dindugal, 300 km from Mysore. Nandraj turns to Haider for help. Meanwhile in Bengal, Robert Clive wins the Battle of Plassey and becomes the master of the EIC and Bengal.

1758: Murar again breaks rank with the Peshwas, and does not join the Mysore war by the Peshwas. Haider fights and negotiates ransom

1761: In three years, Haider ousts Nandraj, imprisons him and becomes the ruler of Mysore. Murar and Haider clash at Chikkaballapura, the former wins. Meanwhile, the Marathas lose the Battle of Panipat. Nanasaheb Peshwa retreats to Poona and dies later. The brave Peshwa Madhavrao comes to power.

1762: The Anglo-French war ends. The French hand over Pondicherry to the British and their army is disbanded. Mercenaries and soldiers join Haider's army for employment and make his forces stronger.

1761–1769: Murarirao, now bolstered by his faith in young Peshwa Madhavrao, goes head to head with Haider on four occasions.

1771: The Marathas go on a rampage and take large tracts of territories, almost reach Mysore. But Haider keeps eluding them. Haider sets trap for the Marathas but in a turn of fortune, escapes with a dozen horses and his son Tipu Sultan.

1772: Murarirao advises the Marathas to finish the job. Haider was left with only three forts: Srirangapatnam, Bangalore and Bidnur. The Marathas and Murarirao lay siege to Srirangapatnam. Haider discusses peace and a treaty, agrees to ransom of Rs 50 lakh and appoints Murarirao his guarantor, pays ransom in full. Murarirao does not trust Haider. Brave Peshwa Madhavrao dies. The equations change again.

1773: Raghunath assumes guardianship of young Peshwa Narayan Rao; then assassinates him and becomes Peshwa himself. Meanwhile, Murar learns of Haider's plans to attack him.

1775: Haider lays siege to Gutti.

1776: Murarirao is captured at the ripe age of seventy-two.

Notes

Prologue

1 Refer to Annexure 7, 'A Tribute to Bhujangrao Ghorpade'.

Why This Book

1 Chakravyūha (Sanskrit: चक्रव्यूह) is a military formation used to surround enemies, depicted in the Hindu epic, the Mahabharata. It resembles a labyrinth of multiple defensive walls. As per the Mahabharata, just a handful of Pandavas, such as Arjuna, Krishna and Pradyumna could get in and out of it.

2 Historian Jadunath Sarkar says this about Santaji in his book *Military History of India* (M.C. Sarkar and Sons, 1960), p. 159: 'Santaji had an inborn genius for handling large bodies of troops spread over wide areas, changing his tactics so as to take prompt advantage of every change in the enemy's plans and conditions . . .' He also calls him an 'old hero of Maharashtra'.

3 There are several books about Santaji Ghorpade. The popular ones are Kaka Vidhate's *Santaji* (Prafullata Prakashan, 2006) and the other is Jaysingrao Bhausaheb Pawar's *Senapati Santaji Ghorpade* (Marathidesha Foundation, 2019).

4 Published first in 1925, this extract is from Vol. 15, p. 551, published by the Calcutta Oriental Press.

5 The place he lived in during peacetime. Murarirao's father Sidhoji had control over all three places–Gutti, Sandur and Gajendragadh.

6 In his book, *A Profile in Courage in 18th Century Deccan* (Ruvari Press, 2010), M.Y. Ghorpade exalts the glory of Murarirao in the

preface. He narrates that historians Govind Sakharam Sardesai and Jadunath Sarkar visited Sandur in 1936 and spoke to his father. They referred to information available from English, French, Persian, Kannada and Marathi sources, including the literature on Clive, Dupleix and the Anglo-French conflict, personal diaries and *Peshwa Daftar*, which contained many letters written by Murarirao. The above description was written by Sardesai in a paper published in the *Modern Review* in May 1940.

7 Rao Bahadur Govind Sakharam Sardesai, popularly known as Riyasatkar Sardesai, was a historian from Bombay Presidency, India. Through his *riyasats* written in Marathi, Sardesai presented an account of over 1000 years of Indian history until 1848. He also wrote the three-volume *New History of Marathas* in English.

8 In Hindi, there is a proverb, '*thali ka baingan*', which means someone who falls on a particular side where it benefits them. In Murarirao's case, this was intentional.

9 A good reference is the academic work *History of Modern Deccan, 1720/1724–1948: Political and Administrative Aspects*, published by Abul Kalam Azad Oriental Research Institute with contributions by historians Anant R. Kulkarni and M.A. Nayeem.

10 The chouth was a tax or tribute, considered a 'tax for protection' levied by the Marathas on those lands that were seen as under nominal Mughal control. This was approximately one-fourth of the land revenue. Sardeshmukhi—literally translated to 'above the Deshmukh' was an additional tax of 10 per cent of land revenue, collected to assert that the Maratha Kingdom's rights were superior to that of the local chieftains.

11 The book *A History of the Maratha People: From the Death of Shahu to the End of the Chitpavan Epic* by Charles Augustus Kincaid, Dattatyara Balavanta Parasanisa (S. Chand, 1925), says, 'Murarirao Ghorpade would not acknowledge the Peshwas.'

12 Get a real flavour of this narration in Annexure 7, 'A Tribute to Bhujangrao Ghorpade', Indrajeet Ghorpade's grandfather.

13 We have spoken to historians and provided an estimate.

14 These royal women also had to be perpetually prepared to be captured as spoils of war, given that by and large, they travelled with their men wherever they went.

15 Ira Mukhoty, *Daughters of the Sun* (Aleph Book Company, 2018), a biography of Mughal women.

16 The daughters of the Mughals remained unmarried because, with multiple wives, each Islamic ruler would have several offspring. Finding suitable husbands for all of them wasn't always possible. The wealth of the Islamic rulers could not be matched by the other Muslim families in India, so finding a suitable groom for all of them was a genuine challenge. One would have to look at far-flung Central Asia to find such men. However, this would pose another problem, as after marriage, the daughters' offspring, who would be born in a powerful family, might raise a claim to the throne! This would disrupt the line of succession!

Chapter 1: The Bhosales and the Ghorpades

1 Table 1.1 is a broad timeline illustrated by Indrajeet Ghorpade to depict successive generations of loyalty.

2 Some might see this as an oversimplification. For e.g., scholar Prachi Deshpande, in her book *Creative Pasts: Historical Memory and Identity in Western India, 1700-1960* (Columbia University Press: 2007) maintains that the Ghorpades of Mudhol cast Shivaji in their chronicles as an adventurer upsetting all that was established. On pages 43 and 44, she talks about them being 'unconvinced' of Shivaji's centralizing claims. However, in his book *Scaling the Heights–Mired in Their Own Blood: Stories of Loyalty and Treachery from Medieval Deccan* (Ruvari: 2010), Manohar Malgonkar says that despite the fact that the Ghorpades and other Maratha clans served the sultans in the fifteenth century, and 'gave of their best', things changed after Maloji Ghorpade chose to renounce the service of the sultans in the seventeenth century, under the influence of Shahaji Bhosale (p. 48). Table 1.1 illustrates this succession of loyalty. On page 13, he says one cannot eliminate some elements of 'claims and counterclaims' causing bickering between the 'Ghorpade brothers themselves' in the later years. Nonetheless, they did not generate 'lasting bitterness or family feud'.

3 The family line of Chhatrapati Shivaji Maharaj.

4 Manohar Malgonkar's book, *Scaling the Heights–Mired in Their Own Blood: Stories of Loyalty and Treachery from Medieval Deccan* (Ruvari: 2010).

5 Eminent historian Vishwanath Kashinath Rajwade (1863–1926) added an introduction to a latter-day edition of Jayaram Pindye's work *Radha Madhav Vilas Champu*. The precise year is not known, even though the book is freely available even today. Jayaram Pindye was Shahaji's poet. A *champu* is a composition made of both prose and poetry. As per Vishwanath Kashinath Rajwade, this champu was composed by Jayaram Pindye between 1653 and 1658. It is a detailed character description of Shahaji Maharaj.

6 Sketch available in the book placed on page 8.

7 Refer to Annexure 1 for more information.

8 For these 300 years, the Deccan was ruled by Sultanates and Bahamanis.

9 As it is known in the present day.

10 Sujan Singh, a proud man with military training, who gave his skills on hire and built a home away from home.

11 Kathleen Kuiper, ed., *The Culture of India* (The Rosen Publishing Group, 2010), p. 34.

12 John Vincent Ferreira (1965), *Totemism in India* (Oxford University Press), pp. 191, 202. 'Together with the Marathas, the Maratha Kunbi belonged originally, says Enthoven, to the same caste . . . the Marathas are largely of a non-Aryan origin. . . . The Kunbi cultivators are also Marathas but of a somewhat inferior social standing. The Maratha claim to belong to the ancient 96 Kshatriya families has no foundation in fact and may have been adopted after the Marathas became with Shivaji a power to be reckoned with.'

13 A town in Karnataka.

14 Remember that even the 'Shaka Vansh' from Central Asia had got assimilated into Indian society by then. They had set up their base in several places including Takshila, Mathura, Nasik and Ujjain in India.

15 Southern parts, Gujarat, Punjab.

Chapter 2: His Mother's Pet

1 Shahaji Bhosale (1594–1664), a military leader of India, who served the Ahmadnagar Sultanate, the Bijapur Sultanate and the Mughal Empire at various points in his career.

2 Shiledar was a term used for a soldier's position in India's Maratha Confederacy (1630–1818).
3 Historian Sadashiv Martand Garge puts his birth at 1625.
4 Manohar Malgonkar, *Scaling the Heights–Mired in Their Own Blood: Stories of Loyalty and Treachery from Medieval Deccan.*
5 When Sujan Singh first came to the Carnatic, he started his work under the Bahamani Sultans.
6 Kanara, also known as Karavali, is the stretch of land in the south-western coast of India, alongside the Arabian Sea in the present-day Indian state of Karnataka.
7 Persian State Papers of the Adil Shahi Government which are preserved in the Sayyidiya Library of Haiderabad have been referenced by historian Jadunath Sarkar.
8 Easily the most illustrious Maratha king. Shivaji Maharaj (1630–80) never saw the Mughals as people he could tolerate. Therefore, even though his father Shahaji spent his military life in the service of the Deccan Sultanates, Shivaji–influenced deeply by the religious beliefs of his mother and his study of various Hindu epics–broke away from his father's path with the vision of Hindavi Swarajya.
9 Dennis Kincaid, civil servant in British India and novelist says, 'While most well-to-do Hindus had come to accept Muslim domination as inevitable and had been seduced by the luxury and comfort of Muhammadan courts, Shivaji spent his earlier childhood among men not yet subdued, among wild tribesmen and in lonely forest villages. Other young Hindus of his rank lived as neighbours with Muhammadan gentry and if they were despised and sometimes persecuted, they accepted such inconveniences without too much complaint; but to Shivaji, the Muhammadans were the people who had taken his mother away and who followed him relentlessly, the ogres of his childhood.'
10 Jadunath Sarkar, *House of Shivaji* (Orient Longman, 1978).
11 His descendants ruled Thanjavur until the British East India Company took over in 1855.
12 Marathi for mother.
13 Mardani khel is an armed Indian martial art from Maharashtra, involving the use of the uniquely Indian patta (sword) and vita (corded lance).

Chapter 3: Multiple Marriages, Multiple Heirs

1 The idea of the human mind as a tabula rasa or blank slate dates back to ancient Greece. Several different thinkers and philosophers have used the term, though not always with the same meaning. The phrase is now generally associated with the human mind in infancy before an individual has had any experiences.

2 Muhammad Ghori was a ruler from the Ghurid dynasty based in the Ghor region of what is today central Afghanistan. He ruled from 1173 to 1206.

3 This is called the second Battle of Tirauri (1192).

4 Scholars and historians express surprise often that the Hindus accepted a name for themselves and their place, given by other people. It was the Arabs and Iranians who coined the term 'Hindu' for people who lived on the other side of the Sindhu River. They named the place 'Hind' (by Ishtakri, AD 590, and Al-Birūnī, AD 1020) and from it was derived, 'Hindustan'.

5 The Battle of Talikota was fought between the Vijayanagara Empire and an alliance of the Deccan sultanates in 1565. Despite the Vijayanagara Army being larger, they were comprehensively defeated.

6 The seventeenth century marked a period of decline for many Hindu kingdoms, as the Mughal Empire's power grew and other Islamic powers rose in the Deccan. The Vijayanagara Empire eventually declined in the seventeenth century, and the Rajput kingdoms also experienced a period of political instability

7 Inspired by James W. Laine's *Shivaji: Hindu King in Islamic India* (Oxford University Press, 2003).

8 Santaji Ghorpade is arguably the most famous member of the Ghorpade clan so far and much literature is available about him, including a rousing biography (Marathidesha Foundation, 2019) by the veritable Jaisinghrao Pawar himself.

9 Some people call this Sambhaji (1657–1689) Sambhaji II as Shivaji's own brother was also named Sambhaji. He was the second Chhatrapati of the Maratha Empire, ruling from 1681 to 1689.

10 A few historians suggest that this rebellion was purely staged between father and son to weaken the Mughals. Shivaji was an astute and crafty ruler and was fully capable of doing something like this.

11 This is the second house arrest, which started in December 1679.

12 It could not have been easy to guard Sambhaji. Manohar Malgonkar has given Sambhaji adjectives such as headstrong, prickly and capricious. He had already escaped from similar situations earlier.

13 It is believed that Shivaji himself preferred Rajaram, despite the fact that Sambhaji was declared the prince at the time of his own coronation. According to Manohar Malgonkar, Shivaji Maharaj was trying to curb Sambhaji's waywardness and loose living. He even sent Sambhaji to the ashram of his guru Ramdas at Sajjangad.

14 Although the Vedic ideal of marriage favoured monogamy, we find the royal personages having more than one wife. Over time, this became a way to make alliances with other states or noble families and to ensure that they would have plenty of heirs.

15 Ramdas was a noted seventeenth-century saint and spiritual poet of Maharashtra, who in Shivaji's later life, provided him with counsel.

16 Indeed, in his Sanskrit letters to Ram Singh (son of Mirja Raja Jay Singh), Sambhaji referred to Aurangzeb as 'Yavanadham' (the worst of the Muslims) and had advocated the unity of all Hindus to restore and maintain the Hindu character of the Indian subcontinent.

Chapter 4: Sambhaji's Valiant Death

1 Even though 'Baba' was the term for father, warrior families preferred the term 'Sarkar'.

2 'Bal' is a term of endearment that means son in Marathi.

3 The Shirkes, who had a family feud with Sambhaji, had given Mukarab Khan the information that Sambhaji Maharaj was staying in Sangameshwar along with Kavi Kalash. Mukarab Khan's son Ikhlas Khan went inside the haveli and dragged Sambhaji Maharaj and Kavi Kalash by their hair and twenty-five of Maharaj's chief followers and their wives were made prisoners.

4 The authentic Islamic biography of Aurangzeb by Muḥammad Sāqī Musta'idd Khān (*Maasir-I-Alamgiri*, Persian, ed. Bibliotheca Indica, Asiatic Society of Bengal, 1871), translated into English by Sir Jadunath Sarkar (Calcutta: Royal Asiatic Society of Bengal, 1947) has a chapter titled 'Capture and execution of Sambha'.

Aurangzeb ordered the captives (Sambhaji Maharaj and Kavi Kalash) to be put in chains and manacled. The author writes, 'The Emperor's devotion to Islam ordered that Sambhaji Maharaj should be made to wear a wooden cap (a sign of a criminal) and as he enters the camp, there should be drum beating and trumpets pealing so that Muslims might be heartened and infidels (Hindus) will be disheartened. The prisoners were taken in this avatar around the entire camp and then put in the dungeons of Bahadurgad the same day. The next day, Kavi Kalash's tongue was cut out. The following few days, Sambhaji was asked to surrender to Islam but he never accepted it. The eyes of both these men were gouged out. They were introduced to the tortures of the worst forms. After suffering a lot of torture, Sambhaji Maharaj and Kavi Kalash were hacked to death limb by limb.

5 The book *Ambedkar Beyond Constitution* (Blue Rose, 2022) by Jagan Chamber suggests that when Sambhaji's body was mutilated and thrown into the river by Aurangzeb, both Marathas and Brahmins were so terrified of the Mughals that none of them came forward to give a funeral to Sambhaji. It was then that Govind Mahar (Gaikwad), an untouchable of the village Vadhu Budruk, showed courage to collect the pieces of Sambhaji's body, stitched them and honourably performed the last rites. Sambhaji's tomb was erected by the Mahars at that place. There are other versions that say that Marathas performed the last rites.

6 In his book *Aurangzeb* (Vikas Publishing House, 1988), Muni Lal writes, 'Aurangzeb's tyranny and treachery sent a wave of desperate anger throughout the territories ruled by Sambhaji. Every Maratha became a Soldier and Every Maratha House a Fort.'

7 John F. Richards, *The Mughal Empire*, *The New Cambridge History of India*, Vol. 5 (Cambridge University Press, 1996, 1993).

8 Satish Chandra, *Medieval India: From Sultanat to the Mughals, Vol. 2* (Har-Anand Publications, 2005), pp. 255–56.

9 After Sambhaji's death, Rajaram Bhosale was crowned at Raigad on 12 March, in the year 1689.

10 Sambhaji's own son, Shahu, was still a boy of seven and considered too young to be head of state at such a dangerous time.

11 Sambhaji died on 11 March 1689. The siege began on 25 March 1689.

12 The fort was eventually captured in October, but only after a tenacious struggle and some treachery by Zulfiqar Khan. Before this capture, Santaji had struck Zulfiqar Khan's besieging army at Raigad and taken away five elephants and other valuables.

13 These were pre-*wada* times, so the structure was not exactly that of a wada but a precursor to it.

Chapter 5: The Ghorpades Set Out for Revenge

1 The distance by foot from Raigad to Gingee would have been over 1100 km by foot! This was a very brave expedition. The map on page 20 shows their route.

2 Keshav Purohit, who accompanied Rajaram, has left an eyewitness account of this perilous adventure in his Sanskrit work, *Rajaram Charitam* (1690). His account is also corroborated in a Persian work, *Masire-Alamgiri* (1871), which graphically describes various events connected with the journey.

3 The Carnatic was the bone of contention between the Marathas and the Mughals for many years. Aurangzeb had tried various times to capture it but the Marathas didn't let him. Though not discussed frequently, Gingee, at one corner of the Carnatic was the centre of Maratha activities for a decade.

4 Annexure 5 details the Marathas' proficiency with weapons.

Chapter 6: Santaji the Rebel

1 Cosme da Guarda, a Portuguese traveller and the first systematic biographer of Shivaji, who wrote his *Vida E Accoeno Do Famoso e Felicissima Sevagy: Life of the Celebrated Sevagy* in 1695, a year before Sabhasad's chronicle (Bakhar) on Shivaji was completed.

2 Cosme da Guarda says of Shivaji that, 'Such was the good treatment Shivaji accorded to people and such was the honesty with which he observed the capitulations that none looked upon him without a feeling of love and confidence. By his people he was exceedingly loved. Both in matters of reward and punishment he was so impartial that while he lived he made no exception for any person; no merit was left unrewarded, no offence went unpunished; and this he did with so much care and attention that

he specially charged his governors to inform him in writing of the conduct of his soldiers, mentioning in particular those who had distinguished themselves, and he would at once order their promotion, either in rank or in pay, according to their merit. He was naturally loved by all men of valor and good conduct.'

3 Rajaram had three sons, Raja Karna (died in 1700) with Sagunabai (his mistress), Shivaji II with Tarabai, Sambhaji II with Rajasbai.

4 Head of the army.

5 One of Dhanaji's subordinates.

Chapter 7: Loyal from a Distance

1 Read Annexure 1 for how the Ghorpades got their name.

2 Tarabai ruled from 1700 to 1708 as Queen Regent to Shivaji II, Rajaram's son. She was a warrior, leading her army into battle and kept the Maratha flag high. Prominent historian Jadunath Sarkar credits Tarabai's administrative genius and strength for the survival of the Maratha Empire in this extremely difficult period.

3 'I'm alone and I'm going away alone. I know not who I am and what I am doing' were Aurangzeb's last words. He lived over ninety years. He died of natural causes, those being terminal illnesses that had gotten to him. This was probably because of all the wars and endless travels that he had to be part of.

4 After the death of Aurangzeb in 1707, the twenty-seven-year war between the Marathas and the Mughals ended. Shahuji was released by the Mughals. Naturally, as the heir of Shivaji's older son, he claimed the Maratha throne.

5 Mughal historian Khafi Khan famously wrote about Tarabai, 'She won the hearts of her officers, and for all the struggles and schemes, the campaigns and sieges of Aurangzeb up to the end of his reign, the power of the Mahrattas increased day by day.'

6 Tarabai's son was Shivaji II.

7 Ajit R. Jadhav, *Proudh Gandharva & Sons* (Ultimate Associates, 2021).

8 *Marathi Riyasat*, Vol. 1, p. 14.

9 The fatal civil war between the two families that convulsed Maharashtra would have been over if Tarabai had accepted Shahu's gesture of ceding the whole country south of Warna to her and her son. Instead, it continued for twenty-three years, up to 1731.

10 H.N. Sinha, *Rise of the Peshwas* (Allahabad: Indian Press, 1954).
11 Ajoba means grandfather. Bahirji had three sons. Only the third son, Sidhoji, survived. At the time of his death, Bahirji was identified with Gajendragadh and Santaji's surviving family was identified with Kapshi.
12 In 1713, Shahu made Balaji Vishwanath his Peshwa (chief minister). This was the beginning of the Peshwa system. Balaji Vishwanath managed to win over Tarabai's most powerful supporter Kanhoji Angre, and helped engineer a palace coup in 1714, whereby Rajaram's other wife Rajasbai and son Sambhaji II assumed power in Kolhapur. Tarabai and her son Shivaji II were thrown into Panhala's prison, where she spent sixteen years, and her son eventually died.
13 Son of Rajasbai. Logically, this would be Sambhaji III.

Chapter 8: Not So Mad, After All

1 John Zubrzycki, *The Shortest History of India* (Picador India, 2022).
2 Palaiyakkarars, or Poligar, Palegara in Andhra Pradesh, Karnataka and Tamil Nadu refers to the holder of a small kingdom as a feudatory to a greater sovereign.
3 *Thorle Shahu Maharaj Hyache Charitra*, pp. 3–6.
4 Tiger claw or 'baghnakh' attained considerable importance after Shivaji Maharaj killed Afzal Khan with it. In such a weapon, five claws are attached to the pointed plates of steel, lining the palm of the hand. The weapon is fastened by rings at the wrist and fingers.

Chapter 9: A Matter of Faith

1 Orally shared by the Ghorpade family.
2 Author of *A History of Gingee and Its Rulers*, Annamalai University, 1943.
3 Robert Orme was one of the earliest British historians of India. Son of a British East India Company physician and surgeon, he entered the service of the Company in Bengal in 1743. He was regarded as an authority on India.

Chapter 10: Sidhoji and the Mahalaxmi Temple

1 His thesis on 'Maratha architecture, 1650 A.D. to 1850 A.D.' was accepted by the University of Poona for the degree of doctor of philosophy in 1957.

2 Counted among the major eighteen Puranas of Hinduism. It is composed by Maharishi Vedavyasa. This Purana has seven sections, 697 chapters and 55,000 verses. The Padma Purana was first narrated by Brahmaji to Pulastya Rishi and Pulastya Rishi to Bhishma. In the Padma Purana, the entire origin of the universe has been narrated by Lord Brahma.

3 Amar Nath Khanna, *Pilgrim Shrines of India, Mythology, Archaeology, History and Art (Hindu, Jain, Buddhist, Sikh, Jewish, Christian & Sufi)* (Aryan Books International, 2003).

4 The Kadamba dynasty was an ancient ruling dynasty of South India that originated in Banavasi in present-day Karnataka state. They ruled over large parts of south India from 345 CE to 525 CE.

5 Jawaharlal Nehru, a founding father of modern India, writes in his *Discovery of India*, first published in 1946, that Aurangzeb was 'a bigot and an austere puritan'. He trounces the sixth Mughal king as someone who 'put back the clock' and ended up destroying the Mughal Empire. Perhaps Nehru's most damning blow was to pronounce Aurangzeb too Muslim to be a successful Indian king: 'When Aurangzeb began to oppose [the syncretism of earlier Mughal rulers] and suppress it and to function more as a Moslem than an Indian ruler, the Mughal Empire began to break up.'

6 There is another view to this. During Aurangzeb's time, 'Hindus' of the day often did not even label themselves as Hindus. They prioritized a medley of regional, sectarian and caste identities (e.g., Rajput, Maratha, Brahmin, Vaishnava). As many scholars have pointed out, the word 'Hindu' is Persian, not Sanskrit, and only became commonly used self-referentially during British colonialism. The Mughals, too, emphasized differences between groups of 'Hindus'. For example, Mahabat Khan, who led Mughal efforts in the Deccan for a short period in the early 1670s, preferred 'Rajputs and Hindus' among the Mughal nobility, even while fighting the Marathas (who apparently did not count as 'Hindu' in this instance). Further, Audrey Truschke writes in *Aurangzeb: The*

Life and Legacy of India's Most Controversial King that Aurangzeb never oversaw a large-scale conversion programme that offered non-Muslims a choice between Islam or the sword . . . He did not perpetrate anything resembling a genocide of Hindus. In fact, Aurangzeb appointed Hindus to top positions in his government.

7 One of Aurangzeb's sardars.

8 The idol was missing for this period. According to the Ghorpade family, the only possible explanation is that some well-wisher was saving it from plunder.

9 Aarti is a sacred act of devotion, offering light and hymns to deities as a culmination of an elaborate ritual of worship.

Chapter 11: Murarirao, the Chief of Gutti

1 Estimate.

2 This fort was built during Chhatrapati Shivaji's reign.

3 Sanduru (often written Sandur) is a town in the present-day Bellary district in Karnataka. It is the administrative seat of Sanduru Taluka.

4 Refer Annexure 2 for some more context on the Peshwas.

5 Surya namaskar, also known as sun salutation, is a sequence of twelve yoga poses performed in a continuous manner.

6 Books written on palm leaf.

7 A tribal community of gypsies or banjaras, the Lambanis are known for their spectacular handcrafted embroidery.

8 P.L. Saswadkar, 'Career of an Eighteenth Century Veteran Maratha General of the South,' Bulletin of the Deccan College Research Institute, Vol. 38, No. 1/4, 1978, pp. 147–53, JSTOR, http://www.jstor.org/stable/42931061.

9 From a personal conversation in Kolhapur with the present-day Chhatrapati in 2022.

Chapter 12: Aurangzeb's Breadcrumbs—The Nizam Becomes a Power in the South (1671–1748)

1 Faujdar under the Mughals was an office that combined the functions of a military commander along with judicial and land revenue functions.

2 Map Illustrating South India in the Eighteenth Century. Source: Charles Joppen, *Historical Atlas of India* (London: Longmans, Green & Co, 1907)

3 He was of Uzbek origin.

4 His mother was the daughter of the prime minister of Shah Jahan and his father, Feroze Jung, was a leading military general and noble of the Mughal Empire during the reign of Emperor Aurangzeb.

5 Jaswant Lal Mehta, *Advanced Study in the History of Modern India 1707-1813* (New Dawn Press Incorporated, 2005).

6 Sourced by historian Amena Begum.

- Khair-un-Nisa Begum who eventually married Rustum Jung. More about her son Muzafar Jung later.
- Padsha Begum who became wedded to Khaja Baba Khan.
- Mukarama Banu Begum (who was referred to as Kali Begum), who was wedded to Mir Kalan Khan.
- Khajista Banu Begum *urf* Khan Bahadur Saheba.
- Mohasina Begum—very little is known about her.
- Banu Begum, who eventually became the wife of Ikhlas Khan.

7 From 1707 to 1719, no fewer than seventeen aspirants jockeyed for the Mughal throne.

8 N.S. Ramaswami, *Political History of Carnatic Under the Nawabs* (1984).

Chapter 13: The Nizam's Departure to Delhi

1 Prof. A.R. Kulkarni, *The Marathas* (Diamond Publishing, 2008).

2 The Treaty of 1719 between the Marathas and the Mughals was signed by Mohammad Shah and Balaji Vishwanath. The treaty recognized Shahu as the king of the Maratha kingdom and gave the Marathas the right to collect chauth and sardeshmukhi in six provinces.

3 Royal decree or edict.

4 On 20 February 1722, there was a grand audience held by the Mughal Emperor, when the Nizam was appointed Wazir and received the usual robe, a dagger, an ornamental pen-case and a diamond ring of great value.

5 *History of Indian Nation: Medieval India* (N.P.: K.K. Publications, 2022).

6 The Mughals that Bajirao saw were very different from the powerful Mughal Empire that Shivaji faced.
7 Ghaziuddin, the eldest son of Nizam-ul-Mulk, who was born in 1710, was, of course, the apple of his father's eye, and he spent the best part of his youth in the personal company and discipline of his father. He was associated with the imperial court at Delhi as a *mansabdar* from an early age, and enjoyed the title of Firoze Jang.
8 The Battle of Sakharkheda.

Chapter 14: The Nizam's Back and Forth with the Marathas

1 He thanked Shahu Maharaj for Bajirao's support against Mubarak Khan, but also addressed a letter to the Emperor, wherein he assured him that he would maintain peace in the Deccan and also try to control the Maratha expansion beyond the Narmada.
2 Palkhed lies between Paithan and Aurangabad.
3 Mungi Shevgaon Treaty of 1728.
4 The long-standing dispute with Sambhaji II was resolved by the Treaty of Warna in April 1731, which demarcated Satara and Kolhapur, while the Nizam too promised not to interfere with the Maratha campaigns.
5 Maharashtra State Gazetteers: Aurangabad district, 1977.
6 The Nizam plotted with Dabhade to remove the Peshwa altogether from the Maratha Court and away from Shahu Raje. Surprisingly, a fair number of prominent chiefs serving Shahu Raje readily agreed to this. Names like Udaji Pawar and his brother Anandrao, Pilaji Gaikwad and the Banday brothers, Chimnaji Damodar and others aligned themselves with the Nizam, not knowing that his evil motive was to decide the fate of the Deccan, Malwa and Gujarat in his favour.

Chapter 15: Connecting Back to the Ghorpades

1 She had come to stay permanently in Gajendragadh.
2 As per page 123 of Manohar Malgonkar's book, *Scaling the Heights–Mired in Their Own Blood: Stories of Loyalty and Treachery from Medieval Deccan*, in a letter sent by Sambhaji II to Sidhoji Ghorpade in 1727, there is a somewhat mysterious reference to

Sambhaji agreeing to grant Sidhoji Ghorpade the sardeshmukhi, or 10 per cent of the revenue of the entire province of Berar and a few villages in the vicinity of Nasik, in return for his help in the coming campaign. In fact, neither Berar nor the environs of Nasik were of Sambhaji's to make such an offer. What Sambhaji was promising Sidhoji was a part of what the Nizam had promised him in return for his help against Shahu. It will be recalled that both factions in the Maratha civil war had sought the rights of chauth and sardeshmukhi of the Deccan from the Mughal Emperor. And the Nizam, as the Viceroy of the Emperor, had offered to intercede with him on behalf of his ally Sambhaji, in return for Sambhaji's help in finishing off Shahu. Sambhaji, in turn, was offering a part of what he was hoping to get as a reward to Sidhoji, contingent on their aid.

3 As per page 124 of Manohar Malgonkar's book, *Scaling the Heights—Mired in Their Own Blood: Stories of Loyalty and Treachery from Medieval Deccan*, a document dated in January 1729 mentions that Shahu Maharaj had invited Sidhoji Ghorpade to join one of his column commanders, Naro Ram Mantri, in the field, and that Sidhoji had agreed to it. Nonetheless, when it was realized that Sidhoji had no intention of honouring it, Shahu suggested a compromise arrangement that Sidhoji should send his son Murarirao to serve in Shahu's court. Writes Shahu to Sidhoji: 'You and Kusaji Bhosle have met, and it was agreed between you that Murarji Ghorpade would be sent to serve the Master. He should be sent accordingly. The Master will see to everything.'

4 A letter sent by Shahu to Sidhoji Ghorpade on 14 November 1730 expresses his delight at the arrival of Murarirao and Sagunabai in Satara. This was possibly the last letter Shah addressed to Sidhoji Ghorpade.

5 Murarirao's domain was peppered over an extensive stretch of the Carnatic, a belt that ran at least 240 km between its two extremes. The westernmost portion, a small and compact area around the fort of Gajendragadh, he entrusted to the care of his younger brother, Daulatrao, so that he could concentrate on the other parts of his domain, particularly on the forts of Sandur, Koppal and Gutti. Koppal, it might be recalled, had been captured by Sidhojirao and which, under the terms of the Varna treaty, the Ghorpades had been called upon to deliver to a nominee of Sambhaji of Kolhapur

(since the seat of the ruler had now been shifted to Kolhapur). As there had been no such handing over, Murarirao had retained possession of the fort. After all, he could always make it out that he was holding the fort on behalf of the Kolhapur domain anyway.

Chapter 16: More Headaches for Nizam-ul-Mulk

1 The Nawayath, as described by eighteenth-century soldier, historian and East India Company administrator Mark Wilkis means 'newcomers' in Persian, referring to Arab emigrants in India.
2 This dates back to the period of the Kutb Shahs of Golconda.
3 H.D. Love, *Vestiges of Old Madras*, Volume 1, 1988.
4 J.D. Gribble, *History of the Deccan* (Mittal Publications, 1990).
5 Dost Ali was the Nawab from 1732 to 1740.
6 Richard Benyon (1698–1774) was a British merchant and colonial administrator who served as the President of Madras from 23 January 1735 to 14 January 1744.
7 His main strength was that he had assiduously cultivated the friendship of the French who had lately established their trading posts at Pondicherry and Karaikal on the east coast. It would seem that Chanda Sahib had visited Pondicherry and been greatly impressed by its defence system.

Chapter 17: A Problem Named Chanda Sahib

1 Legend has it that Chanda Sahib took a brick and covered it with a cloth.
2 J.L. Mehta, *Advanced Study in the History of Modern India 1707-1813* (New Dawn Press, 2005).
3 In 1720, Peshwa Balaji Vishvanath had obtained from Nizam Hussain Ali the right to collect chauth and sardeshmukhi from Arcot and Trichy. The payment of these taxes having fallen in arrears, the Marathas decided to utilize the opportunity to collect them. Further, they cherished an ambition to extend their imperial sway right up to Kanyakumari.
4 K. Rajayyan, *The Marathas at Trichiopoly—1741-43*, Bhandarkar Research Institute.
5 Ibid.

6 In a February 2020 paper published in *Oxford Academic* titled 'Anatomy of a Massacre: Nadir Shah in Delhi', Abhishek Kaicker writes, 'In 1739, the Iranian ruler Nadir Shah spearheaded a rapid invasion of the Mughal realm, which culminated with his occupation of the Mughal capital of Shahjahanabad (Delhi) and the extraction of a vast tribute from the Mughal king Mohammad Shah and his nobles. Nadir Shah's brief time in Delhi is remembered for his sanguinary massacre of the city's inhabitants.'

7 As per an extract from A. Dow's *History of Hindustan Vol. 2*, 'The King of Persia, finding himself in possession of Delhi, called the Nizam and Sadat Khan into his presence and addressed them in the following extraordinary manner: "Are not you both the most ungrateful villains to your King and country? Who after possessing such wealth and dignities, called me from my own dominions, to ruin them and yourselves? But I will scourge you all with my wrath, which is the instrument of the vengeance of God." Having spoken these words, he spat upon their beards, the highest affront possible to Mussalman and turned them, with every mark of indignity, from his presence.'

8 King Vyankoji was an adventurous warrior. He entered Thanjavur victoriously on 12 January 1676 and a couple of months later, he performed his *Rajyabhishekam* (crowning and anointment ceremony) on 5 March 1676, much like his half-brother Shivaji Maharaj.

Chapter 18: The Nizam's Harem

1 Rekha Pande, *Facets of Muslim Women in the Deccan* (USA: Lexington Books, Rowman and Littlefield, January 2024). Rekha Pande is the professor emeritus of history and women's studies at the Henry Martin Institute International Centre for Research, Interfaith Relations and Reconciliation, Hyderabad. She was former head, department of history and former head, Centre for Women's Studies, University of Hyderabad.

2 In those days, the jewellery had no diamonds, as per Indrajeet. It was a whole lot of gold and a mix of precious and semi-precious stones.

3 Soma Mukherjee, *Royal Mughal ladies and their contributions* (Gyan Publishing House, 2001).

4 There is a painting from 'Lot 42' at Christie's which is titled 'A Princess Hunting, Possibly Haiderabad, Deccan, India, Mid-18th century'. The description goes thus: 'Opaque pigments on paper, the princess rides a white horse and shoots at a herd of deer, assisted by cheetahs and attendants, others watching the hunt from behind a fence, laid down on cream card with gilt floral borders.'
5 Case in point being that wherever Babar and Humayun went, their wives, daughters and unmarried sisters also went along.
6 An army of ladies and hermaphrodites who were trained in arms and ammunition, who accompanied the Mughal princesses, if they ever decided to venture outside.
7 Ladies.
8 Muntazim Bahadur Mukund Wamanrao Burway, *Life of Subhedar Malhar Rao Holkar* (State Printing Press, 1930).
9 The 'Shajarah-i-Asafiyah' posted on page 63 has a mention of all the women in the Nizam's life.
10 On the fourth day of the wedding, the bride visits her parents' home accompanied by her new husband. Her parents treat the newlywed couple with a lavish lunch and give them various gifts. This is followed by Jumagi on Friday (Jumma). This is the fifth day and families from both the bride's and the groom's family and relatives invite the new couple and make a jumagi with gifts and delicious foods.
11 Even now, they stand as Falaknuma, Chowmohallah, Basheerbagh, Khurshidjah and Devdi.

Chapter 19: The Foreign Foursome

1 Amar Farooqi, *The Colonial Subjugation of India* (Aleph Book Company, December 2022).
2 Muslim pilgrims wanting to go to Haj relied on Portuguese shipping at this time. Before boarding a vessel, they needed a passport issued by Portugal.
3 Amar Farooqi, *The Colonial Subjugation of India*.
4 Giles Milton, *Nathaniel's Nutmeg* (London: Holder and Stoughton, 1999).
5 On 22 August 1639, English official Francis Day obtained a grant of a 3-mile-long strip of land for the East India Company from the local ruler, Damarla Venkatadri Nayaka, the Nayaka of Wandiwash.

6 As per the rules of the Nayaka, the Europeans in the area were not allowed to decorate their houses with any colour other than white. Hence, this area came to be called the 'White Town'. The surrounding areas were populated by Indians who came in large numbers to partake in the commercial activities. Because of frequent riots between the local population and the Europeans, their respective areas were demarcated as 'White Town' and 'Black Town'. Fort St George, White Town and Black Town were together called Madras. Andrew Cogan and Francis Day can be considered the founders of Madras.

7 The British were masters of both diplomacy and warfare. In the seventeenth century, their Prince Charles the Second was up for marriage. And there was no dearth of offers. After all, who wouldn't want to marry the future King of England at that time? Charles the Second strategically made an announcement, in Parliament no less, that he was ready to settle down. Offers for dowry came pouring in. Obviously, they settled for the fattest dowry. It was the Portuguese who clinched it. Catherine Braganza's hand came along with 3,00,000 pounds, Tangier and 'Bom Bahia' (Bombay) on the western coast of the Indies.

8 Vol. 4 is the Mughal period. It is planned by Lt Colonel Sir Wolseley Haig and Sir Richard Burn at the Cambridge University Press, 1937.

9 John Zubrzycki, *The Shortest History of India* (Picador India, 2022).

10 Ibid., p. 65. Half a century later, Robert Clive, one of the heroes of our story, would use the same farman to justify the overthrow of Bengal's Nawab and seal the beginning of British rule in India.

11 Also referred to as the Compagnie des Andes Orientales.

Chapter 20: The Emergence of French Ambition

1 The Dutch War (1672–78) aimed to establish French possession of the Spanish Netherlands after having forced the Dutch Republic's acquiescence.

2 Thomas Pitt was an English merchant, colonial administrator and politician who served as the president of Fort St George from 1698 to 1709.

3 Henry Dodwell, 'Dupleix and Clive', *Beginning of Empire* (Taylor & Francis Publishers, 2013).

4 The French secured good terms of ransom for English prizes, while the English also remitted the proceeds of the French prizes to Bengal for the French investment. Dupleix returned from his voyages on the Atlantic and Indian oceans, anxious to take a part in the world of enterprise and commerce. His father responded by obtaining for him a high post in the service of the Company of the Indies at Pondicherry.
5 Born at Landrecies in 1697, he was groomed by his father for the world of commerce.
6 It was tough for Dupleix to convince the French Governor at the time, Pierre Christoph Le Noir, about his vision, because of the poverty prevalent in Pondicherry. However, in a short time, Dupleix succeeded in amassing a considerable fortune and demonstrated that the company's agents who came before him had drifted into a life of sloth.
7 Henry Dodwell, 'Dupleix and Clive', *Beginning of Empire*.
8 J. Talboys Wheeler, *Madras in the Olden Time*, 1882.
9 Ibid., p. 125.
10 Manohar Malgonkar, *Scaling the Heights–Mired in Their Own Blood: Stories of Loyalty and Treachery from Medieval Deccan*.

Chapter 22: Duty Calling Murarirao

1 This refers to a collection in the Government Oriental Manuscripts Library in Chennai, which has a large collection of manuscripts and rare, early print material in languages such as Tamil, Kannada, Telugu, Sanskrit and Tamil Grantha.
2 In this context, Indrajeet specifically defines a killedar as a keymaster who maintained the fort's defence and ensured its security.
3 Also called Shahaji or Savai Shahji.
4 K.R. Subramanian, *The Maratha Rajas of Thanjavur* (self-published, 1928).
5 The British did become the laughing stock, after putting a bogus son on the throne of Thanjavur.
6 Pratap Singh came to the throne in 1739, and he ruled until 1763. He allied with Muhammad Ali, the Nawab of the Carnatic, and aided the British East India Company against the French East India Company in the Carnatic Wars and the Seven Years' War.

He was the last king to be addressed by the directors of the British East India Company as 'His Majesty'. In 1762, a tripartite treaty was signed between Thanjavur, the Carnatic and the British by which he became a vassal of the Nawab of the Carnatic.

7 Press list of ancient Dutch Records 1657–1825 (No. 282).

8 One may recall that Shivaji himself had come to an understanding with his step-brother Vyankoji over his holdings in Thanjavur and Mysore. Clearly, the larger goal was to unify the Deccan states under the rule of a native Hindu ruler and protect it from outsiders like the Muslims and Mughals.

9 Manohar Malgonkar, *Scaling the Heights–Mired in Their Own Blood: Stories of Loyalty and Treachery from Medieval Deccan.*

10 To achieve that goal, he was prepared to make astonishing sacrifices such as walking away from the brink of military glory and letting down his associates. It was just one of those quirks of fate that the only time the Marathas had a real chance of establishing their rule in the South, Raghuji should have been at the helm.

Chapter 23: The Nizam Meets Murarirao

1 The properties given thus were usually split into numerous pieces in order to prevent the more powerful among the Paigahs from entertaining any thought of carving out an empire for themselves. The system, which continued relatively unchanged until 1950, ensured a steady source of income for the state treasury and the Nizam. The Nizam had other sources of revenue as well, which included the lion's share of gold unearthed in his dominions, diamonds and gems from the Golconda mines and the income from his vast personal estates.

2 Originally, falconry was needed for survival; using a bird of prey was a tool for putting food on the table. It is widely thought that the sport was restricted to the upper classes. This may not necessarily be true and could be a function of the fact that upper-class lives were recorded more than the lower classes. The Royal Falconer was treated with great respect and was sometimes considered fourth in line of seniority in the court. There is a record of Akbar enjoying falconry as well; this is documented in paintings.

3 There seems little doubt that peregrines are capable of reaching 290 kph, with research indicating their flight path is curved.

This enables them to hold their head straight, thereby reducing aerodynamic drag, while also keeping their prey at the best angle for maximum visual acuity.

Chapter 25: Against All Odds

1 As per G.T. Kulkarni, 'Deccan (Maharashtra) Under the Muslim Rulers From Khaljis to Shivaji: a Study in Interaction, Professor S.M. Katre Felicitation', *Bulletin of the Deccan College Research Institute*, 51/52: 501–510, 1992, JSTOR 42930434, the Marathi language from the era is heavily Persianized. The Persian influence continues to this day with many Persian-derived words used in everyday speech such as *bāg* (garden), *kārkhānā* (factory), *shahar* (city), *bāzār* (market), *dukān* (shop), *hushār* (clever), *kāgaḏ* (paper), *khurchi* (chair), *jamin* (land), *jāhirāt* (advertisement) and *hazār* (thousand).

2 Persian was the language of administration in the Deccan sultanates, with some documentation in the local vernaculars. Grants of land by the Adilshahi regime are typically bilingual, in Persian and Marathi.

3 Source: family narration.

4 Manohar Malgonkar, *Scaling the Heights–Mired in Their Own Blood: Stories of Loyalty and Treachery from Medieval Deccan.*

Chapter 26: The Anticlimax

1 Bajirao died on 28 April 1740, but news of his death travelled slowly.

2 Ananda Ranga Pillai was from a well-connected, upper-caste business family. As someone who knew Tamil, French and Persian, he became an invaluable member of Dupleix's coterie.

Chapter 27: Murarirao Captures Chanda Sahib

1 In the Battle of Damalcheri.

2 In the year 1739, the Marathas captured Salsette and Bassein by defeating the Portuguese with the leadership of Chimaji Appa (brother of Bajirao I).

3 Manohar Malgonkar, *Scaling the Heights–Mired in Their Own Blood: Stories of Loyalty and Treachery from Medieval Deccan.*

4 This wily wizard will make a comeback soon, even after remaining a prisoner of the Marathas for eight years.

Chapter 28: Diplomacy by Brandy

1 Chhatrapati Shahu remarked to a courtier about this incident, 'He let down the kingdom for the sake of some wine.'

2 He had Chanda Sahib and his eldest son as his prisoners, whom he was determined to hold for a stiff ransom. In the event, they were not released for seven years. And now he was anxious to return to his estates in what is today called Madhya Pradesh.

Chapter 29: The Nizam Wakes Up

1 Perched on the pinnacle of this new rock, the future must have seemed full of promise. The view was incomparably superior to anything to be seen from the pavilion of Gutti even during the rainy months when it was least attractive.

2 Famous diarist and spy.

3 The Peshwa's two main armies were in Bengal.

4 Legend has it that Saheba expertly guided him through this.

5 The discord between Shahu's Peshwa, Nanasaheb, and his only other capable military commander, Raghuji Bhosle, was well known.

Chapter 30: The French Record Some Early Wins

1 *History of Modern Deccan, 1720/1724-1948: Political and Administrative Aspects*, ed. M.A. Nayeem (Abul Kalam Azad Oriental Research Institute, 2000).

Chapter 31: Murarirao Ghorpade and the French Hollow Square

1 Chitnis Bakhar.

2 Manohar Malgonkar, *Scaling the Heights–Mired in Their Own Blood: Stories of Loyalty and Treachery from Medieval Deccan.*

3 A website named ibmathsresources.com features a mathematical explanation of the construct. Imagine that a larger outer square of 20 by 20 men would successively become an inner hollow square of 8 by 8. The total number of men in such a formation would be 336.

4 As per a website titled 'military fandom', the strategic aspect of the hollow square was exceptional. The outer square of men would wait till the approaching cavalry was just 30 metres away. Then they would fire hard. The resulting casualties to the attackers would eventually form piles of dead and wounded horses and their riders, which would obstruct further attacks.

5 The book was a significant contribution to the study of infantry warfare. A long and detailed work, published in 1643, it ran on for 320 pages.

Chapter 32: The Nizam's Successor

1 The two of them went to Pondicherry to celebrate, much to the chagrin of Dupleix, who wanted to consolidate his gains.

2 French for tic tac toe.

3 Muhammad Ali had no real claim to Arcot. He was the son of Anwaruddin, who had been appointed as regent of Arcot by Nizam-ul-Mulk. However, after Nizam-ul-Mulk's death, Anwaruddin killed the young nawab he was to guard and pronounced himself nawab. As fate would have it, Anwaruddin was killed by the French and Chanda Sahib. Naturally, Muhammad Ali was inclined to partner with Murarirao and the British.

Chapter 34: Murarirao Saves Robert Clive

1 In August 1763, Orme published the first volume of his major work, *A History of the Military Transactions of the British Nation in Indostan from the Year 1745*.

2 Manohar Malgonkar, *Scaling the Heights—Mired in Their Own Blood: Stories of Loyalty and Treachery from Medieval Deccan*.

3 Ibid.

Chapter 35: Robert Clive's Honour Roll

1 Major George Bruce Malleson, *History of the French in India* (Cambridge University Press, 1868), p. 290.
2 On the Siege of Arcot, *The History of British India: Volume III* (1858), p. 84.
3 'Clive's Dream before the Battle of Plassey', *Under the Rose: Poems Written Chiefly in India* (1868). (*Ex Eremo*, Henry George Keene, London, 1855).
4 Leslie Stephen, ed. 'Clive, Robert', *Dictionary of National Biography*, Vol. 11 (London: Smith, Elder & Co.).
5 As per an ICMR report by the Government of India dated January–March 2008, opium was brought to India by the Arab traders in the ninth century via the west coast and was primarily used for medicinal purposes. By the next century, opium use was widespread and included social functions. By the turn of the fourteenth century, recorded mention of opium as a product and its cultivation along the west coast at Cambay and Malwa was reported amply. Historically, the use of cannabis products predates the use of raw opium. Founder of the first Mughal dynasty, Babar (1524–1530), encouraged poppy cultivation and the sale of opium became state monopolies. Soon, it became an important article of trade with China and other eastern countries. By 1757, the British East India Company took over the opium monopoly and the British attempted to popularize its use to increase revenue. Opium-growing stretched for 500 miles in Bengal with more than a million registered farmers growing opium plants for the East India Company in 5,00,000 acres of prime land.
6 The Black Hole refers to a small lock-up in Fort William, which the British had built for minor offenders. It measured only 18 ft by 14 ft 10 in and had two small windows. In 1756, Siraj-ud-Daula attacked the British at Fort William when they didn't respond to his warnings to stop fortifying it against the French. He hauled 146 British prisoners, including two women and several wounded men, at sword-point for the night into the fort's 'black hole'. The heat at that time of year was suffocating and the prisoners trampled on each other to get near the windows. They fought over the small supply of water they had been left, while begging for mercy from the guards. It is generally believed that 123 of the 146

prisoners died. The story inspired patriotic fervour and rage at Indian perfidy in generations of Britons, even though each version seems to have a different count of prisoners.

7 Speech in the House of Commons (14 December 1757), quoted in Basil Williams, *The Life of William Pitt, Earl of Chatham, Volume II* (1914), p. 24.

8 Read Annexure 4 for insights into Robert Clive's later life.

Chapter 37: The Marathas Wake Up Again

1 Anwar Haroon, *Kingdom of Haider Ali and Tipu Sultan, Sultanat-e-Khudadad*, 2013.

2 Manohar Malgonkar, *Scaling the Heights–Mired in Their Own Blood: Stories of Loyalty and Treachery from Medieval Deccan.*

Chapter 39: Senapati

1 Refer map of 'Peninsular India of the Eighteenth Century' on page 76.

2 *History of Hyder Shah and Tippoo Sultan, His Highness Prince Gholam Mohamed* (W. Thacker and Co.,1855).

3 The Maratha affairs at Poona always had some kind of problem. Balaji Baji Rao's second son, Madhavrao, became Peshwa in his seventeenth year, while Raghunathrao (the younger brother of Balaji Baji Rao and the eldest surviving member of the Peshwa family) became Regent and de facto ruler of the state. Raghunathrao was ambitious and was egged on by his even more ambitious wife, Anandibai. Now, Anandibai seldom saw eye to eye with the Peshwa's mother, Gopikabai, who naturally wanted her son Madhavrao to have a greater say in managing the affairs of state. These personal rivalries had disastrous consequences on the health of Maratha power in Pune. But to his credit, Madhavrao was truly a brave tactician and contributed immensely to regaining lost Maratha pride.

4 Eloy Joze Correa Peixoto's Portuguese book, *History of Nawab Haidar Ali Khan Bahadur from 1718–1779*, has this description. The word *topas* means Indian Christian (loosely South Asian seamen) and *caffree* means Negro (also 'kaffir') and refers to an

African native brought to Ceylon as a slave or mercenary soldier by the Portuguese, Dutch or British. Even though the date of original publication is unknown, it is provided as reference material in the K.N.V.S. Collection at the Mythic Society, Bangalore. Eloy Joze Correa Peixoto was one of Haider Ali's European military hires.

Chapter 41: Missed Opportunities

1 After the death of Madhavrao, the Maratha court was divided between Raghunathrao and Barbhai (the council of twelve ministers) factions. Barbhai was formed to protect the young son of Narayanrao Peshwa, known as Sawai Madhavrao, from the intrigues of Raghunathrao and thwart the British designs for the Maratha Empire. In this scenario, the Carnatic front became secondary. Murarirao was left alone.

Chapter 43: Murarirao's Survivors

1 Excerpted from Manohar Malgonkar's *Scaling the Heights–Mired in Their Own Blood: Stories of Loyalty and Treachery from Medieval Deccan.*

Epilogue: Murarirao's Present-Day Relevance and the Expedition to Gutti

1 Guttikota is how the locals refer to the Gutti Fort.
2 Son of Anjana, Hanuman.
3 Shiva.
4 Mother of Parasurama.
5 Sathyabhama, consort of Lord Krishna.
6 Eight-sided protection.
7 Dr H.S. Brahmananda, *Gutti Fort* (Anantapuram: Rayala Kala Gosti, April 1983).
8 *Gutti History and Culture*, B. Venkata Rami Reddy National Award-winner, Telugu University, Reprint 1994 August.
9 The Gutti Fort had many occupants down the ages. It was passed down from the Chalukya King Vikramaditya to the Vijayanagara Empire, the Qutb Shahi dynasty, the Mughals and finally Murarirao

in 1746, who made it his permanent residence eight years later. In 1775, Haider took over the fort and finally it fell to the British East India Company.

10 Both Gutti and Srisailam are in Andhra Pradesh.

11 Quite rare: only one other temple of this kind is in Ujjain.

12 The East India Company took over Gutti after a fierce battle in 1799. At the time, Major General Sir Thomas Munro was the Governor of Madras Presidency. The battle was long and bloody, with both sides suffering heavy losses. Hence, a European cemetery was set up at Gutti. It is widely believed that Thomas Munro had a kind side to him and worked for the welfare of the people.

Annexure 1: Bhosales and Ghorpades, Brothers-in-Arms

1 Monitor lizard.

2 It was his son Bhim Singh who received this via a sanad.

Annexure 2: The Rise of the Peshwas

1 The first six were Shamraj Nilkanth Rozekar, Moro Trimbak Pingle, Nilkanth Moreshwar Pingle, Parsram Trimbak Pratinidhi, Bahiro Moreshwar Pingle and Balakrishna Vasudev.

2 V.D. Mahajan, *Modern Indian History* (S. Chand and Company, 2022).

3 Ibid.

Annexure 3: An Extract from an Essay about Nizam-Ul-Mulk

1 Yusuf Husain, *The First Nizam: The Life and Times of Nizamut-Mulk Asaf Jahi* (Asia Publishing House, 1963).

Annexure 4: Robert Clive, Opium and Murarirao

1 William Dalrymple, *The Anarchy: The Relentless Rise of the East India Company* (Bloomsbury, 2019).

2 Richard-Davenport Hines, *The Pursuit of Oblivion: A Social History of Drugs* (Orion Publishers, 2012).

3 A hard-nosed opportunist, would Clive have not known the value of opium and the potential of its trade? However, it was only after Plassey and 1773 that the British discovered the trade. They proceeded to establish a monopoly on opium cultivation in the Indian province of Bengal. So this possibility is out. Much later, Britain would be in control of the major opium-growing regions of Patna, Benaras, Bihar and Malwa.

4 George III to Lord North (21 May 1773), quoted in *The Correspondence of King George the Third with Lord North from 1768 to 1783*, Vol. I, ed. W. Bodham Donne (1867), p. 135.

Annexure 5: The Weapons of the Marathas

1 Portions in this Annexure are extracted from *Sainik Samachar* Volume 17, Issues 1–26, 1970. Contributed by Ministry of Defence, Government of India.

2 This Prof. Sen is quoted in Chapter 9 of the book *Mahrattas, Sikhs and Southern Sultans of India: Their Fight Against Foreign Power*, G.N. Pant (2001). The book is edited by Harbans Singh Bhatia and published by Deep and Deep.

3 John Henry Grose, a British traveller and writer affiliated with the British East India Company, was known for his travel account of India.

4 Colonel Tone commanded a regiment of the Peshwa's army. In 1798, he wrote of the Marathas: 'The three great tribes which compose the Martha caste are the Kunbi or farmer, the Dhangar or shepherd, and the Gawli or cowherd; to this original cause may perhaps be ascribed that great simplicity of manner which distinguishes the Martha people.'

5 Royal Armoury of Madrid

6 David Edgerton, *The Rise and Fall of the British Nation: A Twentieth-Century History*.

7 Ibid.

8 Captain William Gordon was Mangal's commanding officer and close friend.

Annexure 7: A Tribute to Bhujangrao Ghorpade

1 This is a famous quote attributed to Walt Streightiff, loosely described as an educator; though not much is known about him.

2 I was quite the brat and often got wounded with all my running around! My loving mother with kind eyes and golden hair would then apply a paste of some leaf and a turmeric base on the wound. To most boys, their mother will always be the most beautiful woman in the world. Mine certainly was. I loved playing with her hair and she always let me.

3 Ajoba is a Marathi word that means grandfather.

4 Kakka or Kalkappa was the main bodyguard. He was a dependable man with glorious white hair and a handlebar moustache, who wore a turban with a brooch and was rather immaculately turned out. And his menacing gun had a finality to it.

5 Ramrao was the bodyguard, who trained under Kakka, as age caught on with the latter. So, for a while, both of them were there. Ramrao was rough in his manner and packed a double-barrelled shotgun in the innards of his dhoti. Don't ask me where!

6 Vithappa was the man Friday.

7 This is an opinion that belongs to Kalkappa and is not endorsed by the authors.

8 A shortened, conversational version of Murarirao's name.

9 One version, verified by historian Amena Begum, confirms that Nizam-ul-Mulk had six daughters. See page 252 for their names.

10 Indrajeet believes that the letters written by Murarirao, a man who loved writing letters, must be available in some archive or in hidden parts or burnt parts of the Nizam's belongings. As for the letters written by Saheba, the family believes that they were destroyed when Haider plundered Gutti.

11 There was a long gap, before he married again to Ranubai. He had two sons from her: Venkatrao and Narsingrao, who were born much later in his life, when he was in his fifties. There is a reference that, in the mid-1770s, the sons were in their teens.

12 The Marathas received the legacy of culture form Thanjavur. As historians have often stated, the brides from Thanjavur were very classy, cultured and educated.

References

Original References

1. Unpublished Original Sources–Mackenzie Collection no. from the Deccan College Historical Museum Rumal 98 (file 2) II. Selections from Peshwa Daftar, Volumes 20, 26, 28, 37. (Bombay 1930–34).

Additional References

1. M.Y. Ghorpade, *The Grand Resistance* (Ravi Dayal).
2. Santaji: *Kaka Vidhate* (Prafullata Prakasan).
3. Sardesai, *New History of the Marathas*, Vol. II.
4. Saqi Mustaid Khan, *Maasir-i-Alamgiri*.
5. Khafi Khan, *Muntakhabu-l-Lubab*.
6. G.S. Sardesai, *Marathi Riyasat*.
7. G.S. Sardesai, *Historical Genealogies* (Bombay 1957).
8. N.K. Sinha, *Hydar Ali III Edition*.
9. R. Orme, *History of British Transactions in Indostan*, Vol. 1, 1803.
10. C.K. Srinivasan, *Maratha Role in the Carnatic*, 1944.
11. S. Gopalan, *Bhonsle Vamsha Charitra*, Thanjavur, 1951.
12. Kaushik Roy, *War, Culture and Society in Early Modern South Asia*, 30 March 2011, pp. 1740–1849; ISBN 9781136790874, retrieved 11 December 2014.

English Articles in Periodicals

1. G.S. Sardesai, 'The Role of Ghorpades in Maratha History', *Modern Review*, May 1940.
2. S.U. Kamat, 'The Chitradurga Chiefs and the Merathas', paper read at the Maratha History Seminar, Kolhapur, 1970.
3. A. Srinivasachari, 'Murarirao Ghorpade', *Indian Historical Quarterly*, Vol. XV, No. 4, December 1939.
